MEN AND SEX

MEN AND SEX

New Psychological Perspectives

EDITED BY

Ronald F. Levant

Gary R. Brooks

John Wiley & Sons, Inc.

New York • Chichester • Weinheim • Brisbane • Singapore • Toronto

Library of Congress Cataloging-in-Publication Data:

Men and sex : new psychological perspectives / edited by Ronald F.
    Levant, Gary R. Brooks.
        p.   cm.
    includes index.
    ISBN 0-471-16903-X (cloth : alk. paper)
    1. Men—United States—Sexual behavior.   2. Men—United States—
Psychology.   3. Gay men—United States—Sexual behavior.   4. Sex
(Psychology)—United States.   5. Intimacy (Psychology)—United
States.   I. Levant, Ronald F.   II. Brooks, Gary R., 1946–
HQ28.M44   1997
306.7'081—dc21   97-12813

Printed in the United States of America

10 9 8 7 6 5 4 3 2 1

To Wilma Levant, Carol Slatter, Caren Levant, and
Adrian and Jeremy Shanker;
and to Patti, Ashley, and Allison Brooks.

Editors and Contributors

Ronald F. Levant, Ed.D. earned his doctorate in Clinical Psychology and Public Practice from Harvard in 1973. He is currently Associate Clinical Professor of Psychology in the Department of Psychiatry at Harvard Medical School (Cambridge Hospital), and in independent practice.

Dr. Levant's focus on reconstructing the male role grew out of his efforts to support fatherhood, an enterprise that began with a research program that he established in 1975, when he joined the faculty of the Counseling Psychology Program at Boston University. He subsequently served as the founder and director of the Boston University Fatherhood Project from 1983–1988.

Dr. Levant has played a leading role in the American Psychological Association (APA) in setting up organizational structures that focus on a re-examination of masculinity, which includes serving as founder and chair of the Division of Psychotherapy's Task Force on Men's Roles and Psychotherapy, founder and chair of the Division of Counseling Psychology's Special Interest Group on Men's Studies, and as co-founder and the first president of the Society for the Psychological Study of Men and Masculinity, Division 51 of APA.

Dr. Levant has authored, co-authored, or edited 10 books and 60 refereed articles and book chapters in the areas of family psychology and the psychology of men. His publications include *Between Father and Child*, co-authored with John Kelly (Viking/Penguin, 1989/1991); *Masculinity Reconstructed*, co-authored with Gini Kopecky (Dutton/Plume, 1995/1996); and *A New Psychology of Men*, co-edited with William Pollack (Basic Books, 1995). He has served as guest editor for special issues of *The Counseling Psychologist*, *Psychotherapy*, *The Journal of African American Men*, and serves on the editorial boards of seven journals and as editor for the *Journal of Family Psychology*.

Dr. Levant has also served as president of the Massachusetts Psychological Association, president of the APA Division of Family Psychology, chair of the APA Committee for the Advancement of Professional Practice, member of the APA Council of Representatives, and is presently a member-at-large of the APA Board of Directors.

Gary R. Brooks, Ph.D. received his doctorate from the University of Texas at Austin in 1976. For the past 21 years, he has been a psychologist at the O.E. Teague Veterans Center, Temple, Texas, and is currently the chief of Psychology Service. He is an associate professor in Psychiatry and Behavioral Sciences with the Texas A&M University Health Sciences Center, adjunct faculty member at Baylor University, and instructor of Men's Studies with Texas Women's University. Dr. Brooks is also an Executive Board Member of the National Organization of Men Against Sexism (NOMAS), co-founder and president of Division 51 of the American Psychological Association Society for the Psychological Study of Men and Masculinity (SPSMM) and past president of APA's Division of Family Psychology.

Dr. Brooks is nationally recognized for his writing and training in the areas of psychotherapy for men, couples, and families. In 1996 he was honored as "Practitioner of the Year" by SPSMM. He has written numerous articles and book chapters and has been invited to present Continuing Education Workshops across the country. He is the author of *The Centerfold Syndrome*, published by Jossey-Bass (1995) and co-author of *Bridging Separate Gender Worlds* published by APA Press (1997).

Earl L. Backman, Ph.D. currently serves as a university ombudsman at Northern Arizona University and has more than 20 years of experience as a senior university administrator. Previous positions include assistant to the president, director of International Studies, and academic dean. In addition, Dr. Backman has taught at four universities, is the author of one book and numerous articles, and has served as a national consultant and trainer. He currently specializes in conflict resolution, gender communication differences, workplace dysfunction, and the development of supervisory management skills. Earl and Linda R. Backman have, together and separately, offered educational and training programs for individuals and educational institutions; and together conduct national searches for key administrative positions at colleges and universities.

Linda R. Backman, Ed.D. is a licensed psychologist with a doctorate in Counseling Psychology and maintains a private practice. With more than 18 years of experience as a psychotherapist, Dr. Backman specializes in relationship and gender issues, worker's compensation and chronic pain issues, conflict resolution, and hypnosis/spiritual crisis. Additional experiences include providing psychotherapy services in a large multispeciality medical clinic, establishing an agency to assist bereaved parents, teaching part-time in a university, writing, consulting, and presentations at regional and national meetings. With Earl Backman, Linda currently provides couples therapy and conducts workshops and presentations on a variety of couples issues and co-therapy techniques.

Glenn E. Good, Ph.D. received his doctorate from the Ohio State University. He is currently an associate professor and director of Training for the Counseling Psychology Program in the Department of Psychology at the University of Missouri-Columbia. He has written more than 33 articles, chapters, and books, and has made more than 70 presentations at national and international conventions. He has been involved with men's issues since 1972, and is president-elect of the Society for the Psychological Study of Men and Masculinity (Division 51 of the American Psychological Association). He also maintains a private practice in Columbia, Missouri.

Joni E. Johnston, Psy.D. earned her doctorate in Clinical Psychology at Florida Institute of Technology and is a licensed clinical psychologist in Texas and a managing partner at The Growth Company. Dr. Johnston has served as host and producer of Mental Health Matters and as an expert witness for the Texas Attorney General's Office in sexual harassment litigation. Dr. Johnston has also served on the board of directors on Mental Health Association of Greater Dallas, as Program Chair of the Media Psychology Division of the American Psychological Association. She is a member of the Texas Psychological Association, member of the National Speaker's Association, and member of the National Association of Radio and Talk Show Hosts. Dr. Johnston is the winner of the Media Award for Mental Health Matters. She is the author of *Appearance Obsession: Learning to Love the Way You Look* (Health Communications, 1994) and the upcoming *Lessons From the Other Side of the Couch*. She has authored articles on sexual harassment and gender diversity in publications including the *Texas Employment Law Newsletter, E.A. Magazine,* and *E.A.P. Digest.*

David Lisak, Ph.D. is an associate professor of Psychology at the University of Massachusetts-Boston and director of the Men's Sexual Trauma Research Project. He conducts and supervises research on the long-term effects of childhood abuse in adult men, and on the relationship between early abuse and the later perpetration of interpersonal violence. He has been studying the impact of male gender socialization in the lives of traumatized men. His research has been published in the *Journal of Traumatic Stress,* the *Journal of Interpersonal Violence, Psychotherapy,* and other journals. In addition to his research and teaching, Dr. Lisak maintains a private practice specializing in the treatment of men and serves as an expert witness in death penalty cases in which child abuse issues are raised.

Don-David Lusterman, Ph.D. is in private practice in Baldwin, New York. He founded the program in family counseling at Hofstra University in 1973. Dr. Lusterman was the founding executive director of the American Board of Family Psychology (now part of ABPP). He is an ABPP Diplomate in Family Psychology, a fellow of the APA and of the American Association for Marriage and Family Therapy, and he was named APA Family Psychologist of the Year in 1987. He is the co-author (with the late Jay Smith) of *The Teacher as Learning Facilitator: Psychology and the Educational Process* (1979) and author of numerous articles and book chapters. He is also a consulting editor for the *Journal of Family Psychology* and on the editorial board of the *American Journal of Family Therapy.* He is the co-author (with Richard H. Mikesell and Susan H. McDaniel) of *Integrating Family Therapy: Handbook of Family Psychology and Systems Theory* (1995).

Vernon McClean, Ph.D. is professor of African American and Caribbean Studies at The William Paterson College of New Jersey and has served as consultant to school districts on curriculum transformation on issues of race, class, and gender. A pioneer researcher in the areas of racism and sexism, he is the author of *Solutions to Problems of Race, Class, and Gender* (Kendall/Hunt, 1993). He has contributed to *The Chronicle of Higher Education, Black Issues in Higher Education, The Activist Men's Journal,* the *New York Times,* and other periodicals. He has served as chairperson of the Committee on Eliminating Racism of The National Organization for Men Against Sexism. His current research focuses on the intersection of racism, sexism, and homophobia.

Roy Scrivner, Ph.D. received his doctorate in Counseling Psychology in 1974 from The University of Texas at Austin. Since 1987 he has worked full time as a family psychologist at the VA Medical Center, Dallas, Texas. He is a clinical assistant professor in the Department of Psychiatry Division of Psychology, The University of Texas Southwestern Medical School in Dallas. Dr. Scrivner has presented numerous programs on lesbian and gay issues; his programs and writings have also addressed ethical issues in family therapy. In 1986, he established the Lesbian and Gay Research Fund in the Texas Psychological Association (TPA). He held offices in TPA from 1985 to 1993, including that of president in 1992. In 1987, the Dallas Psychological Association selected him as the Distinguished Psychologist of the Year; and in 1989 the TPA Division of Applied Psychology recognized him "for contributions in Psychology as a Professional Practice." He served on the APA Division of Family Psychology Committee on Gender Concerns, including as co-chair in 1990. In 1993, he founded the Division's Committee on Lesbian and Gay Family Issues and has served as a co-chair of the Committee since its founding. In 1995, he co-authored a chapter on lesbian and gay family psychology, which appeared in R. H. Mikesell, D. D. Lusterman, and S. H. McDaniel (Eds.), *Integrating Family Therapy: Handbook on Family Psychology and Systems Therapy.*

Nancy B. Sherrod is a doctoral student in the Counseling Psychology Program of the Department of Psychology at the University of Missouri-Columbia. She graduated summa cum laude from the University of Colorado. Her research interests include gender issues and factors associated with perpetration of sexual assault.

Wendy E. Stock, Ph.D. received her doctorate in Clinical Psychology from the State University of New York at Stony Brook in 1983. Dr. Stock is academic director the new Psy.D. program at JFK University of Orinda, California. Previously Dr. Stock was on the faculty of Texas A&M University and the Pacific Graduate School of Psychology. Her areas of specialization are human sexuality, feminist issues in clinical psychology, and gender issues. Dr. Stock's research has focused on women's and men's responses to pornography, and on women's experiences of pornography in their lives. Other publications have included feminist analyses of sexual dysfunction and sex therapy, power dynamics in relationships, and sexual coercion. Dr. Stock was invited to present her findings to the Attorney General's Commission on Pornography in 1985, and is currently conducting a community survey of women's experiences of pornography.

Acknowledgments

WE WOULD LIKE to thank our editor, Jo Ann Miller, for her perspicacity and patience throughout the process of compiling and editing this book.

Dr. Levant would also like to thank his colleagues from whom he has learned much about the psychology of men in general and men's sexuality in particular. Joe Pleck has provided an overarching view for understanding the psychology of men. Co-editor Gary Brooks has been a very important colleague and friend; his rigor, dedication, and vision have added immeasurably to the quality of this book. The members of the "Men's Studies Seminar and Play Group," a group that meets once a month to discuss men's studies—and also to enjoy each other's company—have been a source of inspiration and a place to test new ideas: Joel Eichler, Alan Gurwitt, Steve Krugman, David Lisak, Bill Pollack, Jon Reusser, and Bob Weiss. Finally, he has learned from many other colleagues in Gender Studies in general and the Society for the Psychological Study of Men and Masculinity (SPSMM) in particular: Mike Andronico, Bob Brannon, Richard Eisler, Jeff Fischer, Marion Gindes, Glenn Good, Mark Kiselica, Richard Lazur, Richard Majors, Larry Morris, Jim O'Neil, Carol Philpot, Marlin Potash, Jerry Shapiro, Louise Silverstein, Lenore Walker, Marty Wong, and many others. Dr. Levant would also like to express his gratitude to the men who participated in his Fatherhood courses and Reconstructing Masculinity Workshops, and his clients, from whom he has learned an incalculable amount about men's psychology and sexuality.

Dr. Brooks' efforts to articulate the concerns about men's sexuality would have been impossible without the intellectual insights of many critical thinkers. Lenore Tiefer, Wendy Stock, Charlene Muehlenhard, Diana Russell, and Naomi Wolf gave him perspectives he couldn't ignore. Joe Pleck raised questions about the socialization of men, while Bernie Zilbergeld raised questions about men and sexuality. Many others took this lead and sharpened the critique into areas that have been painful to consider, but imperative to confront. Michael Kimmel, John Stoltenberg, Tim Beneke, and Bob Brannon have helped him understand the multiple insults of pornography and objectification of women. In two primary support groups—The National Organization of Men Against Sexism (NOMAS) and Society for the Study of Men and Masculinity (SPSMM)—many men have provided invaluable friendship and encouragement. Dr. Brooks is thrilled to have had the emotional support of Glenn Good, Murray Scher, Vernon McClean, Roy Scrivner, Don-David Lusterman, Jim O'Neil, Mike Andronico, and many others. Finally, Dr. Brooks is deeply grateful to co-editor Ron Levant, colleague, fellow traveler, and friend. His drive and energy made this book possible; his compassion and sensitivity made it personally meaningful.

Contents

PART III—VARIATIONS

INTRODUCTION

Men and the Problem of Nonrelational Sex

RONALD F. LEVANT AND GARY R. BROOKS

I N THE EARLY stages of our work on this book on men and sexuality, a perspective emerged in which we came to view much of what is taken for granted about male sexuality as problematic. This perspective was influenced by Pleck's (1981, 1995) articulation of the gender role strain paradigm, in which he pointed out that contemporary men are burdened by role definitions that are not only impossible for most men to attain but are also psychologically dysfunctional, and that the skills required to attempt to meet these definitions are often forged in the fires of traumatic childhood socialization experiences. Nowhere is this more true than in the area of male sexuality: Many men have impossible expectations of themselves and of their partners; these expectations can lead to behaviors that are dysfunctional. This orientation to sexuality is the unfortunate product of normative male socialization. We use the term *nonrelational sexuality* to describe the problematic character of male sexuality.

Nonrelational sexuality is the tendency to experience sex primarily as lust without any requirements for relational intimacy or emotional attachment. In this mode of sexual experience, targets of sexual desire are objectified and pursued instrumentally to meet a set of needs, which—in addition to the release of sexual tension—include receiving nurturance and affirming a sense of adequacy. Nonrelational sexuality is a self-involved way of experiencing sexuality. This narcissistic quality is revealed in Michael, Gagnon, Laumann, and Kolata's (1994) national survey on the sexual practices of U.S. adults, which found that while 22 percent of the women surveyed report having been forced to do something sexually at one time, only 3 percent of the men surveyed report having ever having done such a thing. This startling statistic reflects the tremendous lack of empathy inherent in a nonrelational approach to sexuality. Some men do not understand how women experience their sexual behavior as coercive. They may have thought they were negotiating for sex, while their women partners felt they were being forced. Although nonrelational sexuality is common, almost normative among men, it is a nonoptimal state of being that arises as a defensive adaptation to men's normative socialization experiences and developmental traumas (discussed at length in Chapter 1).

This book emerged as an exploration of the origins, meaning, and impact of male nonrelational sexuality—an exploration grounded in the available clinical and empirical literature and informed by the gender role strain paradigm. The perspective offered in this book will have implications not only for scientific research in the areas of human sexuality and the psychology of gender, but also for applied areas, such as psychotherapy and parent education.

In offering this perspective, it is not our intent to bash men or to side with women in the gender wars. Nor are we latter-day puritans seeking to promote a sexless society. We are men who value being men, and who consider ourselves empathic with contemporary male experience. Our views about the male experience are a matter of public record (Brooks, 1995; Levant & Kopecky, 1995/1996). We feel it is urgent that we stimulate a thorough discussion of the serious problem of male nonrelational sexuality. We do not view male sexuality itself as inherently dysfunctional; on the contrary, men's relative freedom from sexual inhibitions can add a great deal to relationships. However, male sexuality does become dysfunctional when nonrelational sexuality is the closest men can come to emotional or sexual intimacy.

The well-known divorce statistics, and the less well-known finding that women are leaving marriages twice as frequently as men (G. Pierce, personal communication, April 18, 1994) reinforce the idea that there is a growing "crisis of connection" between men and women (Levant, 1996). The popularity of the book *The Rules* (Fein & Schneider, 1996), which offers "time-tested secrets for capturing the heart of Mr. Right," suggests that women are abandoning the idea that men will ever choose an open, honest, companionate marriage, and that women think they must use men's emotional limitations to manipulate them into committed romantic relationships. Furthermore, the "dark side" of male nonrelational sexuality is extraordinarily costly to women, children, families, and men themselves (Brooks & Silverstein, 1995). Hardly a week goes by without a new scandal that involves the nonrelational orientation to sexuality (as we write this, the current scandal concerns the large-scale sexual harassment and rape of women in the Army).

This has been a difficult book for us to produce. First, there is scant published psychological literature that focuses squarely on the problem of men's nonrelational orientation to sexuality and views it critically. But also, not unrelatedly, we have come to realize that many people find it hard to accept the idea that men's socialization causes them to place a superordinate value on sex and often approach it from a self-involved point of view. Many regard this state of affairs as "natural," as in essential and unchangeable, the result of evolution and hard-wired into the genes. Others prefer to believe that "men are from Mars and women are from Venus" (Gray, 1992), rather than recognize that men's nonrelational sexuality is a direct product of how our society raises our young people. There is widespread aversion to acknowledging the sexual double standard of a masculinity ideology that values the "sexual stud" glamorized in Henry Miller and Harold Robbins novels and a femininity ideology that constrains women's sexuality and enslaves them to myths of perfectible beauty.

This book takes on the topic of men and sex—particularly the problem of nonrelational sexuality—in 10 chapters, organized into three parts: Theory, Problems, and Variations. The first two chapters—"Nonrelational Sexuality in Men" by Ronald Levant and "The Centerfold Syndrome" by Gary Brooks—delineate the theoretical model that organizes the succeeding critical perspectives on men's sexuality.

Levant's chapter provides a broad overview. He discusses the masculinity crisis, reviews the research that suggests that nonrelational sexuality is normative for men, and challenges the view that nonrelational sexuality is natural. Using Pleck's (1981, 1995) gender role strain paradigm as an overarching perspective, and considering our society's prevailing masculinity ideology, Levant describes the normative but traumatic socialization and development of boys. He details the consequences that both potentiate a nonrelational orientation to sexuality by blocking more intimate avenues and those that have a more specific relationship to nonrelational sexuality.

Brooks' chapter provides an overview of a specific form of nonrelational sexuality he has previously identified (Brooks, 1995). In addition to his description of the "Centerfold Syndrome," Brooks analyzes various etiological perspectives of men's sexuality. He reviews hormonal, neuroanatomical, and evolutionary-biology theories, concluding that while these essentialist arguments are critical for an informed interactionist position, they are minimally helpful in guiding future social action.

The six chapters in the Problems section cover the full spectrum of nonrelational sexuality. Chapter 3, "Appearance Obsession: Women's Reactions to Men's Objectification of Their Bodies," by Joni Johnston, deals with the impact objectification has on women and on intimate heterosexual relationships. The author's elaboration of "Appearance Obsession," "a chronic, painful preoccupation with one's physical appearance," provides valuable insights that underscore the importance of helping men develop emotional empathy for women.

The remaining chapters in this section deal with forms of nonrelational sexuality, along a continuum from mild to severe. In Chapter 4, "Repetitive Infidelity, Womanizing, and Don Juanism," Don-David Lusterman provides a gender-aware analysis of these forms of nonrelational sexuality. Rooting these kinds of sexual insatiability in the gender role strain paradigm, this chapter uses case studies to provide in-depth insight. In Chapter 5, "Sex as Commodity: Men and the Sex Industry," Wendy Stock looks at how the different forms of gender role strain potentiate men's participation in commercial sex—including pornography and interactive-media sex. Through a detailed, and at times shocking, discussion of the commercial sex marketplace she helps us recognize the harmful nature of these forms of nonrelational sex. In Chapter 6, "Sexual Harassment and Rape: A View from Higher Education," Earl L. Backman and Linda R. Backman discuss the violence of nonrelational sexuality, with an emphasis on their professional experience in higher education. The Backmans give careful consideration to the means by which traditional male socialization and contemporary culture give men double messages about appropriate sexual behavior toward women. They describe prevention and intervention programs to raise men's consciousness and curb male sexual aggression. In Chapter 7, "Male Gender Socialization and the Perpetration of Sexual Abuse," David Lisak discusses sexual abuse and violations of trust. He examines the part that male gender role and sexual socialization play in such violations of trust, focusing on the emotion-socialization process and the relationship between the inability to experience one's own vulnerable emotions and impairments in empathy. He reviews a considerable body of research on the interaction of childhood abuse, masculine socialization, and the perpetration of sexual abuse. Finally, he presents a case history of how a man on death row found his way back to humanity by coming to acknowledge the painful abuse he had experienced as a child.

Part III, Variations, contains three chapters on male sexual problems in three different contexts: development over the life cycle, ethnocultural context, and sexual orientation.

In Chapter 8, "Men's Resolution of Nonrelational Sex across the Lifespan," Glenn Good and Nancy Sherrod examine the nonrelational view of sex as a culturally prescribed psychosocial developmental stage which most men in North America enter and some successfully resolve.

The authors' developmental model depicts forces that encourage entrance into the nonrelational sexuality stage for men and outlines the developmental tasks associated with resolution of this stage. They then discuss the impact of resolution or nonresolution of this stage on the development of men from young adulthood through later life.

In Chapter 9, "African American Men and Nonrelational Sex," Vernon McClean provides a summary of what is known and what needs to be known about male sexual socialization and experience in the ethnocultural context, focusing on African American men. He considers how the sexual socialization of African American men differs from that of European Americans, and the implications of these differences, discussing a wide range of topics including opposite race fantasy; racism, sexism, and heterosexism; misogyny and abuse (both physical and sexual); and the sexuality of the adolescent black male.

Chapter 10, "Gay Men and Nonrelational Sex," by Roy Scrivner begins by analyzing sexual attitudes and behaviors in the United States, highlighting their conservative nature. Scrivner then discusses the negative effects of these attitudes, and of heterosexism and the traditional male gender role, on gay men's development and relationships. The author presents his Gay and Lesbian Couple Assessment Model (GLCAM) and explores the differences between gay men and heterosexual men and women in attitudes toward casual sexual relations outside of a couple relationship. Finally, he identifies negative consequences related to nonrelational sex.

The Coda, titled "Toward the Reconstruction of Male Sexuality: A Prescription for the Future," by Gary Brooks and Ronald Levant, addresses the future of male sexuality. The authors note the powerful resistance to changing men's sexuality. They outline an agenda for change both at the broad cultural level and at the personal level. They conclude that substantive change is not only necessary and possible, but also in the best interest of all women and men.

References

Brooks, G. (1995). *The centerfold syndrome.* San Francisco: Jossey-Bass.

Brooks, G. R., & Silverstein, L. B. (1995). Understanding the dark side of masculinity: An integrative systems model. In R. F. Levant & W. S. Pollack (Eds.), *A new psychology of men* (pp. 280–333). New York: Basic Books.

Fein, E., & Schneider, S. (1996). *The rules.* New York: Warner Books.

Gray, J. (1992). *Men are from Mars and women are from Venus.* New York: Harper-Collins.

Levant, R. F. (1996). The crisis of connection between men and women. *Journal of Men's Studies, 5,* 1–12.

Levant, R. F., & Kopecky, G. (1995–1996). *Masculinity reconstructed.* New York: Dutton/Plume.

Michael, R. T., Gagnon, J. H., Laumann, E. O., & Kolata, G. (1994). *Sex in America: A definitive survey.* Boston: Little, Brown.

Pleck, J. H. (1981). *The myth of masculinity.* Cambridge, MA: MIT Press.

Pleck, J. H. (1995). The gender role strain paradigm: An update. In R. F. Levant & W. S. Pollack (Eds.), *A new psychology of men.* New York: Basic Books.

PART I

THEORY

CHAPTER 1

Nonrelational Sexuality in Men

RONALD F. LEVANT

M ASCULINITY IS IN a state of crisis. This state of affairs is principally the result of the collapse of the basic pattern by which men have traditionally fulfilled the code for masculine role behavior—the good provider role—and the concomitant intensification of gender role strain (Levant, 1997a). In particular, there has been an intensification of what Joseph Pleck (1995) has termed discrepancy strain, the strain that results when one fails to meet the expectations of the code. In this climate, many men are confused and demoralized, and others react defensively to even a hint of criticism. Still others have responded by attempting to forge new definitions of masculinity.

I have proposed an approach to the reconstruction of masculinity in which we identify and honor those parts of the traditional masculine code that are still valuable, in order to provide a basis for male pride, and then specify those aspects that are anachronistic or dysfunctional and find ways to help men change these (Levant & Kopecky, 1995/1996). These latter aspects include men's difficulties in experiencing emotional empathy and in being attuned to their own emotional processes, the tendency for their vulnerable emotions to be transformed into anger, rage, and violence, and their inclination to limit themselves to a nonrelational orientation to sexuality.

This chapter focuses on one aspect of traditional masculinity that I believe is anachronistic and dysfunctional today: The nonrelational orientation toward sexuality to which many men limit themselves. This point of view is explored from various perspectives throughout the book.

An earlier version of this chapter was presented in a symposium, "Men and Sex: Biological Lust or Relational Love?" at the 103rd Annual Convention of the American Psychological Association in New York, New York, Monday, August 14th, 1995.

Nonrelational sexuality can be defined as the tendency to experience sex as lust without any requirements for relational intimacy, or even for more than a minimal connection with the object of one's desires. In this mode of sexual experience, objects of sexual desire are objectified, and at times are in fact objects (as in pornographic books and videos), which are pursued, in the agentic fashion so characteristic of men, to meet a set of needs—including the need to release sexual tension, the need for closeness, connection, and nurturance, and needs for affirming one's sense of adequacy as a man (Brooks, 1995).

An examination of nonrelational sexuality is timely because certain aspects of the traditional male sexual code have, come under intense scrutiny and severe criticism. The public deconstruction of male entitlement and abuse of power in heterosexual relationships began in 1991 with Anita Hill's allegations of sexual harassment against Clarence Thomas and the subsequent Senate Hearings, and continued with the William Kennedy Smith and Mike Tyson rape trials, the "Tailhook" and subsequent sexual-harassment-in-the-Navy scandals, Woody Allen's family problems, the allegations against Senator Bob Packwood and President Bill Clinton, the O. J. Simpson trial, and the Army sexual harassment and rape scandal.

Despite the condemnation of certain forms of male sexual abuse (such as harassment and rape), there persists in our society the view that men's nonrelational orientation to sexuality is "natural." These cases are often viewed as the acts of a few bad men, rather than as more extreme points on the continuum of nonrelational sexuality along which most men lie (Brooks & Silverstein, 1995). Hence, we first need to address the issue of how we understand nonrelational sexuality in men. Is nonrelational sexuality "natural," or is it socially constructed and socially learned? Moreover, if nonrelational sexuality is viewed as dysfunctional in today's world, are there still valuable aspects of the traditional male sexual code that should be preserved? Finally, if nonrelational sexuality is socially constructed, is there any evidence of change in the postfeminist era? These three issues will be discussed next.

A Critical Perspective on Male Sexuality

NONRELATIONAL SEXUALITY IS NORMATIVE FOR MEN

The research evidence supports the view that nonrelational sexuality is normative for men in our society. A set of findings suggests that men tend to experience sexuality as unconnected lust, which has no fixed requirement for emotional intimacy, in contrast to women's tendency to experience sexuality as an expression of relational intimacy. For example:

1. Men report thinking about sex more often than do women: 54 percent of men, as compared to 19 percent of women, think about sex every day or several times a day (Michael, Gagnon, Laumann, & Kolata, 1994; see also Leitenberg & Henning, 1995).
2. Men tend to have more explicit sexual fantasies whereas women tend to have more emotional/romantic fantasies (Leitenberg & Henning, 1995).
3. Men report masturbating more frequently than do women (Michael et al., 1994; Oliver & Hyde, 1993).
4. Men report purchasing more autoerotic materials: 41 percent of men as compared with 16 percent of women admitted purchasing such materials in the past 12 months (Michael et al., 1994).
5. Men hold more permissive attitudes toward casual sex than women. Symons and Ellis (1989) found that college men were four times more likely than women to say they would have sex with an anonymous member of the opposite sex who was as attractive as their current partner if there were no risks involved; women were two and a half times more likely to say that they would not. Oliver and Hyde (1993) found the overall effect size for sex differences in attitudes toward casual sex to be large ($d = .81$).
6. Men report having had more sex partners than do women (Billy, Tanfer, Grady, & Klepinger, 1993; Michael et al., 1994).
7. Men report having had more varied sexual experiences than do women (Billy et al., 1993; Michael et al., 1994).

Is Nonrelational Sexuality Natural?

The findings that indicate that nonrelational sexuality is normative for men are taken by some as evidence that nonrelational sexuality is "natural" and "the way things are"—suggesting that it is an essential and unchangeable aspect of being a man. Some evolutionary psychologists suggest that male promiscuity is not only natural but actually confers adaptive advantages by increasing the odds of reproductive success (Buss & Schmitt, 1993). To quote Archer:

> Sexual selection theory identifies women as the discriminating sex when it comes to mate selection. The other side of the coin is that men will show a greater preference for sex without commitment and for multiple partners. (1996, p. 913)

The debate between social constructionism and evolutionary psychology will be taken up in Chapter 2, here we simply note that an alternative view of evolutionary psychology has emerged that is more compatible with the views presented in this chapter (Hrdy, 1990; Silverstein, 1993). This alternative view of evolutionary psychology is supported by both primatological data (Haraway, 1989; Smuts, 1985; Sperling, 1991) and archeological evidence (Taylor, 1996).

Some psychologists not identified with the evolutionary perspective view men's nonrelational orientation to sexuality as natural. For example, Bernie Zilbergeld (1992), in what can be seen as an attempt to validate men's nonrelational orientation to sexuality, identified a set of characteristics that define "men's style of sex." These characteristics are:

1. Sex is very important to men (p. 162).
2. For men, sex has intrinsic value (p. 162).
3. Men use sex as a way of getting close (of showing love) (p. 163).
4. Men sexualize all sorts of situations and behaviors (p. 163).
5. Men tend to get aroused by aspects of female anatomy that they see (p. 164).
6. Men are more likely to be sexual initiators (p. 165).
7. Men tend to view sexual arousal as a runaway train; once in motion, it should not be stopped or deflected until it reaches its destination (p. 166).
8. Men tend to get aroused quickly (p. 166).
9. Men are goal-oriented in sex (p. 167).
10. Men tend to orgasm quickly and easily (p. 168).
11. Men don't necessarily want to be emotionally or physically close after sex (p. 168).
12. Men are concerned with sexual performance (p. 168).
13. Men are interested in a variety of sexual partners for the sake of variety (p. 169).
14. Men don't like to admit sexual problems, especially their own (p. 169).

In contrast to the conventional wisdom, certain perspectives in evolutionary psychology, and others who uphold the status quo, this volume takes the position that although men's nonrelational orientation toward sexuality might be *normative* in our society, it is not *natural* as in "of our nature," and, therefore it is not essential nor unchangeable. Rather, we view men's nonrelational orientation toward sexuality as the result of a set of socialization practices informed by a particular ideology of gender that arises from a particular gender-based power structure.

THE GENDER ROLE STRAIN PARADIGM

The perspective that informs this chapter and unifies the volume is the gender role strain paradigm (Pleck, 1981, 1995)—a social constructionist perspective on the psychology of gender. The strain paradigm does not assume that masculinity and femininity are the same thing as, nor are they essential to being male or female, respectively, but rather sees these definitions of gender as historically relative and socially constructed. In addition, the strain paradigm proposes that, to the extent that parents, teachers, and peers subscribe to a particular gender role ideology extant in a society or historical era, children will be socialized accordingly. The strain paradigm further asserts that molding children to develop personality and behavioral traits that fit prescribed gender roles creates several types of strain: Discrepancy-strain, which results when one fails to live up to one's internalized manhood ideal; dysfunction strain may result even when one fulfills the requirements of the male code, because many of the characteristics viewed as desirable in men can have negative side effects on the men themselves and on those close to them; and trauma-strain, which results from the ordeal of the male role socialization process, which is now recognized as inherently traumatic (Levant, 1996; Pleck, 1995).

Prior to the late 1960s in the United States, what has been termed "traditional gender role ideologies" prevailed (Thompson & Pleck, 1995). Hence, male children brought up in the postwar era were reared to conform to traditional norms of masculinity, of which Levant et al. (1992), identified seven:

1. Avoiding all things feminine;
2. Restrictive emotionality;
3. Toughness and aggression;
4. Self-reliance;
5. Achievement and status;
6. A nonrelational orientation toward sexuality; and,
7. Fear and hatred of homosexuals.

Traditional gender ideology serves the purposes of a patriarchal society by encouraging the socialization of males to develop those characteristics that are functional for attaining and maintaining power, such as toughness, competitiveness, self-reliance, and emotional stoicism. Women, however, are socialized in the opposite way—to foster attachment, emotional expressiveness, and caretaking—attitudes and skills that are functional for creating closeness and maintaining relationships. In a patriarchal society, men are given certain prerogatives vis-à-vis women, are allowed certain "rewards" for their hard work (such as objectified sex), and even more, are judged on their manliness by their sexual conquests. Hence, a nonrelational orientation to sexuality for men fits quite well with traditional masculinity ideology and patriarchal society.

WHAT IS VALUABLE, WHAT IS PROBLEMATIC ABOUT MALE SEXUALITY?

Taking a critical perspective on nonrelational sexuality does not mean that male sexuality, as traditionally defined, must be seen as inherently dysfunctional. Men's relative freedom from sexual inhibitions and unbridled lustiness can add a great deal to relationships. This is particularly the case as long as our society continues to socialize women to suppress their lust. However, male sexuality becomes a problem when nonrelational sexuality is the only way that men can relate intimately or sexually. The exclusive reliance on nonrelational sexuality is a state of being that is less than fully optimal in today's world, where men must meet women on an equal plane.

As with many other human traits, men vary in the extent to which they are limited to a nonrelational orientation to sexuality. There is a continuum of nonrelational sexuality. At one end there are mild, "take-it-or-leave-it," forms, in which a man is not limited to nonrelational sexuality but at times enjoys unconnected lust. Second, there are moderate forms, in which a man must fantasize about tantalizing sexual experiences in order to make love to his wife, or may be unable to experience a deep human connection other than through sexual acts, or may be troubled by certain features of his wife's body that do not conform to the cultural ideal, or may be the victim of the "Centerfold Syndrome" (Brooks, 1995). Third, there are more severe forms, such as repetitive infidelity, compulsive womanizing, and Don Juanism; or compulsive involvement with pornography, phone/computer/compact-disc sex, strip shows, "gentlemen's clubs," and prostitution; or sexual paraphilias, addictions, compulsions, and rituals (the latter as portrayed by Jack Nicholson in the popular film *Carnal Knowledge*). At the far end, there are the most severe forms, in which nonrelational sexuality, fused with aggression, animates sexual aggression against women and children in such forms as sexual harassment, rape, and child molestation.

THE TIMES, ARE THEY CHANGING?

The times may be changing in regard to nonrelational sexuality, at least as far as attitudes are concerned. A survey of 120 male undergraduates at a large northeastern university, using the Male Role Norms Inventory (Levant et al., 1992), found that the respondents rejected the traditional male role norm of Nonrelational Attitudes Toward Sexuality. Although this was a convenience sample of undergraduate males, and hence may not be representative of the population at large, it is at least indicative that attitudes may be changing. Here are the participants' responses to the specific items on the Inventory:

1. They disagreed that "A man should always be ready for sex."
2. They agreed that "A man should love his sex partner."
3. They disagreed that "Men should always take the initiative when it comes to sex."
4. They disagreed that "A man shouldn't have to worry about birth control."
5. They disagreed that "For a man, sex should be a spontaneous, rather than preplanned, activity."
6. They disagreed that "For men, touching is simply the first step toward sex."
7. They disagreed that "Hugging and kissing should always lead to intercourse."
8. They disagreed that "A man shouldn't bother with sex unless he can achieve an orgasm."
9. However, in a bow to traditionality, they did agree that "It is important for a man to be good in bed," and disagreed that "A man doesn't need to have an erection in order to enjoy sex."

The Socialization and Development of Nonrelational Sexuality

In this section, we present a theoretical model describing how traditional male-gender role socialization and normative developmental traumas can result in nonrelational sexuality. It is assumed here that such socialization and developmental experiences have been informed by traditional gender ideology, which made more sense in an earlier, harsher era, such as the period from industrialization through the Great Depression and the two world wars (Gilmore, 1990; Rotundo, 1990). It is also assumed that training male children to be tough, aggressive, competitive, and emotionally stoic is inherently traumatic (Levant, 1996). This theoretical model describes how traditional gender role socialization and normative developmental traumas impede men from being comfortable in, and enjoying, intimate emotional relationships, which in turn potentiates a nonrelational orientation to sexuality. The model also demonstrates how these socialization and developmental influences specifically mold male sexuality along detached, objectified, and agentic lines. Since my database consists primarily of clinical and research experience with white, middle class, heterosexual men, my comments cannot be generalized beyond that population.

MALE EMOTION SOCIALIZATION

Due to what seem to be biologically based differences, males start out life more emotionally expressive than females. Haviland and Malatesta (1981), reviewing data from 12 studies (11 of which were of neonates), concluded that male infants are more emotionally reactive and expressive than their female counterparts. Boys remain more emotional than girls at least until six months of age. Weinberg (1992, p. vii) found that six-month-old boys exhibited "significantly more joy and anger, more positive vocalizations, fussiness, and crying, [and] more gestural signals directed towards the mother . . . than girls."

Despite this initial advantage in emotional expressivity, males learn to tune out, suppress, and channel their emotions, whereas the emotion socialization of females encourages their expressivity. These effects become evident with respect to verbal expression by two years of age, and facial expression by six years. Dunn, Bretherton, and Munn (1987) found that 2-year-old females refer to feeling states more frequently than do 2-year-old males. Buck (1977) assessed the ability of mothers of 4- to 6-year-old boys and girls to accurately identify their child's emotional responses to a series of slides by observing their child's facial expressions on a television monitor. The older the boy, the less expressive his face, and the harder it was for his mother to tell what he was feeling. Buck found no such correlation among the girls: Their mothers were able to identify their emotions no matter what their age. Buck concluded that between the ages of 4 and 6 "boys apparently inhibit and mask their overt response to emotion to an increasing extent, while girls continue to respond relatively freely." (See also Allen & Haccoun, 1976; Balswick & Avertt, 1977; Brody & Hall, 1993; Stapley & Haviland, 1989.)

The Socialization of Emotion

How can we account for this "crossover in emotional expression" (Haviland & Malatesta, 1981, p. 16), such that boys start out more emotional than girls, and wind up, as adults, much less so? Using a social learning model, Levant and Kopecky (1995/1996) propose that four socialization influences result in the suppression and channeling of male emotionality. The mechanisms of emotion socialization include selective reinforcement, direct teaching, differential life experiences, and punishment:

1. *Mothers* work harder to manage their more excitable and emotional male infants (Haviland & Malatesta, 1981; Malatesta, Culver, Tesman, & Shephard, 1989).
2. *Fathers* take an active interest in their children after the thirteenth month of life (Lamb, 1977), and from that point on socialize their toddler sons and daughters along gender-stereotyped lines (Grief, Alvarez & Ulman, 1981; Lamb, Owen, & Chase-Lansdale, 1979; Schell & Gleason, 1989; Siegal, 1987).
3. Both parents participate in the gender-differentiated *development of language* for emotions. Parents discourage their son's learning to express vulnerable emotions (such as sadness and fear); and, while they encourage their daughters to learn to express their vulnerable and caring/connection emotions (such as warmth and affection), they discourage their expression of anger and aggression (Brody & Hall, 1993; Dunn, Bretherton, & Munn, 1987; Fivush, 1989; Fuchs & Thelen, 1988; Greif et al., 1981).
4. Sex-segregated *peer groups* complete the job. Young girls typically play with one or two other girls, and their play consists of maintaining the relationship and telling each other secrets, thus fostering their learning emotional skills of empathy, emotional self-awareness, and emotional expressivity. In contrast, young boys typically play in larger groups in structured games, in which action skills such as learning to play by the rules, teamwork, stoicism, toughness, and competition are learned (Lever, 1976; Maccoby, 1990; Paley, 1984).

The Effects of Male Emotion Socialization

The suppression and channeling of male emotionality by mothers, fathers, and peer groups has four major consequences:

1. Men develop a form of empathy or "action empathy," which can be defined as the ability to see things from another person's point of

view, and predict what they will *do* (Levant & Kopecky, 1995/1996).
On the other hand, men do not develop (as fully as do women) emotional empathy, which can be defined as taking another person's perspective and being able to know how they *feel*, through the vicarious
experiencing of the other person's emotions (Brody & Hall, 1993;
Eisenberg & Lennon, 1983; Hall, 1978).

2. Men become strangers to their own emotional life, and many develop
   at least a mild form of alexithymia (which literally means "without
   words for emotions") (Allen & Haccoun, 1976; Balswick & Avertt,
   1977; Brody & Hall, 1993; Levant & Kopecky, 1995/1996; Stapley &
   Haviland, 1989).
3. Men experience and express more aggression than women (Eagly
   & Steffen, 1986; Frodi, Macaulay, & Thome, 1977) and also tend to
   transform their vulnerable emotions into anger that is expressed
   aggressively (Levant & Kopecky, 1995/1996; Long, 1987).
4. Men suppress and shunt their caring/connection emotions through
   the channel of sexuality (Brooks, 1995; Hudson & Jacot, 1991; Levant
   & Kopecky, 1995/1996).

It is not difficult to see how the first three of these results of the
emotion socialization process would make it difficult for men to be
emotionally intimate, which would tend to potentiate a nonrelational
orientation to sexuality. Lacking an ability to read the emotions of
the women in their lives, to say nothing of the inability to read their
own emotions, would obviously make emotional intimacy difficult;
further, men's tendency to transform vulnerability into anger would
tend to make their wives fearful or angry and serve to keep them at a
distance. The suppression and channeling of caring/connection emotions through sexuality has a more specific relationship to the development of nonrelational sexuality, which we will examine in a bit
more detail.

The Suppression of Caring/Connection Emotions and Their Re-Emergence in Sexuality

Boys experience sharp limitations on the expression of caring/con-
nection emotions. Many men recall that their first experience with
these limitations occurred in the context of their relationships with
their fathers, for, in the traditional postwar family, hugs and kisses between father and son typically came to an end by the time the boy was
ready to enter school, as illustrated in the following anecdote (told to
me by men, participants in my course):

> The son, six-years-old, was tucked in bed by his mother and then asked for his father. The father came in the bedroom and said "Good night, Billy." Billy reached out for a good night hug and the father responded stiffly: "No, Billy, men don't hug and kiss."

I have heard similar stories from dozens of men, who recalled how their fathers abruptly withdrew affection at an age the father considered "too old for that stuff."

Pre-adolescent boys also get the message from their peers that it is not socially acceptable to express affection to, or receive affection from mothers (lest they be a "mama's boy"), girls (a peer might taunt, sing-song fashion: "Johnny loves Susie"), or boys (where anything but a cool, buddy-type relationship with another boy can give rise to the dreaded accusation of homosexuality). Socialization experiences of this type set up powerful barriers to the overt expression of caring/connection emotions, which thus get suppressed, and even repressed.

Later, in adolescence, interest in sexuality suddenly accelerates due to the combined effects of hormones and culture. Boys become aware of their sexuality, experience nocturnal emissions ("wet dreams") and masturbation, and become intensely interested in the release of their sexual urges. Prevailing images of women as sex objects (which are layered on top of the misogyny of boy culture) give boys' emerging objectification of girls a cultural imprimatur. Acting on messages from peers and the culture at large, adolescent boys also develop the need to prove themselves as men by "scoring" with girls, adding an additional layer of self-involvement, which serves to further undermine the relational aspect of sexuality. Boys' deficits in emotional empathy reinforce this self-involved objectification of girls by preventing boys from realizing how it might feel to the girls who are the object of their lust. The long-suppressed caring/connection emotions get swept along in this turbulent stream, but well outside of awareness. As a result, sexuality for boys becomes, at the conscious level, unconnected and nonrelational. For example, Michael et al. (1994) found that only half as many men as women reported that affection for their partner was the reason for having sexual intercourse for the first time.

Zilbergeld (1992) describes how teenage boys learn about sex. An absence of realistic, compassionate portrayals of sexuality combined with ubiquitous fantasy images of sexy women foster the development of unconnected lust:

> The message is clear: For men sex doesn't have to be connected to anything except lust, and it doesn't matter much toward whom it's directed. . . . The female in his fantasies is simply a tool to gain release.

And then to do it again, and again, and again. Next time it will probably
be with a different female. And he certainly doesn't have to like the girl
to have sex with her. (pp. 34–35)

Throughout adolescence, the caring/connection emotions remain an
underground, unconscious aspect of the sexual experience, reinforced
in this position by fear of the shame that results from violations of the
traditional code of masculinity. As an unconscious element of boys' experience of girls, these emotions merge with other unconscious aspects of males' experience of females, to be described in the next
section. Later in adulthood, the caring/connection emotions begin to
surface, taking the form, as described by many men, of feeling most
closely connected to their wives while making love.

NORMATIVE DEVELOPMENTAL TRAUMAS

Normative developmental traumas include the early separation from
mother during the separation-individuation phase, required for the socialization of boys, and what Hudson and Jacot (1991, p. 37) have
termed "the male wound."

Separation from Mother

The gender role socialization of boys includes the requirement of an
early and sharp separation from their mothers during the separation-
individuation phase of early childhood. Girls, on the other hand, can
prolong the symbiotic attachment to their mothers and avoid experiencing this emotional rupture (Chodorow, 1978). At an early age, boys
are given the prize of themselves as separate individuals; in return,
they are required to give up their close attachments to their mothers.
Hence, as boys grow up, yearnings for maternal closeness and attachment (which never completely go away) become associated with the
fear of losing their sense of themselves as separate. When such yearnings for maternal closeness begin to emerge in awareness, they often
bring with them terrifying images of the loss of the sense of self. Consequently, many adult men feel much safer being alone than being
close to someone, a phenomenon that Pollack (1995) has termed "defensive autonomy." This may be experienced as a fear of engulfment,
which often motivates male emotional distancing in marriage.

On the other hand, those yearnings for maternal attachment go underground and may get expressed in marriage in the form of a husband's (often unconscious, certainly unacknowledged) dependence on

his wife. This latter point was illustrated in a *New Yorker* magazine cartoon, a woman seated at the dinner table says to her husband, "That's right, Phil. A separation will mean—among other things—watching your own cholesterol."

Pollack (1995) has referred to the early separation of boys from their mothers as the "traumatic abrogation of the holding environment." This loss of the holding environment, which robs boys of the tranquility of childhood, is never acknowledged, much less mourned, leaving men vulnerable to developing what Boszormenyi-Nagy and Ulrich (1981) refer to as "destructive entitlement"—the unconscious belief that people in one's adult life are required to make up for what one didn't get as a child.

The consequences of this early separation from the mother contribute to men's difficulties with emotional intimacy:

1. As a result of defensive autonomy, men tend to find distance more comfortable than closeness in their relationships with women.
2. Due to unmet needs for maternal attachment, men will depend on the women with whom they are in relationship for basic nurturance, yet often have no awareness of their needs.
3. As a result of destructive entitlement, reinforced by the sense of male privilege that results from the patriarchal social structure, men have unfair expectations of the women with whom they are in relationships—often expecting to be cared for with no requirements for reciprocity.

It is not hard to see how these results of normative developmental traumas, like the results of the emotion socialization process, would make emotional intimacy difficult and potentiate nonrelational sexuality. In addition, Hudson and Jacot (1991) have described how "the male wound" (p. 37) leads to the elaboration of additional defenses that have a more specific relationship to the development of nonrelational sexuality.

The Male Wound

Working from a developmental model that has a "neighborly relation with psychoanalysis" (p. x), Hudson and Jacot (1991) described how men's early childhood separation experiences create a source of unease and dislocation that they call the "male wound." As a result of this wound, men tend to fear the loss of the sense of self at times of emotional closeness (a phenomenon similar to defensive autonomy), which is dramatically heightened in states of intense fusion that occur at moments of sexual union. However, men are drawn to intimate sexual experience because it represents a chance to "magically to recover a primitively symbiotic comfort" (p. 118). The choice, therefore, is:

> Either the male holds himself back from intimate experience, treating the people he desires as objects; or he abandons himself to it, thereby exposing himself to anxiety, even psychic annihilation. In the first mode, he is less than wholly human; a copulatory gadget. In the second, like a cortex without its skull, he is exposed to intolerable extremities of psychic pleasure and psychic pain. In the first case, he retains his sense of agency, and sees himself in instrumental terms, seeking intense but containable discharges of pleasure. In the second, he will experience a collapse of agency, and the need, thereafter, to effect repairs; to gather himself back together as a being who has boundaries to maintain and a life of threats to endure. (Hudson & Jacot, 1991, p. 118)

Hence, the fear of closeness that results from the male wound conflicts with the intense desire for sexual union, creating ambivalence and anxiety, and therefore the need for intrapsychic defenses. The resulting defenses represent a compromise between both sides of the ambivalence, serving to allow men to participate in sex without losing control. The result is a male sexuality that is detached, objectified, and agentic—or, in short, nonrelational.

This defensive aspect of male sexuality not only lies at the base of the nonrelational orientation to sexuality, but also sets the stage in some men for compulsive and even violent forms of sexuality. A man, unable to experience emotional intimacy (or "primitive comfort"), agentic in orientation, with his imagination stimulated, will be susceptible in ways that a woman is not to elaborations and displacements of sexual desire, resulting in the development of at least moderate forms of nonrelational sexuality:

> He is more likely than the female to displace his desire for a person onto part of that person or onto an object; and he is more likely to act out such desires in literal terms, rather than simply fantasizing about them. (Hudson & Jacot, 1991, p. 118)

Men who travel down the path of nonrelational sexuality to even moderate levels often find that their preferred forms of sexual activity tends to alienate women, thus cutting them off from opportunities to attain even a fleeting sense of "primitive comfort." As a result:

> he is likely . . . to infuse his behavior with misogynous resentment or hatred. He may resort inappropriately to violence or become promiscuous. He may also become a pervert. (Hudson & Jacot, 1991, p. 118)

Conclusion

Using a critical perspective on male sexuality in this chapter, I discuss how nonrelational sexuality is normative for men, but challenge the idea that it is, therefore, natural. The nonrelational orientation to sexuality to which many men are limited is an unfortunate but predictable result of growing up male in our society, where male gender role socialization has been informed by traditional masculinity ideology. Men tend to be limited in their capacity to fully participate in and truly enjoy intimate emotional relationships, due to the effects of male emotional socialization and normative developmental traumas. This potentiates a nonrelational orientation to sexuality. In addition, particular socialization experiences (namely, the suppression and channeling of caring emotions into sexuality) and specific results of normative developmental traumas (namely, the male wound and the resulting defenses) serve to specifically mold male sexuality along detached, objectified, and agentic lines. I have also posited that nonrelational sexuality, which exists in mild and moderate forms, lies at the basis of more serious problems such as sexual compulsions and sexual aggression against women and children.

This perspective on male nonrelational sexuality raises a number of issues. First, it highlights the need for research on these matters. Several areas where research might be particularly helpful include:

1. Developmental research specifically focused on the socialization and developmental influences that lead to nonrelational sexuality in men, with particular attention to the development of sexuality in adolescent boys.
2. Investigations of current parenting practices to determine to what extent parents are still influenced by traditional masculinity ideology and the sexual double standard.
3. Investigations of the sexual fantasies, preferences and practices of adult men at different stages of the life cycle, and among men of different ethnocultural groups, different social classes, and different sexual/affectional orientations.
4. Further investigation of the attitudes of young adult men, to determine the generalizability of the findings of Levant et al. (1992) that young men reject traditional male sexual attitudes. If these findings are found to generalize to the wider population of young adult men, investigate the factors involved in their rejection of the traditional code. Finally, investigate the relationship between sexual attitudes and sexual behaviors among young adult men.

Second, there is a need to educate men, parents, teachers, and others about the problems and limitations of the nonrelational orientation to sexuality, and that—though it is normative—it is not natural. In communicating with men about this issue, care must be taken to be empathic with men's experiences, and to keep in mind that none of us had any choice over whether we would be socialized to the mandates of traditional masculinity ideology.

Finally, clinical work with men might be informed by the perspective put forth in this chapter. For example, many of the midlife men I see in my practice tell me: (a) sex is among the most important aspects of their lives, if not *the* most important; and (b) they are disappointed in their sex lives. These two complaints reflect both the tendency of the male sexual code to overvalue sex, and the tendency of nonrelational sexuality to be self-defeating, by either alienating our sex partners, or by making us dissatisfied with our sex partners because they fall short of our fantasies. Working with men to develop emotional skills such as empathy and emotional self-awareness helps them resolve these complaints by broadening their horizon, such that they become more comfortable with, and come to truly enjoy, relational intimacy (Levant, 1997b; Levant & Kopecky, 1995/1996).

References

Allen, J. G., & Haccoun, D. M. (1976). Sex differences in emotionality: A multidimensional approach. *Human Relations, 29*(8), 71–722.

Archer, J. (1996). Sex differences in social behavior: Are the social role and evolutionary explanations compatible? *American Psychologist, 51*, 909–917.

Balswick, J., & Avertt, C. P. (1977). Differences in expressiveness: Gender, interpersonal orientation, and perceived parental expressiveness as contributing factors. *Journal of Marriage and the Family, 39*, 121–127.

Billy, J. O. G., Tanfer, K., Grady, W. R., & Klepinger, D. H. (1993). The sexual behavior of men in the United States. *Family Planning Perspectives, 25*(2), 52–60.

Boszormenyi-Nagy, I., & Ulrich, D. N. (1981). Contextual family therapy. In A. S. Gurman & D. P. Kniskern (Eds.), *Handbook of family therapy*. New York: Brunner/Mazel.

Brody, L., & Hall, J. (1993). Gender and emotion. In M. Lewis & J. M. Haviland (Eds.), *Handbook of emotions*. New York: Guilford Press.

Brooks, G. R. (1995). *The centerfold syndrome*. San Francisco: Jossey-Bass.

Brooks, G. R., & Silverstein, L. S. (1995). Understanding the dark side of masculinity: An interactive systems model. In R. F. Levant & W. S. Pollack (Eds.), *A new psychology of men*. New York: Basic Books.

Buck, R. (1977). Non-verbal communication of affect in preschool children: Relationships with personality and skin conductance. *Journal of Personality and Social Psychology, 35*(4), 225–236.

Buss, D. M., & Schmitt, D. P. (1993). Sexual strategies theory: An evolutionary perspective on human mating. *Psychological Review, 100*, 204–232.

Chodorow, N. (1978). *The reproduction of mothering: Psychoanalysis and the sociology of gender.* Berkeley: University of California Press.

Dunn, J., Bretherton, I., & Munn, P. (1987). Conversations about feeling states between mothers and their children. *Developmental Psychology, 23*, 132–139.

Eagly, A. H., & Steffen, V. J. (1986). Gender and aggressive behavior: A meta-analytic review of the social psychological literature. *Psychological Bulletin, 100*(3), 309–330.

Eisenberg, N., & Lennon, R. (1983). Sex differences in empathy and related capacities. *Psychological Bulletin, 94*(1), 100–131.

Fivush, R. (1989). Exploring sex differences in the emotional content of mother child conversations about the past. *Sex Roles, 20*, 675–691.

Frodi, A., Macaulay, J., & Thome, P. R. (1977). Are women always less aggressive than men: A review of the experimental literature. *Psychological Bulletin, 84*(4), 634–660.

Fuchs, D., & Thelen, M. (1988). Children's expected interpersonal consequences of communicating their affective state and reported likelihood of expression. *Child Development, 59*, 1314–1322.

Gilmore, D. (1990). *Manhood in the making: Cultural concepts of masculinity.* New Haven, CT: Yale University Press.

Greif, E. B., Alvarez, M., & Ulman, K. (1981, April). *Recognizing emotions in other people: Sex differences in socialization.* Paper presented at the meeting of the Society for Research in Child Development, Boston.

Hall, J. A. (1978). Gender effects in decoding nonverbal cues. *Psychological Bulletin, 85*(40), 845–857.

Haraway, D. (1989). *Primate visions.* New York: Routledge & Kegan Paul.

Haviland, J. J., & Malatesta, C. Z. (1981). The development of sex differences in nonverbal signals: Fallacies, facts, and fantasies. In C. Mayo & N. M. Henly (Eds.), *Gender and non-verbal behavior.* New York: Springer-Verlag.

Hrdy, S. B. (1990). Raising Darwin's consciousness: Females and evolutionary theory. *Zygon, 25*, 129–137.

Hudson, L., & Jacot, B. (1991). *The way men think: Intellect, intimacy, and the erotic imagination.* New Haven, CT: Yale University Press.

Lamb, M. E. (1977). The development of parental preferences in the first two years of life. *Sex Roles, 3*, 475–497.

Lamb, M. E., Owen, M. J., & Chase-Lansdale, L. (1979). The father daughter relationship: Past, present, and future. In C. B. Knopp & M. Kirkpatrick (Eds.), *Becoming female.* New York: Plenum Press.

Leitenberg, H., & Henning, K. (1995). Sexual fantasy. *Psychological Bulletin, 117*(3), 469–496.

Levant, R. F. (1996). The new psychology of men. *Professional Psychology, 27,* 259–265.

Levant, R. F. (1997a). The masculinity crisis. *Journal of Men's Studies, 5,* 221–231.

Levant, R. F. (1997b). *Men and emotions: A psychoeducational approach.* Newbridge Assessment and Treatment of Psychological Disorders Series. New York: Newbridge Communications.

Levant, R. F., Hirsch, L., Celentano, E., Cozza, T., Hill, S., MacEachern, M., Marty, N., & Schnedeker, J. (1992). The male role: An investigation of norms and stereotypes. *Journal of Mental Health Counseling, 14*(3), 325–337.

Levant, R. F., & Kopecky, G. (1995/1996). *Masculinity reconstructed.* New York: Dutton/Plume.

Lever, J. (1976). Sex differences in the games children play. *Social Work, 23*(4), 78–87.

Long, D. (1987). Working with men who batter. In M. Scher, M. Stevens, G. Good, & G. A. Eichenfield (Eds.), *Handbook of counseling and psychotherapy with men.* Newbury Park, CA: Sage.

Maccoby, E. E. (1990). Gender and relationships: A developmental account. *American Psychologist, 45,* 513–520.

Malatesta, C. Z., Culver, C., Tesman, J., & Shephard, B. (1989). The development of emotion expression during the first two years of life. *Monographs of the Society for Research in Child Development, 50*(1/2, Serial No. 219).

Michael, R. T., Gagnon, J. H., Laumann, E. O., & Kolata, G. (1994). *Sex in America: A definitive survey.* Boston: Little, Brown.

Oliver, M. B., & Hyde, J. S. (1993). Gender differences in sexuality: A meta-analysis. *Psychological Bulletin, 114*(1), 29–51.

Paley, V. G. (1984). *Boys and girls: Superheroes in the doll corner.* Chicago: University of Chicago Press.

Pleck, J. H. (1981). *The myth of masculinity.* Cambridge, MA: MIT Press.

Pleck, J. H. (1995). The gender role strain paradigm: An update. In R. F. Levant & W. S. Pollack (Eds.), *A new psychology of men.* New York: Basic Books.

Pollack, W. S. (1995). No man is an island: Toward a new psychoanalytic psychology of men. In R. F. Levant & W. S. Pollack (Eds.), *A new psychology of men* (pp. 33–67). New York: Basic Books.

Rotundo, E. A. (1990). *American manhood: Transformations in masculinity from the revolution to the modern era.* New York: Basic Books.

Schell, A., & Gleason, J. B. (1989). *Gender differences in the acquisition of the vocabulary of emotion.* Paper presented at the annual meeting of the American Association of Applied Linguistics, Washington, DC.

Siegal, M. (1987). Are sons and daughters treated more differently by fathers than by mothers? *Developmental Review, 7,* 183–209.

Silverstein, L. (1993). Primate research, family politics, and social policy: Transforming "cads" into "dads." *Journal of Family Psychology, 7*(3), 267–282.

Smuts, B. (1985). *Sex and friendship in baboons.* Chicago: Aldine.

Sperling, S. (1991). Baboons with briefcases: Feminism, functionalism, and sociobiology in the evolution of primate gender. *Signs, 17,* 1–27.

Stapley, J. C., & Haviland, J. M. (1989). Beyond depression: Gender differences in normal adolescents' emotional experiences. *Sex Roles, 20*(5/6), 295–308.

Symons, D., & Ellis, B. (1989). Human male-female differences in sexual desire. In A. S. Rasa, C. Vogel, & E. Voland (Eds.), *The sociobiology of sexual and reproductive strategies* (pp. 131–146). London: Chapman & Hall.

Taylor, T. (1996). *The prehistory of sex.* New York: Bantam Books.

Thompson, E. H., & Pleck, J. H. (1995). Masculinity ideology: A review of research instrumentation on men and masculinities. In R. F. Levant & W. S. Pollack (Eds.), *A new psychology of men.* New York: Basic Books.

Weinberg, M. K. (1992). *Sex differences in 6-month-old infants' affect and behavior: Impact on maternal caregiving.* Doctoral dissertation, University of Massachusetts, Amherst.

Zilbergeld, B. (1992). *The new male sexuality.* New York: Bantam Books.

CHAPTER 2

The Centerfold Syndrome

GARY R. BROOKS

IN HIS ARTICULATION of the gender role strain paradigm, Pleck (1981, 1995) noted that contemporary men are plagued by role prescriptions and proscriptions that are both internally inconsistent and, in many ways, psychologically dysfunctional. The inconsistent and dysfunctional aspects of the male gender role are nowhere more obvious than in the area of male sexuality. In this chapter, I describe the Centerfold Syndrome, a set of psychosexual attitudes and behaviors that is characteristic of most heterosexual men (some more than others) as well as reflective of the many ways in which normative male sexuality is problematic.[1]

The historical domination of "hegemonic masculinity" (Carrigan, Connell, & Lee, 1987), androcentrism, and the view of women as the "subordinate sex" (Bullough, 1973) have all worked to obscure many of men's problems. A "male" standard was held up as appropriate and healthy, while women's ways of being were viewed as inherently inferior. Teifer observed:

> Almost everywhere, standards of mental health, for women as well as for men, have been established by men and often reflect cultural and social norms in which inequality, discrimination, and the undervaluation of women are an accepted pattern of life. (1988, p. 8)

This "male defining" dynamic has been especially operative in the area of sexual mental health. For decades the literature has accepted the idea that men are naturally more comfortable, spontaneous, and

---

[1] Because I have the greatest familiarity with the sexual experiences of heterosexual men, I have conceptualized the Centerfold Syndrome with that population in mind. This is not intended to marginalize gay or bisexual men, nor to suggest that this sexual pattern has no applicability to them.

enthusiastic about sexual activity, while women tend to be repressed and conflicted (Zilbergeld, 1978, 1992). As a result, sex therapy has traditionally focused on helping women overcome their sexual repressions and become sexually "free." Sex therapy for men has tended to be "phallocentric" (Stock, 1988), that is, reserved for helping men improve sexual performance by overcoming impotence or premature ejaculation.

In the past two decades, this situation has begun to change. Spurred by the work of feminist critics, men's studies advocates have begun to look at past assumptions about men's lives and begin to question what was formerly accepted as natural and essential. In the area of men's sexuality, there has been considerable effort to define the social construction of men's sexuality (Fracher & Kimmel, 1987).

The Social Construction of Men's Sexuality: A Brief Overview

In arguing that sexuality is socially constructed, Gagnon and Simon (1973) were leaders in viewing sex as a learned set of behaviors combined with the cognitive interpretations of those behaviors. Gagnon wrote:

> In any given society, at any given moment, people become sexual in the same way as they become everything else. Without much reflection, they pick up directions from their social environment. . . . Sexual conduct is learned in the same ways and through the same processes; it is acquired and assembled in human interaction, judged and performed in specific cultural and historical worlds. (1977, p. 2)

In *The Socialized Penis*, Litewka (1974) described three primary elements of male sexuality: (a) objectification, where generalized women are a "concept, a lump sum, a thing, an object, a non-individualized category"; (b) fixation, where men fixate on certain portions of a woman's anatomy; and (c) conquest, where sex is seen as an adversarial contest.

Gross (1978) provided one of the most thorough and influential descriptions of the contemporary male sexual role. In this analysis, the prominent themes were (a) sex as central to men's lives and critical to men's sense of self; (b) sex as isolated from other aspects of life and relationships; (c) sexual feelings viewed as acceptable, while other feelings viewed as unmanly; (d) a close affinity between sex and aggression;

(e) sexuality conceptualized within a success and achievement framework; (f) sexual inexperience considered a stigma; and (g) sexual activity pursued in spite of the possible negative emotional and moral consequences.

Zilbergeld (1978, 1992) offered the "fantasy model of sex," which included a number of "fantastic" and dysfunctional myths about sexuality. Consistent with Litewka and Gross, Zilbergeld described a normative construction of men's sexuality that calls for men to value intercourse over other forms of sexual contact, to value "performance" over emotional connection, to value orgasm over sensual pleasure, and to resist the suggestion that men's sexuality is problematic in any way.

Conceptualizing the Centerfold Syndrome

My own thinking about men's sexuality has been organized around a constellation of attitudes and behaviors that I label "The Centerfold Syndrome" (Brooks, 1995). Like much of the theoretical work in the area of gender studies, mine also has been informed by a confluence of sources—gender studies literature, clinical experience, and my personal struggles with masculine socialization. Although this "research" method lacks the empiricism of "pure science," it is quite consistent with feminist theory and research methodology and is a natural outgrowth of gender-sensitive psychotherapy (Gilbert, 1980; McLean, 1996; Solomon, 1982), for example:

> An important aspect of being a "real man" is not thinking about being a man—being completely at ease with one's masculinity, and getting on with the job of dealing with practical matters. Recent studies seem to indicate that men are largely unconscious not only of their own motivations and the roots of their prejudices, but also of the range and variety of attitudes within their own sex. (McLean, 1996, p. 13)

I have found that (Brooks, 1990, 1992, 1995) successful work with men depends on recognition of my own gender socialization issues, as well as eschewing habits of viewing male clients through an overly objective lens. When I think about men's issues, I now think about "us," rather than "them."

I was raised as a man, with a close, if sometimes rocky, relationship with my father. I was intensely influenced by the stated and unstated expectations of my own "male chorus" (Pittman, 1990). For more than 20 years, I have worked as a therapist in several settings, where I have heard a wide array of men share their most intimate ideas about women and sexuality. For the past 12 years, I have supplemented that field research with avid consumption of the men's studies literature. Informed by experiences of other men, I've made determined efforts to "deconstruct" my own masculine socialization, trying to understand what drives men. Since sexuality has seemed to be a critical component of the masculine experience, much of my thinking has centered in this area. The Centerfold Syndrome is a product of this analysis.

ELEMENTS OF THE CENTERFOLD SYNDROME

The Centerfold Syndrome is a pervasive distortion in the way men are taught to think about women and sexuality. It is an outgrowth of the social construction of male sexuality and the dysfunctional ways that men initially relate with women and intimacy and later encounter women in the sexual arena. Although men are programmed to relate with women in ways consistent with the Centerfold Syndrome, these patterns are not exclusively the result of early training, as they are assiduously reinforced by the many destructive ways that contemporary culture portrays women.

It makes sense to think of the Centerfold Syndrome as having five principal elements. Since I have not yet conducted an empirical validation (such as a factor analysis of men's responses to a structured interview about their sexual attitudes and behaviors), these are not "scientifically" validated as discrete factors. The Centerfold Syndrome is presented not as a formal clinical syndrome, but rather as a useful distillation of ideas about the problems of men in encounters with women and sexuality. The five elements are:

1. *Voyeurism.* Although there is considerable discussion about the etiology and politics of the behavior, there is little doubt that "looking at" is a central feature of men's sexuality. Looking at women's bodies is a significant part of men's daily activities. The literature supports this impression.

Knoth, Boyd, and Singer (1988) found that teenage boys, in comparison with teenage girls, are far more likely to be aroused by a visual stimulus, such as a picture of a nude and have more visual graphic sexual fantasies. Girls, on the other hand, were more sexually responsive to romantic fantasies and more likely to be aroused by a partner in emotive interaction. Men, by far, are the largest consumers of nude magazines and autoerotic materials (Michael, Gagnon, Lauman, & Kolata, 1994). In fact, pornography has been described as "the largest entertainment

industry in America" (Gaylor, 1985). Six of the 10 best-selling magazines
are male entertainment magazines; and, there are more sex emporiums
than there are McDonald's franchises (Gaylor, 1985).

2. *Objectification.* Closely related to voyeurism is the objectification of
women and their bodies. Just as the Centerfold Syndrome calls for men
to be observers, it also calls for women to be the observed. Women become objects as men become objectifiers. In reviewing sex differences in
sexual fantasy, Ellis and Symons (1990) noted that "men are more likely
to view *others* as the objects of their sexual desires, whereas women are
more likely to view *themselves* as the objects of sexual desire" (p. 529).

Objectification of women and their bodies is closely tied to gender
politics in two critical ways—the authorization to "look at" and the con-
tainment of women as persons. Watching—that is, looking at someone—
is an act with deep political meaning. The powerful watch the less
powerful, while the powerless avoid eye contact and watch covertly. In
patriarchal culture, only men are allowed "authorized images" (Beneke,
1990) of naked bodies.

Considerable attention has recently been given to objectification as
a suppressive political strategy. Griffin commented:

> At the very core of the pornographic mise-en-scene is the concept of
> woman as object. A woman's body forms the center of a magazine. She
> spreads apart her thighs and stares into the camera. Her tongue licks
> her lips. Her eyes reflect back nothing. She is not human. . . . For the
> pornographic camera performs a miracle in reverse. Looking on a living
> being, a person with a soul, it produces an image of a thing. (1984, p. 36)

Wolf (1991) has been one of the most influential writers describing
how the "beauty myth" and "beauty pornography" are utilized to oppress women. "What it is doing to women today is a result of nothing
more than the need of today's power structure, economy, and culture to
mount a counter-offensive against women" (p. 13).

3. *Masculinity validation.* One of the most problematic aspects of
masculinity, as understood from the gender role strain perspective, is
that it is an elusive state. That is, men are programmed to seek out ill-
defined ideas of true masculinity and forever seek overt signs that they
"measure up." Unfortunately, even when they do live up to some masculine standard, men are never really sure that their manhood is established, since any failure can be cause for re-evaluation of manliness.

Pleck (1981) described several particularly powerful ways that men
are dependent upon women. Among those is the dependence of men
for "masculinity validation." "In traditional masculinity, to experience

oneself as masculine requires that women play their prescribed role of doing the things that make men feel masculine." (Pleck, 1981, p. 420).

While this masculinity validation dynamic has many components, it is especially relevant to the Centerfold Syndrome. In some very graphic ways, men are taught that a woman's body and its sexual responsiveness are direct avenues to feelings of virility. The sex manuals of the 1960s taught men to become preoccupied with women's orgasms. Zilbergeld (1978) noted that several myths of male sexuality centered on this need for sexual validation from women's bodies—"a man must take charge and orchestrate sex; good sex is a linear progression of increasing excitement terminated only by orgasm" (pp. 44, 54). Men have learned that a dramatic response from a woman's body—erect nipples, gyrating hips, a shuddering orgasm—can be interpreted as unambiguous evidence of manliness. Conversely, a cold, listless, or indifferent response from a woman's body usually leaves a man feeling ineffectual, inadequate, or resentful.

4. *Trophyism.* Men experience their masculinity in comparison with other men. The most dominant masculine worldview is a hierarchical one, with men competing to acquire manhood tokens that are considered to be in short supply. The most worthy tokens go to the worthiest men—the "winners," the "masters of the universe" (Wolfe, 1988, p. 8).

Gilmore (1990) provided critical insights into the process of manhood socialization with his cross-cultural study of masculinity "rites of passage." Gilmore found that almost all cultures have some form of manhood rituals, whereby young boys are expected to demonstrate courage, physical prowess, or emotional stoicism, before being accorded manhood status. In some cultures, these proofs of manhood included high-risk activities, such as diving in shark-infested waters or enduring extreme physical pain.

In North American culture, young men achieve masculinity status through modern-day "manhood rituals" involving violence, alcohol consumption, high-risk activities, and sexual conquest. The male competition for access to women's bodies begins in adolescence when boys compete to be the first to "score," to achieve the most sexual conquests, to "make it" with the sexiest teenage girl. The women's-bodies-as-trophies mentality, damaging enough in adolescence, becomes even more destructive in adulthood, when the "trophy hunts" of adolescence clash with men's developmental need to "settle down" and select a long-term companion (Levinson, Darrow, Klein, Levinson, & McKee, 1978). While collecting new and different sexual trophies may be celebrated among male adolescents, it is a sign of emotional immaturity in the world of most adults. Here we see some of the baffling contradictions of male sexuality. Nordstrom (1986) has documented that our culture distrusts unmarried men—only happily married men are considered acceptable for many offices of public trust. Our culture vilifies womanizers, yet simultaneously teaches boys to adopt the "James Bond" mentality. Oliver and Hyde (1993) have provided evidence that casual and promiscuous sex continue to be part of many men's sexual role.

Furthermore, the trophyism mentality has an additional major problem. While actual trophies retain their basic physical characteristics, human trophies do not. Women's bodies age, losing their trophylike characteristics, especially in comparison to newer varieties. Hence, the trophy-hunting man, initially satisfied with his trophy wife, must eventually face the maddening reality that his prize will eventually lose her lustre, while other potential prizes will emit near-irresistible allure.

Another aspect of this trophyism mentality makes it especially dangerous. Trophies, once they are won, are supposed to become the property of the winner, a permanent physical symbol of accomplishment and worthiness. This is not so with women's bodies. Women are no longer passive objects and have a growing voice about whom they spend their lives with. From the perspective of the trophy hunter, this is a horrifying trend, as he can never be assured that his trophy will remain his. This is a devastating thought for a trophy-hunting man, one that commonly provokes him to desperate and destructive reactions.

5. *The fear of true intimacy.* Men are created within women's bodies and receive their first experiences of love and security from intimate physical contact with their mother's soft and welcoming bodies (Chodorow, 1978). Fathers' bodies could provide similar sensual pleasures, but they traditionally have been unavailable to young boys, or, when available, have been stiff and threatening.

Though young boys treasure the opportunity to be physically close, both for sensual pleasures and for reassurance in times of vulnerability, they soon encounter social pressures to distance themselves from their mothers' bodies and establish a place alongside the bodies of men. This early developmental injunction was referred to by Pollack (1995) as "traumatic abrogation of early holding environment" (p. 41). This and similar developmental traumas have been thoroughly described by Lisak (Chapter 7). These traumas and subsequent relationship conflicts are endemic to traditional parenting of boys and cause lifelong ambivalence toward women's bodies. This ambivalence comprises the essence of this fifth, and most complex, aspect of the Centerfold Syndrome.

Young boys are conditioned to feel shame over feelings of weakness and vulnerability, encouraged to suppress their needs for sensual physical contact, and expected to develop male body armor with hard muscles and an emotionally stoic exterior. While they try to emulate heroes that are brave, intrepid, fearless, physically aggressive, and emotionally tough, boys cannot ignore that they are still insecure and crave physical comforting. At especially vulnerable times, they may allow nurturers to give some measure of soothing and comforting, but fears of humiliation quickly surface. Frequently, boys discover that some touching and physical closeness are possible through acceptable "boy" activities like sports and horseplay, but they remain continually aware that these sensual pleasures must not be acknowledged.

In short, boys in their childhood learn to associate women's bodies with softness, intimacy, and sensuality, the very qualities that they have been taught to reject. Despite their common exteriors of manic activity and rough play, boys often crave physical closeness and sensuality, but have no way to ask for it and few avenues to experience it.

In adolescence, young men find themselves besieged by two powerful yet contradictory forces—waves of sexual urgency and the extreme prohibitions against emotional intimacy. The sudden appearance of the hormonal pressures of sexuality catches young men unprepared; the fears of intimacy leave them confused and conflicted. Help is rarely available. Usually there is some token guidance in the form of caution about the need to be sexually controlled, but boys recognize that these admonitions are contradicted by their bodies, their peers, their role models, and their culture, where the dominant message is that sex is great and a man should acquire as much of it as possible.

Sadly, young men, who have had minimal preparation for the multiple complexities of sexuality, have also been encouraged to be physically tough and insensitive to emotional issues. Emphasis has been placed on aggressive and competitive skills, with very little emphasis on interpersonal skills of communication, empathy, and nurturing. Young men badly want sexual intimacy, but have learned to fear and suppress their needs for emotional intimacy and sensuality. They learn that the safest form of sex is the "slam-bam-thank-you-ma'am" variety.

It is conceivable that under optimal circumstances, sexual activity might help boys to rediscover these long-suppressed parts of themselves and might help them unlearn their fears of these "feminine" qualities. However, the opposite typically occurs, as young men commonly experience their brushes with sensuality and emotional intimacy as confusing and threatening to their hard-won masculine independence and desire for "sexual freedom." Therefore, sexual needs are given primacy for most young men, while sensuality needs continue to be suppressed.

As young men are learning to wall themselves off from too much emotional intimacy in sex—to develop nonrelational sexuality (Levant, Chapter 1)—they also are taught to sexualize all feelings of emotional and physical closeness. As a result, they cannot experience nonsexual intimacy. Because their closest approximations of emotional intimacy and most intense exposure to sensual pleasure have occurred almost exclusively in the context of rapid-orgasm sexual activity, male adolescents learn to closely associate sex and intimacy. Further, they are poorly tutored in distinguishing the two, as they are being raised in a culture that generally gives minuscule attention to men's sensuality and intimacy needs as it exalts men's sexual needs. Because of this confusion, it should not be surprising that a man who wants to replace his feelings of emotional distance and alienation with ones of closeness and connection, misinterprets the feelings as sexual ones, and assumes that he is just "horny." Men may seek sex when they really want emotional intimacy, sensual pleasure, or physical comforting. Since men are taught to see little connection between intimacy and sexuality, moreover, they will frequently engage in sex when they have no interest whatever in emotional intimacy.

Sometimes the distinction between the desire for sex and the desire for intimacy is irrelevant. In some cases, a sexual relationship may help a man discover his sensuality and intimacy needs, and he may develop a deeply fulfilling relationship with his partner. However, more often than not, this blurring of sexual needs and intimacy needs will create significant relationship constraints. When young men do not learn to distinguish the two sets of needs, they will be highly restricted in their capacity to develop and maintain relationships. For example, intimacy with male peers will incite homophobic panic. Intimate friendships with girls will be contaminated by compulsive sexual overtures. Limited in their pursuit of true intimacy, young men will be prone to overdependence upon sexual partners. Or, to defend against excessive intimacy, they may seek promiscuous sexual activity, rather than risk getting too close to partners. Even when remaining monogamous, young men will be prone to seek emotional distance through fantasy and emotional flight.

Ultimately, this fifth aspect of the Centerfold Syndrome is about how men are taught to suppress their needs for intimacy and sensuality, and come to invest too much emotional and psychological power in some women's bodies. Fearing their potential overdependence, men develop a preoccupation with sexuality, powerfully handicapping their capacity for emotional intimate relationships with men and for non-sexual relationships with women.

Etiology of the Centerfold Syndrome

Discussion of etiological roots of men's sexual behavior is fraught with controversy and is ultimately, as I will argue later, counterproductive.[2] The views most sharply divergent from the social constructionist position just outlined are those characterizing men's sexuality as an outgrowth of men's "essential" human nature.

Essentialists see men's sexuality as composed of a set of basic and innate preferences that characterize all men across the ages—the idea that men's sexuality is hard-wired. Whatever root cause is cited—evolution, genetic make-up, brain structure, hormones, or God's will—the essentialist position holds strongly to the idea that women and men are fundamentally very different. Not always stated, but clearly implied, is the idea the culture should not discount these differences and should make suitable accommodations. Significant change is viewed as either unlikely or many centuries away.

SCIENCE AND POLITICS

Before taking a closer look at the various essentialist etiological arguments, some mention must be made of the cultural context surrounding the science of gender differences. There is a well-established scientific tradition of searching for the biological underpinnings of differences between social groups—races, sexes, or social classes. Generally, these explorations have been initiated by scientists confident of their scientific objectivity, ethical uprightness, and disinterest in the political ramifications of their work. At its best, science has been driven by the innate need to understand one's surroundings or by a desire to eliminate human suffering. But in extraordinary times, science has been subverted by a need to justify political goals or rationalize mistreatment of social groups (Blier, 1984; Fausto-Sterling, 1992; Hubbard, 1990; Reed, 1978). For example, in Nazi Germany during the 1930s, efforts were made to discover the biological inferiority of Jews; African Americans have been blamed for their racial victimization by a line of research that claimed intellectual inferiority.

---

[2] Although I will be discussing etiological explanations for the Centerfold Syndrome in particular, this discussion applies equally well to the broader spectrum of problems defined as Nonrelational Sexuality (Levant, Chapter 1).

Fausto-Sterling (1992) described the 1849 research of physician Samuel Gage Morton, who published measurements of the cranial capacity of 623 human skulls, claiming that Asian and Caucasian brains were the same size, while African brains were somewhat smaller. Even though Morton's findings were later found to have been manipulated, they nevertheless struck a nerve and served as impetus for decades of research into brain differences among racial groups. Fausto-Sterling reviewed the history of research into brain size and found an intriguing pattern—scientists usually found evidence to support their initial expectations. Sometimes, however, they've had to be creative by finding novel ways to get the research to come out right, or by rejecting as flawed research that contradicts their expectations.

Fausto-Sterling's arguments are impressive and raise serious questions about the interaction of politics, values, and science. The solution to manipulated results has been improvement in scientific methods and institution of more rigorous experimental controls. Less likely to be resolved, however, are the more subtle problems created by the preconceptions and "blindspots" that shape the way experimenters frame their empirical questions. For example, Silverstein (1991) argued that research into the effects of maternal employment on children has been seriously compromised by conceptual bias. Because the prominent belief has been that mothers are responsible for children, the research has not focused sufficiently on the father's role in child development.

Fausto-Sterling summarized the problem well:

> there is no such thing as apolitical science. Science is a human activity inseparable from the societal atmosphere of its time and place. Scientists, therefore, are influenced—consciously or unconsciously—by the political needs and urgencies of their society. (1992, pp. 207–208)

Does this apply to the research on biological differences between women and men? Several highly respected feminist scientists certainly think so. Schreiber (1993) quoted Ruth Blier, a neuroscientist at the University of Wisconsin, and Ruth Hubbard, professor emeritus of Biology at Harvard University, who have recently called for greater attention to the political implications of the scientific inquiry into sex differences, suggesting that certain types of research have often appeared during historical periods of upheaval in racial and sexual politics.

Cited as a particularly blatant example of politically motivated research has been the work of J. Phillipe Rushton, a psychologist at the University of Western Ontario (cited by Fausto-Sterling, 1992). Based on poorly conducted scientific inquiry, Rushton claimed that different races have different-sized brains and penises, in an inverse relationship—bigger brain, smaller penis. Rushton also claimed that within each race, women have smaller brains than men. C. Davison Ankney, a colleague of Rushton, joined the argument by examining 1,200 corpses and purporting that women's brains were smaller.

My point right now is not to present this work as good science. It's not. It has received very little acceptance in the scientific community. The point is that sometimes questionable scientific findings are received enthusiastically by a culture hearing what it wants to believe. At times of major change in the roles of women and men, a large segment of the population is ready to have their anxieties assuaged by evidence of men's and women's innate gender differences. Research *is* political. As feminist scientists have adamantly insisted, research into sex differences is especially value-loaded. If women are seen as usurping men's turf, any shred of evidence suggesting innate sex differences may be used by some to justify gender prejudice. In her book, *Politics of Women's Biology*, Hubbard (1990) stated "it is well to be suspicious when objective science confirms long-held prejudice" (quoted in Schreiber, 1993, p. 237).

Well-constructed scientific inquiry has a vital role in guiding political action and public debate that is too often driven by fear, prejudice, and misinformation. Nevertheless, the assumption should not be made that scientific inquiry is without its own political underpinnings, which affects both how problems are conceptualized and how scientific findings are interpreted. It is well-established that scientists have blind spots and often cannot see what is right under his or her nose because current theory doesn't account for the findings (Kuhn, 1962). Therefore, it is vital that researchers who investigate gender differences clearly "spell out their beliefs, to step out from behind the mask of objectivity" (Fausto-Sterling, 1992, p. 10). In this way, it seems, scientists will be held accountable for their findings, not just in terms of their techniques, but in terms that address the broader cultural implications.

HORMONES AND THE CENTERFOLD SYNDROME

Between the third and fourth months of human gestation, the hormone testosterone begins to play the most significant role in prenatal development. Essentially, testosterone "masculinizes" the already formed genetic male embryo. Testosterone is critical; without it, the male embryo will develop as a sterile female.

For many, hormones seem to offer the simplest explanation for male-female differences in general, and sexuality in particular. For centuries, women have been portrayed as irrational and emotional creatures, prone to dramatic mood swings related to hormonal ebbs and flows. Women's menstrual cycle has been blamed for a range of negative female characteristics, ranging from hygienic impurity to premenstrual syndrome. Of late, however, with increased attention to what Brooks and Silverstein (1995) refer to as the "dark side of masculinity" (violence, sexual abuse, substance abuse, and relationship inadequacies), men's hormonal influences have come into question. To some, testosterone has become identified as the principal etiological factor. A range of negative male behaviors have been attributed to what some have jokingly called "testosterone poisoning."

The sociobiologist David Barash (1979) has argued that male hormones are principally responsible for a wide range of behaviors—social dominance, criminal activity, reckless driving, lynchings, genocide, and even warmongering. Similar sweeping claims were made by Goldberg (1973), who asserted that male dominance and political control were a natural outgrowth of hormonal differences between women and men.

Space limitations do not permit an exhaustive review of the many decades of research into the interaction between hormones and sexuality. In brief, the case for hormonal influence has been buttressed by (a) the commonly accepted idea of sexual latency, whereby male sexual interest explodes with the hormonal rushes of puberty; (b) primate research that demonstrated higher levels of sexual aggression among testosterone-injected rhesus monkeys (Kolata, 1976); and (c) the sex literature on treatment of sex offenders through surgical and chemical castration (depo-provera).

After years of research into the interplay between testosterone and sexual behavior, the general consensus seems to be that the relationship is far more complicated than ever thought. First, the previously accepted ideas of an explosion of sexual interest in puberty, have been challenged by more recent developmental research (Rossi, 1985). Erotic behaviors and sexual play occur earlier than previously thought. Overall, the actual pattern of sexual behavior for boys seems to be less one of sudden appearance of sexual interest at 11 to 13, and more one of a steady pattern of increasing sociosexual play throughout childhood. This pattern of increasing sexual interest, when viewed in light of girl's relative lack of sexual play, provides a strong argument that boys are taught to be sexual; their sociosexual play is part of the young male role and is not an exclusive result of surging hormones.

Second, both primate research and the research into treatment of sex offenders with depo-provera has resulted in considerable controversy. Chemical castration doesn't work very well, either with sexually aggressive humans or primates (Kling, 1975; Whitehead, 1981). The existing research has been shown to have major shortcomings in terms of failure to control confounding variables, carefully define target variables, and determine direction of causality. Fausto-Sterling noted:

> For monkeys as well as humans it is probably impossible to sort out "pure" biological effects from those reinforced through interactions with the surrounding environment. The significant effect of hormones may be to induce development of external genitalia, and the subsequent non-reproductively related sex differences in behavior may result from the subtle and not-so-subtle ways in which adults and peers (both monkeys and humans) react to knowing the type of genitalia possessed by each infant. (1992, p. 152)

After carefully reviewing the studies on effects of male hormones on "the human condition," Fausto-Sterling concluded "not a single one of these studies is unequivocal. Several contradict each other, while a number of uncontrolled variables makes others impossible to interpret." She concluded that claims of "clear-cut" evidence into the effects of male hormones are "little more than flights of fancy" (p. 141).

In this regard, Fausto-Sterling is in line with many biologists (Bancroft, 1987; Brown, Moni, & Corriveau, 1978; Kroemer et al., 1976; Lee, Jaffe, & Midgley, 1974; Raboch & Starka, 1973; Stearn, Winter, & Fairman, 1973) who have stated emphatically that while there is a complex relationship between testosterone and sexual interest in women, in normal men there are no consistent correlations between levels of sexual interest and testosterone levels.

NEUROCHEMISTRY, NEUROANATOMY, AND THE CENTERFOLD SYNDROME

Whereas hormones have long been popular explanations of sex differences for those in the biological/essentialist camp, a new physiological site has become fashionable—the brain. Media attention to sex differences in brain functioning has been enormous and most all coverage has trumpeted the same message—neurological science is uncovering basic differences in men's and women's brains that account for most gender differences. The new area of brain research has provided considerable impetus to the essentialist position that sexuality is "hard-wired."

Space permits only a brief overview of the research. Those claiming that there are different male and female brains have focused on several physiological characteristics: (a) total size (Swaab & Hoffman, 1984), (b) medial preoptic area (Swaab & Hoffman, 1984), (c) size of the amygdala (LeVay, 1993), (d) perceptual sensitivity (Moir & Jessel,

1991), (e) specificity versus diffuseness (Kimura, 1992; LeVay, 1993), and (f) development of the corpus callosum (Allen, Richey, & Gorski, 1991; de Lacoste-Utamsing & Holloway, 1982).

A range of carefully controlled comparisons have been made between the brains of rats, primates, and humans, either postmortem or through newly developed methods of Magnetic Resonance Imagery (MRI). Numerous researchers have claimed to have found significant differences and extrapolated their results to suggest explanations of complex interpersonal behaviors.

Among the more well-publicized findings are those suggesting that women's more developed splenium (corpus callosum) allows them greater ability to integrate data from left and right brain hemispheres. Although it is far from clear what this claimed difference would make in behavior, many have suggested that it might cause women to be more intuitive, more able to be emotionally expressive, and more able to integrate sexuality and intimacy needs (Schreiber, 1993). Moir and Jessel (1991) went so far as to claim that there was proof of major differences between women and men in their abilities to perceive and interpret sensory data from the environment. According to them, differences such as greater tactile sensitivity and wider peripheral vision (more rods and cones in the retina) allow women to more readily "grasp the big picture" and respond empathically to others. "The least sensitive woman is more sensitive than the most sensitive man" (Moir & Jessel, 1991, p. 23).

Let's consider the question of whether there are male and female brains. Taken as a group, the last decade's high-tech research studies of brain function are very impressive, making it tempting to see gender differences as rooted in different male and female brains. Perhaps, if our brains are so different, we should not be surprised to find men and women approaching sexuality from dramatically different perspectives. Perhaps the Centerfold Syndrome is just a by-product of the way men's brains are wired. But, once again, what seems to be a compelling case on initial review, collapses on closer examination.

First, and easiest to challenge, are the more extravagant claims of some brain research. Moir and Jessel's (1991) book *Brain Sex* has been particularly outrageous in claiming that the past decade of research into brain sex differences has produced "a remarkably consistent pattern . . . one of startling asymmetry." (p. 5) The authors' claims are grossly out of step with any dispassionate analysis of accumulated evidence and seem to be a prime example of what Schreiber (1993) referred to as a "many-turreted castle of speculation that we are repeatedly induced to accept as established fact" (p. 276).

Of particular concern is Moir and Jessel's (1991) misuse of controversial research about gender differences in perceptual skills. Whatever basis might exist for their assertions (the authors did not provide citations), there certainly cannot be sufficient justification to make such sweeping extrapolations. The capacities to process sound, perceive visual depth, differentiate smells and taste, are radically different processes than those involved in the complex interpersonal behaviors of experiencing and expressing emotion, developing the capacity for empathy and compassion, and becoming socially perceptive or intuitive. Readers cannot help but be insulted when told that the questionable gender differences in perceptual skills constitute major "hard-wiring" differences that fully account for the complex variations in how the genders approach interpersonal situations.

Other critiques of brain research require reference to biological experts. Once again, Fausto-Sterling (1992) has provided a rich analysis of the field and generally debunked the more unfounded assertions. First, Fausto-Sterling refutes the claims of significant sex-based structural differences in the hypothalamus, medial preoptic area, amygdala, and the sexually dimorphic nucleus. She has noted that the very few studies claiming to have uncovered differences were questionably executed, never replicated, and subject to far more within-group difference than between-group difference. The research on differences in the corpus callosum has similarly been dismissed by Fausto-Sterling. She noted that after the original corpus callosum research in 1982, 16 attempts at corroboration have produced no replication of the first study's results.

Even the most dedicated brain researchers acknowledge that the field is very much in its infancy. Although many expect ultimately to find a neurochemical or neuroanatomical basis for sex differences, many scientists are much more cynical. The most relevant point here is only the most zealous brain researchers would hold that the Centerfold Syndrome can be adequately explained by structural differences in men's brains.

SOCIOBIOLOGY, EVOLUTION, SEXUAL SELECTION, AND THE CENTERFOLD SYNDROME

The branch of evolutionary biology most immediately relevant to the etiology of the Centerfold Syndrome is sexual selection theory. According to Buss (1995), sexual selection theory departs slightly from theories of natural selection in that sexual selection is "the causal process of the evolution of characteristics on the basis of reproductive advantage, as opposed to survival advantage" (p. 165).

Sexual selection is thought to occur in two ways: (a) advantages accrued by the best competitors with each sex and (b) creation of "ideal"

characteristics for the other. In other words, any characteristic or behavior pattern that improves likelihood of access to desired mates—
strength, cunning, or social skills—will be perpetuated. Also, when one
sex agrees on what makes the other sex attractive—antlers, plumage, or
earning power—members of the other sex possessing those characteristics will be sexually selected.

The heart and soul of the evolutionary perspective is the following
powerful logic. At this point, women and men differ rather substantially on a number of psychological and psychosexual variables. Men
and women, by virtue of certain irrefutable differences in physical
make-up and role in reproduction, have always faced dramatically
different adaptive challenges. When we make efforts to explain the
differences between women and men, it only makes sense to examine
how the different adaptive challenges throughout human evolution
may have contributed to the observed differences in the present day.

Evolutionary theorists have been exceptionally ambitious and creative in their efforts to theorize how sex-specific adaptive challenges
have led to qualitative differences in how men and women interrelate.
Among the many behaviors and sexual patterns subjected to theorizing are those of rape, promiscuity, parental investment, jealousy, and
preference for visual versus relational sexuality.

Rape, from a purely sociobiological perspective, is viewed as a more
or less natural strategy of males to "maximize fitness"—to project genetic copies of themselves into succeeding generations. Barash (1979),
who studied mallard ducks, and Thornhill (1980), who studied scorpion
flies, both have conceptualized rape as an act whereby males who are
unable to compete for sexual access to desirable females—either because
they are too small, or, in the case of scorpion flies, unable to seduce the
female with the expected prenuptial meal—force themselves sexually
on the female.

Another sociobiologist, Trivers (1972) considered parenting as a behavior that is made more understandable through study of nonhuman
primates. Trivers theorized that "parental investment" in children is
markedly different between sexes because males can impregnate
females with comparatively little energy expenditure, leaving the im-
pregnated female with the enormous energy expenditure of pregnancy
and lactation. According to this analysis, males can be expected to be
promiscuous, seeking to impregnate whenever possible, and to be
parentally irresponsible when children appear, while females have a
vested interest in remaining monogamous and cautious.

Symons (1979, 1987) is the sociobiologist whose work seems to have
the most obvious relevance to theorizing about origins of the Centerfold

Syndrome. Symons has argued that adaptation and sexual selection have caused men to be more desirous of sexual variety, more visually-oriented, and more likely to take advantage of all sexual opportunities. Women, because of parental investment and the need for a more thorough assessment of a partner's ability to provide and protect, are destined to be more reticent toward engagement in sexual activity. Women have had to select the "best" males—men of high status and exceptional competitive abilities, who were willing to invest their resources in a given female and her offspring. Within this perspective, a male's "mate value" is determined by physical and psychological characteristics indicating good genes and likelihood of being a political and economic success. Supposedly, evolution has favored women who are slow to arouse sexually, but has not especially favored women who are visually perceptive. Instead, advantages went to women who could easily enhance themselves as objects of men's visual interest, were skillful at managing and manipulating men's sexual desire, and were skillful at discriminating the nature of men's interest. Females were selected on the basis of being able to evaluate male's desirability on "noncosmetic" cues and to experience sexual arousal primarily from tactile stimulation (which is more subject to conscious control):

> Since human beings, like all higher primates, are fundamentally visual creatures, and since female mate value was closely associated with health and youth, ancestral males were selected to become sexually aroused by visually detected characteristics that were reliable indicators of health and youth (e.g., clear eyes, unwrinkled skin). Clues to male mate value, on the other hand, are more complex and more dependent on psychosocial characteristics, which are not normally detected by stereotyped visual cues. (Ellis & Symons, 1990, p. 534)

According to Symon's reasoning, sexual selection perpetuates the Centerfold Syndrome, since it gives advantages to men who are voyeuristic, objectifying, fearful of attachment and intimacy, and who are willing to compete to acquire the attentions of the "best" females.

Buss (1996) presents an argument that "the destructive emotion of male sexual jealousy," which he describes as a "leading cause of spousal battering and homicide" (p. 161), can be understood through analysis of male-female evolutionary differences. Buss posits that the sex differences in triggers for jealousy—men more upset by sexual infidelity; women more upset by emotional commitment infidelity—are clearly traceable to issues of "paternity uncertainty." "Being cuckolded would have jeopardized years or decades of 'parental' effort" (p. 161).

In summary, we can see that sexual selection theory views the Centerfold Syndrome as a natural by-product of human evolution. To a theorist of this perspective the message is clear—our tastes, whether in terms of what "turns us on" in food or in our objects of sexual desire—are products of our adaptive history; they got us here. According to theorists like Symons and Buss, men enjoy looking at naked women, objectify women, compete for the most desirable women, and resist intimate connection because it is good for them and good for the survival of the species.

Sexual Selection Theories—A Critique

The work of evolutionary theorists has generated enormous excitement and controversy in scientific and professional communities, with reactions varying from exuberant adoption of its tenets to serious questioning of its methodological limitations, gender blindness, and political agenda (Fausto-Sterling, 1992; Haraway, 1989; Hrdy, 1990; Silverstein, 1993; Smuts & Gubernick, 1992).

Three principal types of counterarguments to evolutionary theory can be identified: (a) evolutionary theory is inferior science; (b) evolutionary theory is too narrow and gender-blind; and (c) evolutionary theory has heuristic value, but is somewhat irrelevant and bankrupt of ideas for future action.

Evolutionary Theory Is Deficient

Fausto-Sterling (1992) has provided some of the most impressive critiques of sociobiology and evolutionary theory. Although her criticisms are more complicated than can be fully elaborated here, her basic point is that sociobiology is closer to philosophical and political theory than it is to experimental science. Her objection is that controlled research is impossible. Since no scientific experiment can be designed that deprives humans from social input and developmental learning opportunities, human sociobiology, by necessity, will always be little more than scientific speculation:

> Thus, even if one were to grant a starting premise of human essence, it remains impossible to figure out which essences are adaptations arising under the pressure of natural selection, helping to increase fitness, and which just happened along for the ride. *Human sociobiology is a theory that inherently defies proof.* (Fausto-Sterling, 1992, p. 199, emphasis hers)

To illustrate this point, Fausto-Sterling has provided examples whereby decidedly nonadaptive traits, such as nearsightedness in albino animals of the Arctic, have survived. She notes that nearsightedness is more common in albino (white) animals. Animals survive predators better in snowy niches because they are white, not because they are nearsighted. Some things survive for reasons other than adaptation: Sometimes traits have evolved, sometimes they've just "come along for the ride." Sometimes fortuitous events and not adaptation may account for the presence of a breed of animal with certain traits. Fausto-Sterling therefore cautions, "the lesson from all this is that one must proceed with caution when trying to decide whether the evolution of a particular trait has occurred by natural selection" (p. 173).

A second substantial problem with sociobiology is that it broadly attempts to apply observations made with animals to the behavior of humans, without recognizing the phenomenal qualitative differences in the behavioral processes they describe. Rape in mallard ducks and scorpion flies may well be an attempt of males to get something they couldn't get any other way—access to a desirable and/or fertile female. However, making the shift from this behavior in scorpion flies to human behavior requires an unacceptable conceptual leap. In fact, a compelling argument can be made that the term rape cannot be applied to subhuman behavior without doing serious disservice to the concept and minimizing the multiple layers of meaning of the rape act. Whatever physiological aspects there may be to a rapist's motives, they are dwarfed by the motives related to cultural definitions of men and women, personal senses of meaning and powerlessness, rage, and the pathological desire to exercise control or revenge. Among humans, no complex interpersonal and social behavior like rape can be understood outside its sociocultural context. Similarly, to strip parenting behavior of all meaning except that of parental investment, forfeits any chance of understanding its many complexities. Jealousy, reduced by Buss to represent male rage about parental uncertainty, is certainly more than that. When we study men's socialization, their competition for women as symbolic trophies, and men's reliance upon women for masculinity validation, we realize that jealousy is a multilayered sociocultural phenomena, far more complex than the reproductive reflexes of subhuman primates.

A third problem for sociobiology in its attempt to pinpoint what is "essential" about human nature is the requirement that it identify a number of universal behaviors. To meet this standard, sociobiologists point to things like sexual double-standards, sexually-preoccupied men, the sexual division of labor, and male competitiveness and aggression.

But, as Fausto-Sterling (1992) points out, there is very little evidence of universal human behaviors. Those that come close to being universal are actually very different in their interpretations, dependent on the culture in which they are manifested. For example, though most all human societies have a division of labor by sex, few have exactly the same form. Most all cultures have a standard of female beauty, but there are sweeping differences in what is considered beautiful. Finally, even if we were to find certain near-universal human traits, we cannot know whether they survived because of adaptation of fitness maximization, or if they simply are the product of random genetic events. Even then, we cannot rule out another option.

> Quite early in human prehistory protohumans could have *learned* certain behaviors and taught them to their offspring. If the present-day world-wide population of humans all evolved from a small progenitor stock (on this point there is some, albeit far from unanimous agreement), then certain kinds of behavior might be universal, yet learned rather than genetically programmed. (Fausto-Sterling, 1992, p. 200, emphasis mine)

EVOLUTIONARY THEORY IS OVERLY NARROW

Although evolutionary theory has generally been attacked as inherently anti-woman, some feminists (Hrdy, 1981, 1990; Silverstein, 1993, 1996; Smuts, 1995) see merit in the approach when it is expanded to include women's experiences, that is, when efforts are made to "raise Darwin's consciousness" (Hrdy, 1990). Smuts (1995) closely examined the dominant evolutionary hypothesis about paternity and challenged the central ideas regarding the relationship between paternity certainty and male involvement. She expanded current theory by proposing a "reciprocity" hypothesis, whereby male care of infants would be high when both males and females have reciprocal benefits to offer each other and low when there is no possibility of reciprocal benefits.

Hrdy (1994) has challenged the concept that primate males are predisposed to be more sexually promiscuous than primate females. While Buss has argued that males must be promiscuous to ensure sexual advantage, Hrdy described species in which females "steal" copulations with roving males. In this way, casual sex is shown to be adaptive for females, since it confuses the paternity of infants and makes infanticide less likely in the event that a roving male overthrew the reigning male. Silverstein (1996) points out that estrus females in many species, such as Barbay macaques, savanna baboons, and chimpanzees, regularly solicit virtually every male in their troop. She concludes:

Recent feminist scholarship in primate research has documented the *overlap* in male and female potential for sex, aggression, and parental involvement. Rather than focus on a single variable, more recent theories emphasize the interaction of biological, ecological, and sociological variables. (1996, p. 161, emphasis hers)

EVOLUTIONARY THEORY HAS LIMITED RELEVANCE

Researchers who seek information about root causes of human behavior ultimately face what I call the "so what?" question—that is, what are the practical implications of the findings? For essentialists in general, and evolutionary theorists in particular, this is not a simple question. When sexual dimorphism is claimed, whether due to a difference in neuroanatomy or a difference in "biograms," essentialists have little to offer the culture at large—either accept and appreciate how mother nature created us, or "mess with mother nature" (or both). Sociobiologists and evolutionary theorists differ markedly in their recommendations. Some (Barash, 1979; Symons, 1979, 1987; Wilson, 1978) are more interested in the internal consistency of their theories than the practical questions of how to address gender inequities. For example, Symons rejects the idea that culture plays a significant role in changing men's sexuality:

any more than fast food restaurants cause tastes for sugar, salt, and fat . . . men are not partial to signs of female youth because they read *Playboy.* (1987, p. 119)

Addressing the question of rape prevention, Symons says young boys could be bred with social inhibitions that would "produce men who want only the kind of sexual interactions *that women want* . . . [this program] might entail a cure worse than the disease" (1987, p. 284, emphasis mine).

Wilson (1978) is similarly pessimistic about the potential for greater gender equality (though he claims to favor it):

The amount of regulation required would certainly place some personal freedoms in jeopardy and at least a few individuals would not be allowed to reach their full potential. (p. 132)

Some evolutionary thinkers, however, profess greater hope for potential change and, perhaps, even a degree of gender equality. Buss (1995, 1996), for example, claims to be an "interactionist":

Evolutionary psychology provides a powerful interactionist model. Human behavior cannot be explained without articulating evolved psychological mechanisms *combined with the social and cultural input to those mechanisms.* (1996, p. 162, emphasis mine)

Second, contrary to common misconceptions about evolutionary psychology, finding that sex differences originated through a causal process of sexual selection does not imply that the differences are unchangeable or intractable. On the contrary, understanding their origins provides a powerful heuristic . . . a guide to effective loci for intervention *if change is judged to be desirable.* (1995, p. 167, emphasis mine)

Sadly, even Buss, who appears to be the one nonfeminist evolutionary thinker most open to the interactionist perspective and the one most sanguine about the potential for change, has very little to offer by way of practical suggestions. Though he seems to acknowledge an etiological role for sociocultural variables, he says virtually nothing about how to approach sociocultural change. In fact, like many sociobiologists and evolutionary theorists, Buss seems to accept the idea that fundamental change in sexuality is really *for women.* For example, he strongly opposes excessive criticism of "male" adaptive strategies and sexual style, regardless of the pain they generate in their current contexts.

Those of us who embrace the gender role strain paradigm believe that many aspects of traditional male sexual socialization *are* inherently harmful to men. While *we* are alarmed at how we men are programmed to be sexually promiscuous and compulsively hypersexed, Buss and Symons refer to these patterns merely as "the desire for sexual variety." There's a big difference between seeing compulsive sexuality as a major barrier to fuller emotional functioning and simply dismissing it as a "boys-will-be-boys" interest in occasional trips to the sexual buffet table. If evolutionary theorists wish to be considered true interactionists, they should be as familiar with the new psychology of men and gender role strain theory as they are with their theories of human evolution.

Women's studies and men's studies are branches of academic scholarship that shift attention from *sex* to *gender.* That is, rather than focusing on biology, we examine the multiple ways that cultures enhance or minimize biological sex differences and imbue biologically-driven interactions with nuances of meaning. Sociobiologists (Buss, 1996; Wilson, 1978) have challenged social constructionists to become interactionists by studying and appreciating "our evolved psychological mechanisms" (Buss, 1995, p. 167). While some social constructionists are insufficiently aware of biological and evolutionary givens, sociobiologists, even when claiming to be interactionists, seem appallingly unaware of, and uninterested in the gender role strain model and its implications for gender relations. For example, rather than viewing sexual behavior as inextricably bound up with all other aspects of masculine socialization (e.g., emotion socialization, the good-provider role, homophobia, misogyny), they isolate sex as simply an adaptive strategy for reproduction. Sexual behavior is far more than biology. Fundamental change in men's sexual behavior requires a far more sophisticated appreciation of the social construction of men's sexuality.

Essentialists endeavor to find basic truths and explanations for why things are the way they are. At their worst, they suggest immutable human nature and reify the status quo. Social constructionists focus on contextual and cultural issues. Buss and others are right when they say that social constructionists *must* understand and appreciate certain biological and evolutionary givens. However, the true interactionist, while sobered by the proven truths of the essentials (not just the speculations), still pushes ahead to struggle to find the best possible adaptation between men and women and their environments. For example, even when scientists argue about whether humans are inherently violent, no one seriously suggests that violence be accepted—all call for a maximal effort to create the best possible environment to decrease the likelihood of violence. The case is identical for nonrelational sexuality—whatever the biological or evolutionary factors driving men to act this way, we must do all we can to counter these factors because this sexual behavior is harmful to women *and* men.

Essentialists have done none of this work and have been woefully silent about how to create egalitarian environments. It *can* be done. We now know that just as biology determines social context, social context also changes biology, from testosterone production to brain chemistry:

> Any biological theory about human behavior that ignores the complex of forces affecting behavior as well as the profound two-way interactions between mind and body is scientifically hopeless. (Fausto-Sterling, 1992, pp. 220–221)

Finally, as noted before, there is something relatively moot about the evolutionary argument since the entire sociocultural climate has undergone sweeping and radical change in the past 100 years—a speck of time to evolutionary thinkers:

> Any mechanism—structure, function, or behavior—that is adaptive *on the average* for populations *over long time spans* . . . may become largely

maladaptive when there are radical changes in environmental conditions. When we consider the profound changes in human environmental conditions within *very recent* evolutionary times, it becomes entirely conceivable that some of the mechanisms which evolved of millions of years of mammalian, primate, and human evolution may now be less useful than they once were. Since cultural change has moved much more rapidly than genetic change, the *emotional response tendencies* that have been built into us through their suitability for a long succession of past environments may be less suitable for the very different *present* environment. In this sense there may be some respects in which modern man is obsolete. (Washburn & Jay, 1977)

In summary, even if there were evidence that the Centerfold Syndrome is inherent in men's essence (and there's almost none), that still doesn't change the fact that this pattern of sexuality is badly out of touch with contemporary times, and some of the more obsolete aspects of men's sexuality need to be thoroughly revised. Social constructionists, by far, have the most to say on this matter.

What Causes the Centerfold Syndrome and Nonrelational Sexuality?

Men's sexuality is best understood by examining the social construction of masculinity and sexuality. The basic premise of this position is that sexuality consists of a learned set of behaviors and the cognitive interpretations of those behaviors. People learn to become sexual in the same way as they become everything else. Elsewhere (Brooks, 1995), I have presented an etiological model for men's acquisition of the Centerfold Syndrome. This model adapts the work of Walen and Roth (1987), who view learning as a complex process involving continual interaction between perception, behavior, and evaluation of behavior. My model additionally attempts to incorporate the sociopolitical perspectives of feminism, enriched by the newer perspectives of men's studies.

I make no simplistic contentions that we consider only the *nurture* side of the hoary dualism debate. As an interactionist, I believe that we must carefully consider the evidence being uncovered by biological scientists, endocrinologists, neuroanatomists, and evolutionary theorists. However, as I review my clinical experience with a wide range of men, my review of the sexuality literature, and my own subjective experiences with sexuality socialization, I am awed by the power of the social environment to shape and interpret basic biological reality. Moreover, I am impressed by research demonstrating the bidirectional influence of physiology and social experience. Not only have we learned that hormones affect behavior, but we also now know that hormone levels are also greatly affected by environmental conditions (Purifoy & Koopmans, 1980). Furthermore, the human brain (particularly the cerebral cortex) is far more "plastic" (i.e., structurally alterable) than previously thought (Clark, Allard, Jenkins, & Merzenich, 1988; Pons et al., 1991). Finally, the social constructionist perspective is simply the approach with the most relevance.

If, as I firmly believe, men's sexuality is a product of the way sex has been presented and taught to men, these lessons have been supported by patriarchal politics and pressures on men to prove themselves through exploitation of women's bodies (and their own). This teaching has been grossly deficient in terms of straightforward teaching about sexuality. These circumstances are a tragic result of a culture that profits from manipulating images of women's bodies and grossly impairing men's capacity to develop deeply intimate relationships with women.

Although it isn't easy to change culture, it can be done. In fact, many of the most pressing issues confronting contemporary men are the direct result of the sweeping changes in gender politics of the past three decades. Those of us committed to the "new psychology of men (Levant & Pollack, 1995) are interested in utilizing these sweeping changes to challenge men to develop new masculinities that are more flexible, adaptive, and compassionate to women and to men.

References

Allen, L. S., Richey, Y. M., & Gorski, R. A. (1991). Sex differences in the corpus callosum of the living human being. *Journal of Neuroscience, 11,* 933–942.

Bancroft, J. (1987). A physiological approach. In J. Geer & W. T. O'Donohue (Eds.), *Theories of human sexuality* (pp. 411–418). New York: Plenum Press.

Barash, D. (1979). *The whisperings within.* New York: Penguin Books.

Beneke, T. (1990). Heterosexual porn. In M. Kimmel (Ed.), *Men confront pornography* (pp. 168–187). New York: Crown.

Blier, R. (1984). *Science and gender.* Elmsford, NY: Pergamon Press.

Brooks, G. R. (1990). The inexpressive male and vulnerability to therapist-patient sexual exploitation. *Psychotherapy: Theory, Research, Training, 27,* 344–349.

Brooks, G. R. (1992). Gender-sensitive family therapy in a violent culture. *Topics in Family Psychology and Counseling, 1,* 24–36.

Brooks, G. R. (1995). *The centerfold syndrome: How men can overcome objectification and achieve intimacy with women.* San Francisco: Jossey-Bass.

Brooks, G. R., & Silverstein, L. B. (1995). Understanding the dark side of masculinity: An integrative systems model. In R. F. Levant & W. S. Pollack (Eds.), *A new psychology of men* (pp. 280–333). New York: Basic Books.

Brown, W. (1987). Hormones and sexual aggression in the male: Commentary. *Integrative Psychiatry, 5,* 91–93.

Brown, W. A., Moni, P. M., & Corriveau, D. P. (1978). Serum testosterone and sexual activity and interest in men. *Archives of Sexual Behavior, 7,* 97–103.

Bullough, V. (1973). *The subordinate sex: A history of attitudes toward women.* Athens: University of Georgia Press.

Buss, D. M. (1995). Psychological sex differences: Origins through sexual selection. *American Psychologist, 50,* 164–168.

Buss, D. M. (1996). Paternity uncertainty and the complex repertoire of human mating strategies. *American Psychologist, 51,* 161–163.

Carrigan, T., Connell, B., & Lee, J. (1987). Toward a new sociology of masculinity. In H. Brod (Ed.), *The making of masculinities: The new men's studies* (pp. 63–100). Boston: Allen & Unwin.

Chodorow, N. (1978). *The reproduction of mothering.* Berkeley: University of California Press.

Clark, S. A., Allard, T., Jenkins, W. M., & Merzenich, M. M. (1988). Receptive fields in the body-surface map in adult cortex defined by temporally correlated inputs. *Nature, 332,* 444–445.

de Lacoste-Utamsing, M. C., & Holloway, R. (1982). Sexual dimorphism in the human corpus callosum. *Science, 216,* 1431–1432.

Ellis, B. J., & Symons, D. (1990). Sex differences in sexual fantasy: An evolutionary psychological approach. *Journal of Sex Research, 27,* 527–555.

Fausto-Sterling, A. (1992). *Myths of gender: Biological theories about women and men.* New York: Basic Books.

Fausto-Sterling, A. (1993, October). Sex, race, brains, and calipers. *Discover,* 32–37.

Fracher, J., & Kimmel, M. (1987). Hard issues and soft spots: Counseling men about sexuality. In M. Scher, M. Stevens, G. Good, & G. Eichenfield (Eds.), *Handbook of counseling and psychotherapy with men* (pp. 83–96). Newbury Park, CA: Sage.

Gagnon, J. H. (1977). *Human sexualities.* Chicago: Scott, Foresman.

Gagnon, J. H., & Simon, W. (1973). *Sexual conduct: The social sources of human sexuality.* Chicago: Aldine.

Gaylor, L. (1985, July/August). Pornography: A humanist issue. *The Humanist,* 34–40.

Gilbert, L. A. (1980). Feminist therapy. In A. M. Brodsky & R. Hare-Mustin (Eds.), *Women and psychotherapy* (pp. 245–266). New York: Guilford Press.

Gilmore, D. D. (1990). *Manhood in the making: Cultural concepts of masculinity.* New Haven, CT: Yale University Press.

Goldberg, S. (1973). *The inevitability of patriarchy.* New York: Morrow.

Griffin, S. (1984). *Pornography and silence.* New York: Harper & Row.

Gross, A. (1978). The male role and heterosexual behavior. *Journal of Social Issues, 34,* 87–107.

Haraway, D. (1989). *Primate visions.* New York: Routledge & Kegan Paul.

Hrdy, S. B. (1981). *The woman that never evolved.* Cambridge, MA: Harvard University Press.

Hrdy, S. B. (1990). Raising Darwin's consciousness: Females and evolutionary theory. *Zygon, 25,* 129–137.

Hrdy, S. B. (1994). What do women want? In T. A. Bass (Ed.), *Reinventing the future: Conversation with the world's leading scientists* (pp. 7–25). Reading, MA: Addison-Wesley.

Hubbard, R. (1990). *The politics of women's biology.* Brunswick, NJ: Rutgers University Press.

Kimura, D. (1992, September). Sex differences in the brain. *Scientific American,* 119–125.

Kling, A. (1975). Testosterone and aggressive behavior in men and nonhuman primates. In B. Eleftheriori & R. Spot (Eds.), *Hormonal correlates of behavior.* New York: Plenum Press.

Knoth, R., Boyd, K., & Singer, B. (1988). Empirical tests of sexual selection theory: Predictions of sex differences in onset, intensity, and time course of sexual arousal. *Journal of Sex Research, 24,* 73–89.

Kolata, G. B. (1976). Primate behavior: Sex and the dominant male. *Science, 191,* 55–56.

Kroemer, H. C., Becker, H. B., Brodie, H., Doering, C. H., Moos, R. H., & Hamburg, D. A. (1976). Orgasmic frequency and plasma testosterone levels in normal human males. *Archives of Sexual Behavior, 5,* 125–132.

Kuhn, T. S. (1962). *The structure of scientific revolutions.* Chicago: Chicago University Press.

Lee, P. A., Jaffe, R. B., & Midgely, A. R. (1974). Lack of alteration of serum gonadotrophins in men and women following sexual intercourse. *American Journal of Obstetrics and Gynecology, 120,* 985–987.

Levant, R. F., & Pollack, W. S. (1995). *A new psychology of men.* New York: Basic Books.

LeVay, S. (1993). *The sexual brain.* Cambridge, MA: MIT Press.

Levinson, D., Darrow, C., Klein, E., Levinson, M., & McKee, B. (1978). *The seasons of a man's life.* New York: Knopf.

Litewka, J. (1974). The socialized penis. *Liberation, 18*(7), 61–69.

McLean, C. (1996). The politics of men's pain. In C. McLean, M. Carey, & C. White (Eds.), *Men's ways of being* (pp. 11–28). Boulder, CO: Westview Press.

Michael, R. T., Gagnon, J. H., Lauman, E. O., & Kolata, G. (1994). *Sex in America: A definitive survey.* Boston: Little, Brown.

Moir, A., & Jessel, D. (1991). *Brain sex: The real difference between women and men.* New York: Carol Publishing Group.

Nordstrom, B. (1986). Why men get married: More and less traditional men compared. In R. A. Lewis & R. E. Salt (Eds.), *Men in families* (pp. 31–53). Newbury Park, CA: Sage.

Oliver, M. B., & Hyde, J. S. (1993). Gender differences in sexuality: A meta-analysis. *Psychological Bulletin, 114,* 29–51.

Peplau, L. A., Rubin, Z., & Hill, C. T. (1977). Sexual intimacy in dating relationships. *Journal of Social Issues, 33,* 86–109.

Pittman, F. (1990). The masculine mystique. *Family Therapy Networker, 14*(3), 40–52.

Pleck, J. H. (1981). *The myth of masculinity.* Cambridge, MA: MIT Press.

Pleck, J. H. (1995). The gender role strain paradigm: An update. In R. F. Levant & W. S. Pollack (Eds.), *A new psychology of men* (pp. 11–32). New York: Basic Books.

Pollack, W. S. (1995). No man is an island. In R. F. Levant & W. S. Pollack (Eds.), *A new psychology of men* (pp. 33–67). New York: Basic Books.

Pons, T. P., Garraghty, P. E., Ommaya, A. K., Kaas, J. H., Taub, E., & Mishkin, M. (1991). Massive cortical reorganization after sensory deafferation in adult macaques. *Science, 252,* 1857–1860.

Purifoy, F., & Koopmans, L. (1980). Androstenedione, testosterone, and free testosterone concentration in women of various occupations. *Social Biology, 26,* 179–188.

Raboch, J., & Starka, L. (1973). Reported coital activity of men and levels of plasma testosterone. *Archives of Sexual Behavior, 2,* 309–315.

Reed, E. (1978). *Sexism and science.* New York: Pathfinder.

Rossi, A. S. (1985). *Gender and the life course.* New York: Aldine.

Schreiber, L. (1993, April). The search for his and her brains. *Glamour,* 234–237, 274–276.

Silverstein, L. B. (1991), Transforming the debate about child care and maternal employment. *American Psychologist, 46,* 1025–1032.

Silverstein, L. B. (1993). Primate research, family politics, and social policy. Transforming "cads" into "dads." *Journal of Family Psychology, 7,* 267–282.

Silverstein, L. B. (1996). Evolutionary psychology and the search for sex differences. *American Psychologist, 51,* 160–161.

Smuts, B. S. (1995). The evolutionary origins of patriarchy. *Human Nature, 6,* 1–30.

Smuts, B. S., & Gubernick, D. J. (1992). Male-infant relationships in nonhuman primates: Paternal investment or parenting effort? In B. S. Hewlett (Ed.), *Father-child relations, cultural and biosocial contexts* (pp. 1–30). New York: Aldine de Gruyter.

Solomon, K. (1982). Individual psychotherapy and changing masculine roles: Dimensions of gender-role psychotherapy. In K. Solomon & N. Levy (Eds.), *Men in transition: Theory and therapy* (pp. 247–274). New York: Plenum Press.

Stearn, E. L., Winter, J. S. D., & Fairman, C. (1973). Effects of coitus on gonadotropins, prolactin, and sex steroid levels in men. *Journal of Clinical Endocrinology and Metabolism, 37,* 687–691.

Stock, W. (1988). Propping up the phallocracy: A feminist critique of sex therapy and research. In E. Cole & E. D. Rothblum (Eds.), *Women and sex therapy* (pp. 23–41). New York: Haworth Press.

Swaab, D. F., & Hoffman, M. A. (1984). Sexual differentiation of the human brain: A historical perspective. In G. J. de Vries, J. de Bruib, H. Uylings, & M. A. Corner (Eds.), *Sex differences in the brain: Progress in brain research* (pp. 361–374). Amsterdam, The Netherlands: Elsevier.

Symons, D. (1979). *The evolution of human sexuality.* New York: Oxford University Press.

Symons, D. (1987). An evolutionary approach: Can Darwin's view of life shed light on human sexuality? In J. Geer & W. T. O'Donohue (Eds.), *Theories of human sexuality* (pp. 91–125). New York: Plenum Press.

Teifer, L. (1988). A feminist critique of the sexual dysfunction nomenclature. In E. Cole & E. D. Rothblum (Eds.), *Women and sex therapy* (pp. 5–21). New York: Haworth Press.

Thornhill, R. (1980). Rape in Panorpa scorpionflies and a general rape hypothesis. *Animal Behavior, 28,* 57–65.

Trivers, R. (1972). Parental investment and sexual selection. In B. Campbell (Ed.), *Sexual selection and the descent of man, 1871–1971* (pp. 136–179). Chicago: Aldine.

Walen, S. R., & Roth, D. (1987). A cognitive approach. In J. Geer & W. T. O'Donohue (Eds.), *Theories of human sexuality* (pp. 335–362). New York: Plenum Press.

Washburn, S. L., & Jay, P. C. (1977). In F. A. Beach (Ed.), *Human sexuality in four perspectives* (p. 20). Baltimore: Johns Hopkins Press.

Whitehead, T. (1981). Sex hormone treatment of prisoners. In P. Brain & D. Benton (Eds.), *Multidisciplinary approaches to aggression research* (pp. 503–511). Amsterdam, The Netherlands: Elsevier.

Wilson, E. (1978). *On human nature.* Cambridge, MA: Harvard University Press.

Wolf, N. (1991). *The beauty myth: How images of beauty are used against women.* New York: Morrow.

Wolfe, T. (1988). *Bonfire of the vanities.* New York: Bantam Books.

Zilbergeld, B. (1978). *Male sexuality.* Toronto: Bantam Books.

Zilbergeld, B. (1992). *The new male sexuality: The truth about men, sex, and pleasure.* New York: Bantam Books.

PART II

PROBLEMS

CHAPTER 3

Appearance Obsession: Women's Reactions to Men's Objectification of Their Bodies

JONI E. JOHNSTON

TO UNDERSTAND THE complexity and diversity of women's responses to objectification by men, it is first important to understand the cultural and historical context in which this objectification occurs. Beauty standards, created and enforced through fashion, families, and peers, were the patriarchal dictates denoting what objective form of beauty was considered desirable for a certain time and place (Hansen & Reed, 1986; Wolf, 1991).

From an early age, women have been taught the value of attaining beauty, both in terms of societal approval and personal power. For much of our history these two concepts were intertwined; it was through cultural approval that a woman attained personal freedom.

Historically, beauty standards have served many purposes, not least of which has been political and economic control in a culture that assigns subordinate status to women (Bullough, 1974). It is no accident, for instance, that following the Bubonic Plague of Europe, a catastrophe that eliminated one-third of the European population, the beauty standard for the next 30 years was the pregnant look (Kaiser, 1990). Even if a woman was not pregnant or nursing a child, she was encouraged to look "fertile." For women, "looking" has taken the place of "being" time and time again.

In the United States, beauty standards have vacillated in direct correlation with women's access to civil rights. For example, the "thin" beauty ideal (i.e., "nonfertile"), which first emerged in the 1920s and later in the 1960s, has often been viewed as a rejection of traditional femininity; it has consistently appeared at times when women have made political and economic progress (Hansen & Reed, 1986; Wolf, 1991).

Beauty standards have also defined women's physical freedom. From the crippling thousand-year tradition of Chinese foot binding, to the inhibitions and conflicts many women exhibit around eating today.

Beauty has been a part of traditional female sex-role socialization in every culture throughout time. It has invariably been male-defined (Hansen & Reed, 1986; Wolf, 1991). This beauty mandate has fluctuated in form but not in its sphere of influence. If the cultural objectification of women through beauty standards led only to political and personal bondage, it is likely that women would have made as much progress in this area as in so many others. However, the subtle yet pervasive nature of transmission, the promise of indirect power, and the early internalization of its message have rendered the cultural objectification of women through beauty standards the last bastion of patriarchal control.

Not only have women been taught that femininity is based on beauty, they have also historically been taught that beauty is currency. It has been women's primary, if not only, avenue to power and resources. Women have been taught from an early age that beauty is survival strategy. Women must do everything possible to maximize beauty's power. While the power women obtain is indirect—attained through beauty's influence over those in a position of direct power—it provides women's only security.

Since the 1960s, we have seen an increase in economic and political opportunities for women. At the same time, we have seen a beauty standard that is unprecedented in its complexity and unrivaled in its proliferation. It is estimated, for example, that the average person views between 400 and 600 advertisements a day, between 40 and 60 million by the age of 60 (Nichter & Nichter, 1991). One out of every 11 of these messages has a direct message about feminine beauty. Numerous studies have documented the negative impact of this exposure; there is a direct correlation between amount of exposure to ideal body images and personal body dissatisfaction (Abramson & Valene, 1991; Myers & Biocca, 1992).

Just as women are reared according to the current trend in body objectification, men are exposed to an "ideal beauty" through soft and hard core pornography. All too often, this fantasy ideal beauty distorts men's expectations of women in terms of sexuality and physical appearance. This interplay between women's and men's sex role socialization intertwines sexuality in destructive ways for both men and women.

Appearance Obsession Defined

"Appearance obsession" is a term that I use to describe both the increasing cultural preoccupation with female beauty, as evidenced by the recent escalation in media messages targeted to women around physical appearance, and the painful personal and relationship ramifications of these messages on individual women (Johnston, 1994). Girls are taught from an early age that attractiveness is an intrinsic part of pleasing others and, in turn, of securing love (Brownmiller, 1984; Striegel-Moore, Silberstein, & Rodin, 1986). With this early foundation, it is not surprising that Wooley and Wooley (1984), exploring the impact of cultural standards on teenage girls and boys, found that girls are more influenced by, and therefore more vulnerable to, cultural ideal beauty mandates.

Appearance obsession is the chronic, painful preoccupation with one's physical appearance. It creates never-ending frustration through significant internal pressure to meet unrealistic beauty standards and important goals of perfection.

The purpose in describing this syndrome is not to pathologize what is often a natural, and somewhat adaptive, response to cultural pressures around beauty and sexuality. Rather it is to highlight the painful personal consequences that arise out of these cultural pressures. To some extent, the pursuit of beauty is an understandable response to cultural pressures, because it may be the only way for a woman to get her needs met. The problem arises, however, when beauty and sexuality become too closely linked—love and looks become inseparable. Appearance obsession is often mislabeled as vanity, although it is actually rooted in fear and insecurity.

Appearance obsession is normative in the sense that most American women experience pervasive dissatisfaction with their physical appearance. Appearance obsession occurs regardless of a woman's size, weight, or "objective" physical attractiveness. In a 1985 symposium, Rodin, Silberstein, and Striegel-Moore attempted to define the "normal level of discontent" that women feel toward their bodies. While the jury is still out for adult women, the link between self-image and body image for American teenage girls is clear. By age 13, it is possible to predict a girl's self-esteem by assessing her body image (Lerner, Iwasaki, Chihara, & Sorrell, 1981).

A number of variables influence the degree of body dissatisfaction—age, physical and developmental history, family background, ethnicity, and current developmental level. These variables often dictate the degree to which physical attractiveness becomes psychologically salient to the individual. The psychological importance of cultural beauty ideals is a predictor of depression and low self-esteem among young adult women (Salem, 1990).

Appearance obsession is not a clinical term although, as we shall see, many of the personal and relationship symptoms overlap DSM-IV diagnoses (APA, 1994). This syndrome includes an underlying dissatisfaction with one's physical appearance coupled with a desperate need to improve it. It promotes anorexia nervosa, bulimia nervosa, and the dieting behavior that commonly precedes binge-eating disorder.

Appearance obsession has five general characteristics. First, it is marked by a tremendous need for social approval that is sought through self-improvement behavior around physical appearance. Chronic dieting, overexercise, compulsive shopping, frequent appearance checking, or repeated plastic surgery are some of the behaviors most commonly seen. While the majority of these behaviors are not pathognomonic, the pressured quality that drives these behaviors often causes significant emotional discomfort.

A second characteristic of appearance obsession is a distant and adversarial relationship with one's body. Cognitions regarding one's body are often critical and punitive. These cognitions are likely to escalate in conjunction with changes in mood or in accordance with situational distress. Normal bodily signals are either ignored, misinterpreted, or distrusted. Two of the most fundamental bodily cues, hunger and satiety, are replaced with arbitrary rules, calorie or fat gram counters, or fashion-dictated weight loss goals.

A third characteristic is fragile appearance esteem. Sense of self is so tied to physical appearance that a woman becomes highly vulnerable to changing circumstances in her emotional environment. Unlike most other individual characteristics, such as intelligence, honesty, or creativity, there are no objective measures by which she can measure her physical appearance—her appraisal of her looks is highly dependent on the feedback she receives from others. As an adult woman, this influence often broadens and encompasses internal feedback based on comparison to either an internalized ideal or a threatening environmental stimulus.

This leads to the fourth characteristic of appearance obsession, the translation of feelings into body thoughts. Because body image is so closely linked to self-image, in puberty, affective states can easily become channeled into changes in body perception or satisfaction. Body image distortion, once thought indicative of psychopathology, can now be recognized as an inherent characteristic of being an American woman. In fact, it has been demonstrated that at least 95 percent of all women overestimate their body size, often by as much as 25 percent (Dolan, Birtchnell, & Lacy, 1987).

As body thought replaces the language of feelings, women suffer a loss of affective insight. The capacity to recognize feelings of anger, fear or sadness all too often becomes supplanted by preoccupation with feeling of being "fat," "ugly," or "out of shape." Over time, the underlying feelings become so deeply sublimated that they may elude conscious awareness. A woman's body can become the scapegoat for any number of unpleasant feelings. Efforts to resolve unpleasant events can be translated into efforts to tame, control, mold, or change one's body. Thus, the objectification process becomes internalized and the female body is denigrated or exploited a second time. Appearance obsession is, in many ways, the female counterpart to the centerfold syndrome (Brooks, 1995).

A final characteristic of appearance obsession is image empowerment, the prioritization of external appearance at the expense of comfort, self-acceptance, and intimacy. The premium placed on appearance extends far beyond physical appearance into the arena of impression management. At some level, impression management—the energy and effort one expends on controlling one's social presentation—is a natural part of any interpersonal relationship. For example, we have all been taught to "put our best foot forward" when meeting someone new. But for the many women who struggle with appearance obsession, impression management becomes a harsh measuring stick and is utilized far beyond the bounds of its usefulness. Clinically, clients report a sense of "having to" be a certain way, of consistently acting differently from how they are really feeling, from feeling stuck in a role. Their relationships with others are often characterized by superficiality, a desperate desire for acceptance, and a lack of basic trust in others.

Theoretical Underpinnings and Familial Beginnings

While appearance obsession originates in adolescence, its roots are in infancy. From an early age, a girl receives a substantial amount of feedback about the importance of her looks. She quickly learns to evaluate herself by standards she has not set and to define herself by the responses of others. Just as the dominant culture objectifies her, she learns to objectify herself. She learns to view herself through the eyes of another, always male, always evaluating and judging.

This internalized objectification can ignite a wide variety of behavioral, cognitive, and emotional responses that are pervasive and developmentally harmful. On a theoretical level, a woman's response to cultural objectification of her body is consistent with the gender role strain paradigm (Pleck, 1981, 1995). Although Pleck specifically outlines the gender role strain paradigm as it relates to male socialization, it is particularly salient for women in terms of role expectations about beauty and sexuality.

First, society creates and perpetuates myths around beauty that become internalized as gender role expectations. One of the basic tenets of the gender role strain theory is that the violation of gender role norms leads to negative psychological consequences. A closely related proposition posits that actual or imagined violation of gender role norms lead individual to overconform to them.

Examination of gender role norms and stereotypes about female beauty and sexuality reveals a significant dilemma for women. What happens to the woman who attempts to meet the mandates of a gender role norm that is impossible to obtain? Ninety-five percent of all women will find it impossible to even approximate current beauty ideals. The powerful hold that beauty has on women's psyches is evident. Cash (1995) noted that as much as 25 percent of a woman's self-esteem is based on how she feels about her looks. Thus, the vast majority of women will experience gender role discrepancy strain, that is, an incongruity between what is expected of her and what she can attain. She will inevitably fail to fulfill her role expectations, leaving her with a chronic sense that she is deficient.

A woman who has internalized unrealistic gender role expectations will find her emotional life to be an internal struggle that mirrors the external conflict of cultural mandates and myths—that physical perfection is possible. That a woman has direct and complete control over her body, that men are limited resources for whom women must compete; that a woman is responsible for creating and maintaining the sexual responses of men.

Because of the marked discrepancy between most women's expectations and physical reality, compensatory chronic dieting, compulsive exercise, and frequent appearance checking are common compensating behaviors. Sadly, this desperate attempt to regulate self-esteem, restore a sense of control, and seek love or acceptance is often mistaken for vanity. In this way, women are further paralyzed by this social mandate.

Appearance Obsession and Women's Sexuality

There is one postulate of Pleck's gender strain paradigm that merits question when viewed in relationship to sexuality. In his theoretical overview, he asserts that violating gender norms has more severe consequences for men than for women (Pleck, 1981, 1995). Looking at the varying physical and emotional consequences of intimacy between men and women, this line of reasoning quickly falls short. While the most tangible consequence of violating the female gender role of sexual gatekeeper in a heterosexual relationship is pregnancy, in reality this is only the tip of the iceberg. Just below it lies issues related to sexual satisfaction, sexual assertiveness, and sexual esteem.

Sexual expression by women seems to be especially vulnerable to receiving negative attributions for nonstereotypic behavior. Garcia (1982) found, for example, that androgynous women compared to stereotypic women were more sexually experienced. They also found an inverse relationship existed between the amount of sexual experience and positive evaluations of nonsexual traits for women. The sexual double standard still exists, since the same finding did not apply to men. Clinical implications of these findings will be reviewed below.

The socialization process that perpetuates the internal and external objectification of women's bodies is itself traumatic to her sense of identity and to her sexuality. As she learns to view her body as an object to be viewed, adorned, controlled, and changed, a dichotomy develops between her mind and her body. As she is surveyed, she learns to survey everything she does and everything she is because how she appears to others is culturally linked to what is thought to be success in her life. Her own sense of self is supplanted by a sense of being viewed, evaluated, appreciated as herself by another.

Gender Role Socialization and Emotion: The Language of Feelings

In their overview of the role of gender in emotion, Brody and Hall (1993) identified three gender role patterns of emotional experience and expression that are highly salient in adult male-female interactions. These patterns create a potent combination when couples communicate around beauty and sexuality. They also lay the groundwork for a blurring of body boundaries and for power issues to be debated and carried out in the physical appearance arena.

INTERNALIZING CONFLICT

Tangney (1990), using a behavioral self-report inventory, discovered that women report more shame- and guilt-based experiences than males. Gender researchers agree that women generally report intropunitive emotions, while reporting and displaying less overtly aggressive emotions such as contempt, disgust, or anger (Nolen-Hoeksema, 1990). This gender role discrepancy implies that women are more likely to internalize criticism or conflict, while outwardly sacrificing self-esteem or pride to maintain affiliation or connection.

Self-perceptions of one's physical appearance, more so than any other attribute, are dependent on the feedback of others. Beauty is always relative; there is no unbiased, objective measure one can use to measure one's physical appearance. Since girls are socialized to internalize, rather than externalize, their emotions, they are unlikely to recognize, or question, the agenda of the other. As such, they are likely to respond to comments about physical appearance with self-blame and to perceive any criticism as justified.

Children in general tend to blindly accept the beliefs and values of authority figures. Girls, in particular, are vulnerable because of the strong value attached to beauty, and the continued reinforcement of introjected emotions.

DECODING AGGRESSION

The second gender difference that adversely affects women is a "blind spot" regarding their ability to decode aggressive affective expressions. While there is overwhelming evidence that women are superior to males at identifying emotions based on nonverbal cues of face, body, and voice, there is an exception when it comes to accurate recognition of other-directed emotions such as anger, contempt, or disgust (Rotter & Rotter, 1988; Wagner, MacDonald, & Manstead, 1986).

The gender role socialization of males regarding sexuality appears to provoke significant confusion and anger toward women. It is impossible to ignore the undertones of anger and resentment that resonate throughout Brooks' (1995) description of the characteristics of the centerfold syndrome. This anger and resentment appears to reflect both a societal devaluation of women as well as a personal reaction to women's gender role as the "gatekeeper" of sexuality. It appears that the male gender role of sexual pursuer has its emotional costs, as it dictates responsibility for sexual initiation and conquest without control for (and responsibility for) the outcome. This bind often produces feelings of sexual helplessness and frustration that men commonly divert toward women.

If women indeed have more difficulty detecting nonverbal indicators of anger and other-directed emotions in men, then they are particularly likely to have trouble doing so in the sexual arena. Also as already discussed, there is a social prohibition against female expression of anger. These two patterns create a dangerous situation for women in the sexual arena, particularly when combined with the gender socialization expectation for women to invoke desire in men while simultaneously monitoring and controlling it.

Men are more likely to act out their anger rather than express it directly. Boys use more retaliation and aggression as anger coping strategies than girls do (Eagly & Steffan, 1986; Fabes & Eisenberg, 1991; Whitesell, Robinson, & Harter, 1991). This acting out tendency interacts with female sex role behaviors in a manner that is personally as well as interpersonally destructive.

Objectifying actions and behaviors are likely to be internalized by women rather than recognized as information about the messenger. They are also likely to reflect, and perpetuate, men's power and control over women. Additionally, women are socialized to inhibit expression of other-directed emotions and, therefore, tend to not express anger, contempt, or disgust when experiencing subtle forms of sexual exploitation. Instead they respond with inner-directed coping behaviors, either in the form of efforts at physical improvement or in terms of cognitive reframing ("boys will be boys") or minimizing ("it's no big deal").

Emotion Focus versus Action Focus

A third gender role pattern identified by Brody and Hall is that of male-female differences in "emotion focus" versus "action focus." Boys are generally taught to temper their emotional expression; that is, talk around emotions and focus on emotional control and behavioral response (Fivush, 1989). A long-term impact of this process may well be an eventual loss of self-awareness around experienced emotions, alexithymia (Levant & Kopecky, 1995/1996), and a tendency to act out, rather than experience, emotions.

Girls, on the other hand, receive much more support for the verbal expression of emotions (except anger, disgust, and related emotions, such as contempt) and are exposed to wider displays of emotions from both parents. As a result, they learn very early to interpret and provide emotion cues. However, they are taught much more about how to experience emotions than they are taught how to take action on them.

This greater sensitivity to emotional expression can be a clear social advantage, yet it can also become a personal disadvantage when it is not paired with active coping strategies that foster a sense of control. Girls are usually taught to use emotion-focused coping strategies that include ventilation and catharsis rather than action. They are discouraged from learning action-focused coping strategies. As a result, they learn to adapt or seek self-improvement instead of setting limits or confronting unreasonable expectations. The result can be an overemphasis on self-improvement at the expense of much-needed limit-setting or confrontation. This pattern is complex in the interpersonal arena. For example, women who experience jealousy usually try to improve their appearance. Men, on the other hand, are much more likely to respond to jealousy-provoking situations by distancing themselves from a partner or flirting with another woman (Mullen & Martin, 1994; Nadler & Dotan, 1992).

Objectification and Its Impact on Women

The divergent gender role socialization experiences of men and women can, and do, have adverse consequences in their sexual relationships. Masters and Johnson (1989) estimate that sexual dysfunction occurs in up to 50 percent of all marriages at some point in time. While situation or transient factors may account for some of these, skills deficits and misinformation between the two are often a strong component. At the very least, they are likely to be a complicating factor.

Gender role socialization plays a distinct role in sexual satisfaction in the couples dyad. Interestingly, though not surprisingly, gender role identification leads to differing consequences for men and women. Rosenzweig and Dailey (1989) looked at the relationship between gender-role self-perception and sexual satisfaction in the dyadic relationship and concluded that androgynous sex role self-perception in sexual situations had a much higher consequence for men than for women. This held true for dyadic adjustment as well as sexual satisfaction. For the women's sample, sexual satisfaction and dyadic adjustment was predicted by the presence of high femininity.

Women grow up in a culture that normalizes the objectification of women. Women cannot avoid the impact of this objectification. Increased awareness of the pervasiveness of this objectification has consciousness-raising benefits.

Cairns (1990) said that "women's greatest psychological and sexual barrier to intimacy . . . is an impaired sense of self." Sadly this "impaired sense of self" is the legacy of many women's sexual development. For many women, one legacy of their sexual development has been a splitting of their sexuality, consistent with the many dichotomous aspects of the social constructions of female reality. Female sexuality has consistently been the source of male worship and male denigration (Bartky, 1990; Delaney, Lupton, & Toth, 1988).

For women, the concepts of power and shame around sexuality often become intertwined. From an early age, women are taught that to be desired is to be powerful, yet to submit is sinful and unladylike. Women are held responsible not only for keeping their own sexuality in check, but also the sexual expression of the objectifier. While sexual freedom seems to have dramatically expanded for women, the double standard remains. Women still are expected to be the keepers of moral standards and the bearers of the repercussions of "loose morals."

Objectification affects women's sexuality through the myths this process perpetuates. Since women's sexuality has been defined by men (Danilik, 1993; Stock, 1988), women become confused by the inconsistencies between what they are supposed to experience and what they actually experience. We only have to reminisce about the myth of the vaginal orgasm to see how far afield male-dominance-inspired myths can take us. The rape myth, an outgrowth of male fantasy cloaked for so long as female reality, has done as much damage to female sexuality as have religious inductions of sexual guilt and confusion.

Although objectification affects women long before puberty, it is during the sexual blossoming of puberty that the most damage is done. While the adolescent girl struggles to incorporate her changing body into her emerging identity, she is simultaneously bombarded with mixed messages about her body and its functions. She soon learns that her body is no longer her own. It becomes a public object as she is exposed to sexual comments, suggestions, or gestures from the unlikeliest of sources. The world is no longer safe, and she is taught that she is the gatekeeper of male sexuality. Simultaneously, the attainment of beauty and sexual attractiveness is continuously linked to female power, popularity, love, and success. The adolescent female often comes away with the sense that she must walk a fine line. She must be able to arouse sexual desire in men yet simultaneously keep them in check. She must please, but not provoke.

A young woman's sexual desires, thoughts, and feelings often remain a mystery. If they arise, they are either ignored or chastised. They are certainly not encouraged. She learns that to "be desired" is much more important than to "feel desire." As a client succinctly stated, "I never knew if I wanted men or not, but I sure knew that I wanted them to want me."

A woman also learns that feeling desire can lead to disastrous consequences. If she develops a healthy awareness and appreciation of her own sexuality in adolescence, she is an anomaly. Probably she has benefitted from role models who buffered normative socialization process. For women who analyze it, healthy sexuality usually comes later in life, proceeded by much unlearning and the shedding of cultural and emotional baggage. This is the best case scenario, as it does not begin to address the reparation necessary for someone who has been the direct victim of sexual exploitation and/or abuse.

Women's Sexual Difficulties in Response to Objectification

Other chapters in this book address the consequences of non-relational sex for men. This pattern has many parallel losses for women that are compounding women's disadvantage access to power in relationships. Many women learn to equate sex with safety and security through commitment and monogamy. In a world where women continually feel unsafe, safety and security are valued commodities. In this respect, sex may be used as a means to an end just as men view sex as the outcome of conquest.

Because "being the object of desire" supplants the right to "feel desire," women become "critical spectators." An essential part of herself remains separate to assess how her body looks and how much her partner appreciates it. She becomes preoccupied with how she looks, instead of enjoying how she feels. This spectatorship is a common complaint among women seeking treatment for hypoactive sexual desire.

The culture misinforms women regarding what is normal and healthy female sexuality. The media most often reflects masculine fantasies and desires around female participation and responsiveness. Research has been of little assistance in correcting this information, since most research on women's sexual functioning is based on pathology rather than health (Danilik, 1993).

The effect of misinformation about female sexuality is magnified by a peculiar absence of accurate sex education, particularly for women reaching puberty. Women are not encouraged to, and frequently are discouraged from, seeing sexuality as a natural part of themselves. Masturbation is rarely discussed. Sex, when talked about at all, is generally discussed in the context of a committed, romantic relationship. This socialization is dramatically different from masculine gender role prescriptions touting promiscuity, conquest, and sexual acting out (Gross, 1978). This difference in sexual exploration ultimately contributes to the historical imbalance of power between the genders. When a teenage girl is first aroused by a partner, with little awareness of her own sexuality, she is likely to attribute her pleasure solely to her partner (Friday, 1996). In this way, she is likely to hand over her emotional well-being to the figure who has stirred such a powerful physical response rather than realize that her pleasure is a natural physiological response that she could create herself.

Women are taught that their sexual pleasure is secondary to that of their partner's. Women, therefore, learn how to please men long before they learn to please themselves. This socialization can have a disastrous impact on the women's capacity to experience pleasure and on the potential for mutually satisfying sexual relationships.

The cultural taboos against female sexual expression, drummed into an adolescent girl's head since the beginning of puberty, leave their mark on her psyche and inhibit her sexual activity. As an adult, however, particularly after marriage, these marks are supposed to magically disappear. Literally overnight, she is expected to transform herself into a fully sexual being with expertise in satisfying her mate. Since no preparation has been provided, her sexual desire and responsiveness are erratic. Consistent with their socialization, many women blame themselves for thinking they have "hang-ups" about sex. A partner's objectification and sexual voyeurism, whether through pornography or ogling of other women, worsens matters. Many women experience rage that becomes channeled into shame because of the internalized message that her mate's sexual behavior is a direct reflection on her sexual desirability.

Clinical Implications

Gender role expectations are carried into the therapy office both by clients and therapists. Therefore, therapists working with couples are well-advised to begin their work by looking inward, examining personal values and beliefs about gender roles and power dynamics between men and women. It is only by understanding the remnants of our own socialization that we can begin to foster healing in others. The potential for unwitting abuse is great. A personal anecdote illustrates the subtle ways that our own socialization process can perpetuate sexism and sexual stereotyping in our clients:

> At a recent social gathering I was heartened by this man's faith in marital therapy. He professes that therapy was responsible for saving his marriage. "I learned through therapy that my affair really wasn't all my fault," he says. "My wife and I learned that she had a part to play as well. After all, it had been three years since we had our last child and she was still 20 pounds overweight. No wonder I was tempted." I am saddened, but not surprised, by the shared responsibility assigned to this man's personal choice.

I have heard similar stories from others, including treatment recommendations that a woman wear a sexy nightgown or other strategies to "win a husband back from the other woman." The underlying message is usually the same: women are responsible for stimulating and maintaining their husband's sexual interest and to blame when it wanes or strays.

To be gender sensitive, we must also adopt an attitude of inquiry toward the role of sexuality and beauty in women's lives. A functional rather than diagnostic mentality will allow for greater understanding of the wide spectrum of common, albeit sometimes unhealthy, behaviors that are a part of a woman's personal struggle to reconcile societal messages with her needs for love, recognition and approval.

To be effective clinicians, we must recognize that ideas of female sexuality have historically been defined by men. Measures of "healthy sexuality" have traditionally employed a goal-oriented, objective bias, often, for example, using the ability to achieve orgasm as the primary gauge (Zilbergeld, 1978). Portrayals of female sexuality have most often reflected male fantasy and not female reality. This can easily be illustrated by examining how male sexual fantasies of women dominate the mass media. To overcome the potential bias of our own socialization, we must listen to each woman's personal definition of sexual satisfaction, and let a woman define her sexuality on her own terms. Inevitably this process will allow us to appreciate a broad spectrum of sexual values and avoid imposing values based on our own gender ideology.

A curious, nonjudgmental attitude will allow the clinician to recognize the healthy aspects of even the most pathological or self-defeating behavior, and will help clients understand themselves better. Although power dynamics have changed enough that beauty is less critical to survival, many women still see beauty as their primary avenue to love, approval and acceptance. A clinician who understands the basic socialized needs behind self-defeating behavior will more likely avoid inappropriate labeling or pathologizing the patient. It is crucial that the therapist understand the socialized needs behind a client's behavior if the therapist hopes to open avenues for more effective behaviors.

Clinical Assessment and Individual Treatment

Certain clinical presentations will warrant a more thorough assessment of, and emphasis on, the role of sexuality and body image in a woman's life. While symptoms of eating disorders, sexual victimization, hypoactive sexual desire, or body dysmorphia are obvious hallmarks for body/sexuality exploration and treatment, the spectrum of complaints that lend themselves to an exploration of this area is broad. Symptoms ranging from compulsive shopping to overexercising to psychological factors affecting a physical condition may have a body image component. A woman's body image is likely to be a factor in each of these complaints.

Regardless of a woman's presenting complaint, however, information about her current relationship with her body and her sexuality will be a relevant part of the treatment process. Her relationship with her body, for instance, is a good predictor of her overall self-image. As noted earlier, Cash (1995) estimated that one-fourth of a woman's self-esteem is based on appearance. For many women, however, the percentage is even higher. Therefore, body image assessment, focusing on a woman's daily thoughts, feelings, and actions in relation to her body image, may provide the quickest clue to her overall self-esteem.

A functional analysis requires specific information about a woman's eating patterns, weight fluctuations, exercise habits, shopping patterns, sexual functioning, history of sexual trauma, and other pertinent information. Avoidance behaviors are a critical part of the clinical picture since it is common for many women to avoid situations where they feel that their body will be on public display.

Because of the elements of secrecy and shame, many problems related to body image and sexuality will not emerge without special efforts from the therapist. Therefore, therapists should develop their own comprehensive clinical interview schedule with specific questions focusing on these areas.

Body Dysmorphia: A Brief Look

Appearance obsession, like its closet clinical counterpart, body dysmorphia, can cause enormous interpersonal and emotional difficulties when taken to extreme lengths. But, unlike body dysmorphia, which has three discrete symptoms, appearance obsession occurs on a continuum, with body dysmorphia or an eating disorder falling at one extreme end of the spectrum.

According the DSM-IV (APA, 1994), body dysmorphia is defined as a "preoccupation with some imagined defect in the appearance of a normal looking person." Dissatisfaction with some facial feature is the most common complaint, although virtually any area of the body can be the target of the person's distress. The belief is not of delusional intensity in that the person can acknowledge the possibility that he or she may be exaggerating the extent of the defect or that the defect may not, in fact, be present.

A review of the literature reveals that the level of insight may fluctuate according to the individual's mood and situation, a finding not unlike the fluctuating body image that many women describe. It is the severity of the impairment, and the intensity of the pain, that differentiate appearance obsession from true body dysmorphic disorder, although it is likely that true body dysmorphia is the tip of the iceberg and is part of a much broader phenomenon whose features, though recognizable, are not as compelling.

Body dysmorphia is often chronic, generally beginning in adolescence. Gender ratios vary from an equal number of men and women (approximately 1 percent of the adult population) up to 4 times the higher incidence in women than in men (Rich, Rosen, Orosan, & Reiter, 1992). In a series of body dysmorphic disorder patients, 58 percent had been hospitalized and 29 percent had made suicide attempts. (Phillips et al., 1994). Individuals with body dysmorphic disorder invariably describe significant difficulty in social and occupational functioning.

Patients are ashamed of their concerns and are often reluctant to disclose them for fear of ridicule or of drawing attention to the imagined defect (Phillips, 1991). As such, they may initially present with a variety of vague complaints; in fact, the defect is almost never mentioned during the initial interview (Castelnuovo-Tedesco, 1992). As such, clinicians must be prepared to inquire about specific symptoms and complaints.

Cognitive behavioral treatment strategies are commonly acknowledged as the treatment of choice for body dysmorphic disorder (Rosen, Reiter, & Orosan, 1995). These approaches attempt to modify intrusive thoughts of body dissatisfaction and overvalued beliefs about physical appearance, exposure to avoided body image situations, and elimination of body checking.

Couples Therapy

There is a reciprocal relationship between a woman's body image and her social relationships. Just as her view of her body will have an impact on her heterosexual interactions, so will these male-female interactions influence her body image. The same is true for her sexuality.

To the extent that each person is in touch with, and accountable for, sexual needs and desires, sexuality is ultimately a personal, rather than relationship, concern. However, because of the stature that sexuality often obtains in a romantic relationship, it is inevitably a source of potential conflict or intimacy. This is especially true in light of gender socialization patterns around sexual expression.

Women often experience an invasion of body boundaries when exposed to objectifying comments or actions. Not surprisingly, the damage is more severe when her partner is the one engaging in such behavior. In addition, women feel objectified whenever treated as moral inferiors, and as less than deserving of freedoms that their partners enjoy (Lemoncheck, 1994). For example, husbands who treat wives with affection and respect in everyday interactions, may be quite different when encountering sexual resistance. Many husbands experience this as sexual rejection and respond with implicit or explicit demands or coercion. At these times, wives who expect sex to be a shared experience may feel like a sexual apparatus without feelings or rights.

Women's responses depend upon a number of situational and personality variables. Many women, for example, have become so adapted to societal objectification that the behavior is not noticed. They may feel it is their "duty" to acquiesce to make husbands happy. Some women may take a stand, but suffer guilt and insecurity. Other women voice their rights to refuse sexual participation and prepare themselves to face the negative fallout.

Internal responses, however, are more insidious. Women are often unaware of the long-term emotional impact this behavior causes. Anger that lingers just below the surface causes a gradual emotional disconnection from partners and a marked reduction in sexual interest.

The more her body boundaries are violated, the more a woman may withdraw her sexual expression from her partner. This is one way that power and control issues can be played out between couples in the sexual arena. Her physical body, at least, is something she can exert control over.

Similarly, power and control issues often emerge in the details of couples' sexuality. Negotiations around frequency of intercourse, length of foreplay, and sexual communication must take into account differing sexual desires and preferences that often reflect gender-based values and beliefs. Couples who present with sexual difficulties will benefit from exploration of early role models, teachings, and experiences regarding sexuality.

Adolescence is a critical time, since it is the period when gender roles are enforced to the point of exaggeration. In this developmental stage, we see the social meaning of sexuality and beauty take root in teenager's language. As would be predicted by our assigned gender roles, girls begin using body talk to discuss a variety of emotions and experiences. Boys use sex talk to do the same.

Nichter and Vuckovic (1994) discuss the various roles "fat talk" plays in the negotiation of self and peer group interaction among adolescent females. It is multivocal, and the contextual cues provided by the speaker and the situation are used by the hearer to attach proper meaning. For adolescent girls, ritualized talk about weight serves as a metaphor for expressing distress (Nichter, 1981; Swartz, 1987), calling for support or validation among one's peers, or solidifying affiliation with a group.

At a time when boys are indoctrinated into gender roles regarding sexuality, sex talk may serve similar purposes. Bragging about sexual conquests and referring to women by their body parts is likely to disguise or alleviate underlying feelings of sexual insecurity. Making unwelcome sexual gestures toward females, most likely to be group behavior, is a way to establish affiliation with other males as well as to reestablish a lost sense of control. Unfortunately, this denigration and objectification of women is reinforced by a society that normalizes and encourages it. Many men have trouble getting beyond this way of relating and continue to rely on it to serve needs of validation and power.

Couples can benefit not only from an exploration of how gender role socialization affects their relationship, but also from the establishment of new ground rules regarding sexual interactions. Women must be encouraged to set boundaries and resist attempts by their partners to control their appearance or sexuality. Men must be encouraged to verbalize the vulnerability they often feel toward sexuality and taught to communicate clearly about their sexual needs.

Men will benefit from a better understanding of female sexuality in general, and of their partner's sexuality specifically. In addition, their own sexual satisfaction is likely to increase with a broadening of gender role expectations and a shift toward androgyny. Rosenzweig and Dailey (1989) found that androgyny in men was a predictor of sexual satisfaction and dyadic adjustment.

Female assertiveness and couple communication have been found to be positively related to the incidence of female orgasm (Cotton-Houston & Wheeler, 1983; Hurlbert, 1993; Kuriansky & Sharpe, 1981; Kuriansky, Sharpe, & O'Conner, 1982). Assertiveness may be an even more important role in the treatment of hypoactive sexual desire, a highly frequent problem for women.

While hypoactive sexual desire has traditionally been considered a function of an individual woman's sexual pathology, recent research points to the role of foreplay, or lack thereof, as a direct contributor to decreased sexual interest. Specific strategies that focus on sexual communication as well as techniques that lengthen foreplay, such as the "ladies come first" rule (Darling, Davidson, & Cox, 1991) have been very effective in increasing sexual satisfaction for both partners.

Cultural Implications

When we look at the divergent ways that boys and girls are socialized, we find much that needs to be changed. Social activism, targeting the sexual exploitation of women by the media, is a much-needed priority. A second priority is an awareness of the damage ultimately done to men when they are socialized in a way that limits their ability to experience intimacy.

Family values and societal values mirror each other. There is well-documented evidence that fathers play an important role in shaping gender roles in their children. While women are beginning to see a diversity of female role models in the media, male role models continue to predominantly reflect a Rambo-like approach to sexuality. Active parenting is a first step. Both parents must be helped to avoid gender role stereotyping and to simultaneously foster healthy ideas about how to function as women and men.

Most media portrayals not only perpetuate objectification of women, but also exacerbate male inadequacy by creating a "super sex" model for male performance. Perhaps even more telling is the media's covert endorsement of sexual acting out or other objectifying behavior on the part of its darlings. One has only to look at the paternalistic tolerance surrounding Hugh Grant's sexual exploits to see the perpetuation of the "boys will be boys" attitude.

Women desperately need permission—and role models—to expand their options well beyond stereotypic behavior regarding beauty and sexuality. Men also need new role models. Reshaping gender roles toward androgyny and flexibility will allow couples to negotiate the power and sexual dynamics of their relationship based on their personal needs, goals and interests rather than have them constrained by strict gender role expectations.

A less obvious cultural implication is the need for education about the often-subtle power dynamics that impact dyadic sexual interactions. Boys and girls need to be educated about the responsibilities of sexuality and about the ethics of power. They need to be aware of the pressures of traditional gender role socialization. Equipped with the ability to decode gender role mandates, adolescents may be able to avoid following the erroneous paths of previous generations. They become more able to respond to inevitable peer, family and media pressures that continue to perpetuate female objectification and misinformation about sexuality.

References

Abramson, E. E., & Valene, P. (1991). Media use, dietary restraint, bulimia, and attitudes toward obesity. *British Review of Bulimia and Anorexia Nervosa, 5,* 73–76.

American Psychiatric Association. (1994). *Diagnostic and statistical manual of mental disorders.* Washington, DC: Author.

Bartky, S. L. (1990). *Femininity and domination.* London: Routledge & Kegan Paul.

Brody, L. R., & Hall, J. A. (1993). Gender and emotion. In M. Lewis & J. M. Haviland (Eds.), *Handbook of emotions* (pp. 435–460). New York: Guilford Press.

Brooks, G. (1995). *The centerfold syndrome.* San Francisco: Jossey-Bass.

Brownmiller, S. (1984). *Femininity.* New York: Linden Press/Simon & Schuster.

Bullough, V. (1974). *The subordinal sex: A history of attitudes toward women.* New York: Penguin Books.

Cairns, K. (1990). The greening of sexuality and intimacy. *Sieccan Journal, 25*(2), 1–10.

Cash, T. (1995). *What do you see when you look in the mirror.* New York: Bantam Books.

Castelnuovo-Tedesco, P. (1992). Body dysmorphic disorder. *American Journal of Psychiatry, 149*(5), 718.

Cotton-Houston, A. L., & Wheeler, K. A. (1983). Preorgasmic group treatment: Assertiveness, marital adjustment and sexual functioning in women. *Journal of Sex and Marital Therapy, 9,* 296–302.

Danilik, J. C. (1993). The meaning and experience of female sexuality. *Psychology of Women Quarterly, 17,* 53–69.

Darling, C. A., Davidson, J. K., & Cox, R. P. (1991). Female sexual response and the timing of partner orgasm. *Journal of Sex and Marital Therapy, 17,* 3–20.

Delaney, J., Lupton, M. J., & Toth, E. (1988). *The curse: A cultural history of menstruation.* Chicago: University of Illinois Press.

Dolan, B. M., Birtchnell, S. A., & Lacy, J. H. (1987). Body image disturbance in non-eating disordered women and men. *Journal of Psychosomatic Research, 4,* 513–520.

Dolan, B. M., & Steffan, V. J. (1986). Gender and aggressive behavior: A meta-analytic review of the social psychological literature. *Psychological Bulletin, 100,* 309–330.

Eagly, A. H., & Steffan, V. J. (1986). Gender and aggressive behavior: A meta-analytic review of the social psychological literature. *Psychological Bulletin, 100,* 309–330.

Fabes, R. A., & Eisenberg, N. (1991, April). *Children's coping with interpersonal anger: Individual and situational correlates.* Poster presented at the biennial meeting of the Society for Research in Child Development, Seattle, WA.

Fivush, R. (1989). Exploring sex differences in the emotional context of mother-child conversations about the past. *Sex Roles, 20,* 675–691.

Friday, N. (1996). *The power of beauty.* New York: HarperCollins.

Garcia, L. T. (1982). Sex-role orientation and stereotypes about male-female sexuality. *Sex Roles, 8,* 863–876.

Gross, A. (1978). The male role and heterosexual behavior. *Journal of Social Issues, 34,* 87–107.

Hansen, J., & Reed, E. (1986). *Cosmetics, fashions and the exploitation of women.* New York: Pathfinder.

Hurlbert, D. F. (1991). The role of assertiveness in female sexuality: A comparative study between sexually assertive women. *Journal of Sex and Marital Therapy, 17,* 183–190.

Hurlbert, D. F. (1993). A comparative study using orgasm consistency training in the treatment of women reporting hypoactive sexual desire. *Journal of Sex and Marital Therapy, 19,* 41–55.

Hurlbert, D. F., White, L. C., & Powell, R. D. (1993). Orgasm consistency training in the treatment of women reporting hypoactive sexual desire: An outcome comparison of women-only groups and couples-only groups. *Journal of Behavior Therapy and Experimental Psychiatry, 24,* 3–13.

Johnston, J. (1994). *Appearance obsession: Learning to love the way you look.* Deerfield Beach, FL: Health Communications.

Kaiser, S. (1990). *The social psychology of clothing: Symbolic appearance in context.* New York: Macmillan.

Kuriansky, J. B., & Sharpe, L. (1981). Clinical and research implications of the evaluation of women's group therapy for anorgasmia: A review. *Journal of Sex and Marital Therapy, 7,* 268–277.

Kuriansky, J. B., Sharpe, L., & O'Conner, D. (1982). The treatment of anorgasmia: Long-term effectiveness of a short-term behavioral group therapy. *Journal of Sex and Marital Therapy, 8,* 29–43.

Lemoncheck, L. (1994). What's wrong with being a sex object? In A. M. Jagger (Ed.), *Living with contradiction: Controversies in feminist social ethics.* San Francisco: Westview Press.

Lerner, R. M., Iwasaki, S., Chihara, T., & Sorrell, G. T. (1981). Self-concept, self-esteem, and body attitudes among Japanese male and female adolescents. In S. Chess & A. Thomas (Eds.), *Annual progress in child psychiatry and child development.* New York: Brunner/Mazel.

Levant, R. F., & Kopecky, G. (1995/1996). *Masculinity reconstructed.* New York: Dutton/Plume.

Mullen, P. E., & Martin, J. (1994). Jealousy: A community study. *British Journal of Psychiatry, 164,* 35–43.

Myers, P., & Biocca, F. (1992). The elastic body image: The effects of television advertising and programming on body image distortions in young women. *Journal of Communication, 42,* 108–133.

Nadler, A., & Dotan, I. (1992). Commitment and rival attractiveness: Their effects on male and female reactions to jealousy-arousing situations. *Sex Roles, 7/8,* 293–310.

Nichter, M. (1981). Idioms of distress: Alternatives in the expression of psychosocial distress: A case study from south India. *Culture, Medicine, and Psychiatry, 5,* 379–408.

Nichter, M., & Nichter, M. (1991). Hype and weight. *Medical Anthropology, 13,* 249–284.

Nichter, M., Ritenbaugh, C., Nichter, M., Vuckovic, N., & Aiken, M. (1993). *Weight control and behavior among adolescent girls.* Unpublished manuscript.

Nichter, M., & Vuckovic, N. (1994). Fat talk: Body image among adolescent girls. In N. Sault (Ed.), *Many mirrors: Body image and social relations.* New Brunswick, NJ: Rutgers University Press.

Nolen-Hoeksema, S. (1990). *Sex differences in depression.* Stanford, CA: Stanford University Press.

Phillips, K. A. (1991). Body dysmorphic disorder: The distress of imagined ugliness. *American Journal of Psychiatry, 148,* 1138–1149.

Phillips, K. A., McElroy, S. L., & Gunderson, C. G. (1994). *Body dysmorphic disorder: Data on imagined ugliness.* Continuing Medical Education (CME) Syllabus and Proceedings, American Psychiatric Association 147th annual meeting, Philadelphia.

Pleck, J. H. (1981). *The myth of masculinity.* Cambridge, MA: MIT Press.

Pleck, J. H. (1995). The gender role strain paradigm: An update. In R. F. Levant & W. S. Pollack (Eds.), *A new psychology of men* (pp. 11–32). New York: Basic Books.

Rich N., Rosen J., Orosan P. G., & Reiter, J. T. (1992). *Prevalence of body dysmorphic disorder in non-clinical populations.* Paper presented at the meeting of the Association for Advancement of Behavior Therapy, Boston.

Rodin, J., Silberstein, L., & Striegel-Moore, R. (1985). Women and weight: A normative discontent. *Nebraska Symposium on Motivation, 32,* 267–307.

Rosen, J. C., Reiter, J., & Orosan, P. (1995). Cognitive-behavioral body image therapy for body dysmorphic disorder. *Journal of Consulting and Clinical Psychology, 63*(2), 263–269.

Rosenzweig, J., & Dailey, D. (1989). Dyadic adjustment/sexual satisfaction in women and men as a function of psychological sex role self-perception. *Journal of Sex and Marital Therapy, 15*(1), 42–56.

Rotter, N. G., & Rotter, G. S. (1988). Sex differences in the encoding and decoding of negative facial emotions. *Journal of Nonverbal Behavior, 12,* 139–148.

Salem, S. K. (1990). Perceived body image, importance of ideal body image, self-esteem, and depression in female college students. *Dissertation Abstracts International,* 1–20.

Stock, W. (1988). Propping up the phallocracy: A feminist critique of sex therapy and research. In E. Cole & E. D. Rothblum (Eds.), *Women and sex therapy* (pp. 23–41). New York: Haworth Press.

Striegel-Moore, R., Silberstein, R. L., & Rodin, J. (1986). Toward an understanding of the risk factors associated with bulimia. *American Psychologist, 41,* 246–263.

Swartz, L. (1987). Illness negotiation: The case of eating disorders. *Social Science and Medicine, 24*(7), 613–618.

Tangney, J. P. (1990). Assessing individual differences in proneness to guilt and shame: Development of the Self Conscious Affect and Attribution Inventory. *Journal of Personality and Social Psychology, 59,* 102–111.

Wagner, H. L., MacDonald, C. J., & Manstead, A. S. R. (1986). Communication of individual emotions by spontaneous facial expressions. *Journal of Personality and Social Psychology, 50,* 737–743.

Whitesell, N. R., Robinson, N. S., & Harter, S. (1991, April). *Anger in early adolescence: Prototypical causes and gender differences in coping strategies.* Poster presented at the biennial meeting of the Society for Research in Child Development, Seattle, WA.

Wolf, N. (1991). *The beauty myth: How images of beauty are used against women.* New York: Morrow.

Wooley, W., & Wooley, S. (1984, February). Feeling fat in a thin society: Women tell how they feel about their bodies. *Glamour Magazine,* 198–252.

Zilbergeld, B. (1978). *Male sexuality.* Toronto: Bantam Books.

CHAPTER 4

Repetitive Infidelity, Womanizing, and Don Juanism

DON-DAVID LUSTERMAN

MUCH HAS BEEN written about marital infidelity from a systemic viewpoint (Brown, 1991; Glass & Wright, 1995; Lawson, 1988; Lusterman, 1989, 1995; Moultrup, 1990; Pittman, 1989; Vaughan, 1989). This chapter focuses solely on male role issues and their impact on men's sexual and emotional behavior during marriage. The focus will not be on normative male roles in marriage, but rather on particular acts that most people would consider to be violations of the marital contract with its specification of monogamy.

Marriage begins, at least in Western cultures, with a legal, public, and often religious declaration of marital fidelity. There is little reason to believe that men, more than women, take these vows lightly at the time of marriage. What then accounts for the fact that, while estimates of the frequency of marital infidelity vary from a high of 50 percent (Kinsey, Pomeroy, & Martin, 1948) to a low of 15 percent (Smith, 1993), almost all agree that there is close to twice the frequency of unfaithful behavior among men as among women? Such a remarkable discrepancy cannot be accounted for by one simple explanation. It may be helpful to examine men's marital infidelity from the aspect of studies of men and masculinity.

The general theory of male gender socialization toward nonrelational sexuality has been described in Chapter 1. Using case studies, this chapter focuses on the way in which theoretical constructs such as masculinity ideology, gender role strain (Pleck, 1995), alexithymia (Levant & Kopecky, 1995/1996), and Kuper's concept (1993) of "pathological arrhythmicity" can help us to increase our understanding of repetitive infidelity in men.

Marital infidelity may be clumped into two broad categories:

1. "Pursuit" behavior takes the form of womanizing, one-night stands and Don Juanism. It is, for the most part, planned behavior. Men who endorse the ideology that women are men's playthings feel strongly entitled to these behaviors. Gender role dysfunction occurs when the successful fulfillment of male role expectations has negative consequences for either men who achieve them or those in relationships with them (Pleck, 1995). The most obvious negative effects of pursuit behavior include marital and familial disruption and the risk of sexually transmitted diseases.
2. Affair behavior is more complex and nuanced than pursuit behavior. Unlike pursuit behavior, affairs are almost invariably experienced as spontaneous and unplanned. Most men report that their affairs "just happened" (Brown, 1991, p. 22). Some affairs are short-lived and intense. Some men call these involvements "battery chargers." Others are long-term. Men may experience these as "solutions" to marital problems (e.g., poor sex or fighting).

In most instances, men do not believe that their pursuit behavior or their affairs will endanger their marriages. There is, however, a subcategory of affair behavior which involves "testing the water" before ending a marriage. Such men differ in that they have already begun the psychological, if not the legal, process of divorce.

The following cases illustrate the significance of masculinity ideology and gender role strain in the occurrence of infidelity.

Men's Perceptions of Wives and Mothers

Society believes that women are responsible for relationships, and particularly for the maintenance of marriage (Bernard, 1972; Nordstrom, 1986). Many people still consider a husband's affair to be his wife's fault. When some men hit a lull in their marriage, that is, a period of sexual boredom or loss of interest, they may blame their wives. Because men are trained not to reveal or explore their feelings, they tend not to be introspective about their role in the maintenance of a companionable relationship. Lacking this skill, they are sitting ducks for an affair, even though they are not consciously seeking one.

In many marriages, the man begins by feeling that he is his wife's protector and educator. In return, he expects adoration and service. When such a man's wife matures and seeks greater parity in the relationship, the man may experience this as a loss. He now experiences a type of gender role strain that Pleck (1995) describes as gender role *discrepancy*. His ideology, which focuses on his role as protector, is threatened by his feelings of failure to live up to his role, as well as a failure to reap its benefits. In an affair, such a man can once again play the role of Pygmalion, and receive a flood of adulation from his new Galatea. In a new experience with a woman, whether it be a one night stand, a visit to a prostitute, the activity of a womanizer, or a man in the throes of an affair's beginnings, many men are excited by the feeling of being totally attended to by the woman. "We can let down our guard with women," says Kupers (1993, p. 1). Because they are not men, and therefore possible competitors and judges, we can feel safer with them. "Many men are only able to feel fully alive when they are with a woman who adores them," he continues.

The desire for mothering behavior is a strong motive for some men to marry (Nordstrom, 1986). Often, women happily supply this service early in the marriage, but stop when the normal pressures of life mount and children arrive. The husband may come to feel he has been emotionally abandoned and left to fend for himself. One man, whom his wife believed to be a hard-working, decent guy, although a very poor communicator, announced one day after 30 years that he was leaving. "Why," she asked, "what did I do?" "It's not what you did, it's what you didn't do," he said. "For instance," he continued, "when I would go out in the garden to plant and weed, you would just sit inside. You never came out to be with me or to bring me a cup of iced tea." "How should I have known?" she asked. "You should have known," he replied.

In the early stages of an affair, many men once again feel served, valued, and mothered by a woman. Further, there is a magical quality to the affair. The affair, unlike the marriage, exists in a suspension of time and responsibility. And at first, the object of his newfound love takes a very subservient role. He is absent on holidays, important family occasions, in fact, whenever he must be at home or at work. But she is expected to be "at the ready." As the relationship intensifies, however, and the woman begins to make the same demands for intimacy and commitment as had his wife, the affair often sours.

ENTITLEMENT

A social "readiness" for objectifying women is inherent in our society. Although we are in a period of change, it is still to a remarkable degree socially acceptable to "come on" to women, to eye them, to make suggestive remarks, and, in a wide variety of ways, to objectify them. In much the same way that Western culture imposes a certain ideal of feminine "beauty" on girls (which creates an environment of readiness for eating disorder), so males are trained to a readiness for seeing women as objects of pursuit, objects that can, in one way or another, be "won" (Brooks, 1995). This sense of entitlement is often an important factor in extramarital behavior. The phenomenon of entitlement does not necessarily predict acting-out behavior, but is merely a socially-sanctioned possibility.

Example: One-Night Stands

John is a 35-year-old salesman, specializing in high-tech medical equipment. In the course of his work, he travels a great deal. He was brought to therapy by his wife of 14 years after she discovered that he had frequent one-night stands while on the road. John expressed shock at his wife's distress with his behavior. "We are very happily married," he explained. "We have two adorable kids, a nice house, plenty of money, and, I might add, a nice sex life. Joan doesn't understand that this is a "guy" thing. I bet most of the guys who do what I do for a living have a one-nighter once in a while. It hasn't got the vaguest meaning to me. And it's not like I do it every time I'm on the road. It's a victimless crime—if it's a crime at all." It was difficult for John to understand why his "private" behavior should have any effect on his marriage. John felt an absolute entitlement to his behavior, which was supported by his professional cohorts. Therapy focused on heightening John's consciousness and helping him to develop new listening and empathy skills that enabled him to better understand how his one-night stands affected his wife, including her fear that he would contract and transmit to her a venereal disease. In this, as in similar cases, he did not exhibit any underlying dissatisfaction with the marriage itself. He simply saw his womanizing as socially-sanctioned behavior. Only under the threat of loss of the marriage could he begin to examine some of his assumptions about what it is to be a man, and to make necessary changes to ensure the continuation of his marriage.

Entitlement takes other forms as well. The sociologist Jesse Bernard (1981) describes the traditional male role of "the good provider," tracing what she terms "its historical rise and fall." But in many instances, there has been no meaningful fall in the "good provider" role. Despite the radical increase in dual-earner families, many men continue to view themselves as the *primary* provider, and make a far smaller contribution than their wives to homemaking and childcare. In fact, the male is often the higher earner, either because of a gender-based wage differential between men and women or because many women work only part-time, with their work seen as a less "significant" source of income. Men and women who equate "work" with the production of income are ignoring the important contribution made by women's "home work" to the family's financial well-being.

It is still not at all unusual to hear a husband complain, "I don't know what she wants from me. I'm a good provider, I work hard all day, and bring all my money home." As a recompense, many men expect their home to be their castle. and hold their wives responsible for maintaining a safe and serene environment, in which the home is neat and orderly, the children cared for and well-behaved, and the wife sexually at the ready. One such man, a Vietnam veteran, stated that he saw his work as a battlefield, and his home as R&R. This too is a form of entitlement. Nor is it surprising that, when this sort of man feels that he has lost this entitlement, troubles may ensue. "Unable to appreciate the value of any family contributions except those of the worker-provider, men are especially vulnerable to disruptions to that role, such as those caused by unemployment, disability and retirement (Philpot & Brooks, 1995). Such men are often very vulnerable to extramarital affairs when their expectations are not fulfilled.

Example: Feeling Entitled

Mary Ann was concerned about her husband, Pete, a 26-year-old electrician. She reported that he seemed a little stressed because he'd had a fight with the union steward and was no longer getting the choice jobs, as he had in the past. This upset him, because he felt that he was a superior worker. She also reported that she suspected that he was having an affair, maybe brought on by his stress at work, but he steadfastly denied it. She described her marriage in the earlier years as better than good. They met as teens, and during her high school years, she developed a rare and life-threatening form of cancer that necessitated the removal of an eye. He had been incredibly helpful, always ready to get her to doctor's appointments, pick her up after chemotherapy treatments. She felt he was the kindest person she ever met. They married when she was 20 and he was 21. Within the first year of marriage her brother, with whom she was very close, died. She reported grave difficulty pulling out of her mourning. She became pregnant and, following the delivery, developed a severe, but untreated postpartum depression. Once again, Pete was always there, always helpful. Nothing appeared to be too much for him. He would get up early, be sure the baby was cared for, and rush home after work to shop. She also reported her total loss of interest in sex, which she began to view just as her mother had described it—"a wifely chore." Pete had always seen daily sex as his "right."

Even here, Pete seemed to be exceptionally understanding—he simply backed away and didn't bother her. Only now, she reported, he seemed suddenly distant and cold. He continued to do all the right things, but she sensed that something was wrong. Recently, she noticed strange things. He was coming home later that usual, and immediately rushed to the shower upon his return. He seemed "snippy" when he spoke to her. When the phone rang, he rushed to grab the cell phone and went outside to talk. She tried to explain to him how grateful she felt for his support in her many difficulties, and that she could imagine how angry and hurt he must be feeling because she had had so little energy for the marriage, but all to no avail.

Pete eventually admitted that he was "very involved" with another woman, but that it "wasn't sexual." Furthermore, he said, he had no patience with her expressions of shock and anger toward him. "I'm the good guy here," he said. "I bust my chops to provide for her and the kid. All she really cares for is her goddamned part-time job at the doctor's office. She sure is holding out on me. She even told me that sex is just a chore. I can't forget that."

Although Pete had been very attentive and giving in the sense of "doing things" for her, Mary Ann felt that he had never been able to talk with her, about either himself or the relationship. "He's strong and silent—I used to think that's what I loved about him. Now I think it means that he can do things, but he can't really show love." Pete shot back that he could show plenty of love, but not to someone who was holding out on him. She began to realize that part of her depression was because she felt so alone in the relationship, even though he was so helpful. One day she reported furiously, "I can't believe it, he came in last night, late, pawed at me, turned me over and had sex with me. Is this his idea of making up? I felt almost like he raped me." Tears came to her eyes as she spoke. Pete said, "The tears won't help. You better get it through your head—I'm a guy. You broke the deal. I gave you everything I had, and you couldn't give me the one thing I asked for." Pete eventually left the marriage. He told Mary Ann that in his new relationship, he didn't have to work so hard at it, and that his new friend did all "the girly stuff" that he so much craved.

Fantasy and Curiosity versus Acting Out

Fantasy has been defined as "the realm of vivid imagination, reverie, depiction, illusion." Curiosity is defined as "a desire to know or learn, especially about something new or strange." The word *curiosa* is defined as "books or other writings dealing with unusual, especially pornographic, topics." Certainly it seems a small jump for many men from curiosity to pornography. Yet there is little reason to believe that fantasy, curiosity, or even *curiosa* necessarily produce acting-out sexual behavior. As an example, when former President Jimmy Carter was asked whether he had been involved in any extramarital affairs, he replied, "No, but I have lusted in my heart." The American public found this to be a rather laughable and naive response, and Carter was the subject of much public ridicule. The consensus was that everyone lusts in his heart, so why report it? For many people, curiosity leads to the search for stimuli that permit vicarious experience that is not necessarily available in real life, whether because of circumstance or moral conviction. That's why people go to the movies, read books, and go to art museums. Many nonmurderers read murder mysteries or watch them on the television or in the movies. Many men consume pornography but do not act out with women. In my clinical experience, there are times when quite the opposite is the case. The debate about pornography (see Chapters 2 and 5) blurs the distinction between fantasy and curiosity, on the one hand, and acting out, on the other. There is a type of man who is very action-oriented and thrill-seeking. Such men seem to believe that "what you think about, you must do." For these men, fantasy is not a time of floating free or of experiencing vicariously. Rather, their thought process must result in action.

This distinction between fantasy and acting out is important in understanding certain, but not all, types of extramarital infidelity and is particularly significant in the treatment of compulsive womanizers and "deficit" affairs—affairs that develop out of a man's feeling that he has not yet really lived.

Example: Making Up for Lost Time

Tony, a 40-year-old lawyer, seemed to lead an exemplary life. He had a beautiful wife, an excellent income, two lovely children, a boat that slept six, and all the "toys" that money could buy. Nonetheless, his wife Marie was at the end of her rope. Tony had always turned to her for all the major decisions in his life, from his choice of career to the kind of cars he bought. He still did. They both agreed that they had a great sex life. Tony said that Marie was not only the most beautiful woman he'd ever known, but also the smartest and the most down-to-earth. At home, he was the model father; at work, the model worker. For the past three years, however, he had been involved in a torrid affair with a coworker. In the affair, he was a different person. He and his girlfriend had long days in bed, often high on cocaine. During the times that the affair was "hot and heavy," he often missed days of work, and would show up at home very late.

Tony felt very confused by his own behavior. He knew that Theresa, the other woman, was no good for him. But he also felt powerless to end the relationship. He was the son of a minor player in the "mob," a man engaged in money-lending at exorbitant rates, illegal gambling, and similar operations. Tony said that when he began to date as a teenager, his father's first question each time he came home, was, "Did you get laid?" Tony felt very turned off by his father's womanizing and demands that he follow suit, but he also felt inadequate when he compared himself to his father. In fact, despite his frequent lies to his father that he was "getting it" all the time, he was not. He was not a sportsman and certainly not a ladies' man. Perhaps, because he felt he failed at sports, he didn't have male friends either. He felt that he fell far from the mark. He also deeply resented his mother for taking what his father "dished out." He felt that she was so washed out that she had nothing left for him as a son. So when he met Marie at age 17, her warmth and encouragement were enormously soothing to him. Indeed, it was she who pushed him toward college and later toward law school, despite his father's urging that he enter the "mob."

Following his graduation from law school, Tony's dependence on Marie grew even stronger. Despite his growing success, there was scarcely a day that he didn't telephone her several times for words of encouragement. Although he had always imagined that he would feel better about himself when successful, it hadn't happened. One day he began to ruminate on how disappointed he was that he had never been with other women before the marriage. He wondered what it would be like to have sex with someone else. It was then that he began, as he put it, "the fooling around with a lot of women," that eventually led to his relationship with Theresa.

When he was questioned about his fantasies, thoughts during masturbation, and his feelings when watching pornography, he replied, "I don't have any fantasies, I seldom masturbate, except maybe to get to sleep, and I don't like porn. I just can't get into imaginary stuff." He felt that he needed, as he said, "to screw around for a while" in order to make up for what he felt he had lost as a teenager. At first he would simply find a woman, seduce her into sex, usually while both were drunk or high, and then move on. It wasn't the sex, he said, but the sense of conquest that he craved. "I wanted to be the teenager that I never was. Now I had the success and power to do it. *Carpe diem.*"

In fact, he said, none of the sexual experiences came close to what he had with Marie. Eventually he tired of these encounters, but it wasn't long before he became involved at a much more intense level with Theresa. She represented what he called his "other side," the part of him that was like his father. Theresa took what she wanted. She was ruthless, exciting, completely amoral. When he was with her, he felt out of control, but powerful. He told Marie that now he was having his adolescence, and he wanted her to give him time to get it out of his system. Marie said, "Not in my house!" She told him that he could go, but that she didn't know if she'd be there for him when he wanted to come back. Shortly after, he moved out.

Soon after, he began to see a therapist. In therapy, he was able to get in touch with his own ability to fantasize and with the wounds that his father and mother had inflicted. He realized that fantasy was an important and heretofore repressed part of his life. When he felt safe with his fantasies, he realized that having them did not mean that they required action. He ultimately ended his affair and returned to the marriage. Tony's ideology told him that he had not "measured up" sexually and socially in his adolescence. The difference between his masculine ideal and his life situation exemplify discrepancy strain.

Alexithymia and "Pathological Arrhythmicity"

Levant and Kopecky (1995/1996) borrow the psychoneurological term *alexithymia* and uses it to describe a socially-conditioned inability to "feel, identify, and express feelings" (p. 19). While girls are socialized to feel, name and express their feelings, he points out, boys learn to suppress theirs. This leads to a feeling of numbness. It is not hard to understand that when such boys become men, their alexithymic behavior makes marital communication largely the wife's responsibility. It often leaves the man feeling "out in left field" as he hears his wife's complaints that he is not communicating, doesn't hear her, and is not emotionally expressive toward her unless he is angry or wants sex.

While musing on men's need to label women's cyclicity as "pathological," for example, PMS or "late luteal phase dysphoria," Kupers (1993) playfully proposes the term "pathological arryhthmicity," which he defines as "Too little responsiveness to natural cycles—in fact, to cycles of any kind" (p. 30). He points out that, in the male's drive to succeed, he develops a coping style that involves long work hours with no let-up, working despite illness, vigilance against possible attack, and suppression of tears and laughter. Other symptoms include time obsession, an inability to "let alone emotions take their course," and an inability to enjoy relationships and events that are not task-oriented.

Kupers describes marriage as "an intimate relationship in which each partner will occasionally be dependent on the other, in what one hopes is some kind of reciprocal alternating rhythm. When the man is unable to tolerate thinking of himself as dependent, he tries to make it appear as if his partner is the dependent one." The element of spontaneity is all but absent for such a man; this is a formula for emotional burnout.

Success-oriented men are frequently so addicted to the fast track that they cannot imagine life without it, even though it is evident to others that their work style is the source of their increasing burnout. It is at this point that many men experience a midlife crisis. It is much more likely at that juncture that such a man will change relationships (e.g., have an affair) than that he will change his job. In the affair, he reexperiences pure infatuation, free of the pressure of the many responsibilities that accompany marriage. In the affair, he once again feels "number one." At least at the beginning of the affair, he feels that the third party is totally consumed with him.

Example: Burned Out

Fred, a 59-year-old dentist, had first entered therapy about 10 years before his current visit. At that time, he complained of almost nonstop anxiety and depression. He reported that not only did he have a highly successful practice of his own, but that he had also set up several other offices in which he employed young dentists. Nonetheless, he found himself plagued with worry. If he was overbooked, he felt panicked that he couldn't do it all. If a few patients canceled, he was equally sure that his practice was going under. He expressed amazement at his anxiety. "Never felt this before," he reported. In fact, he said, "I always felt kind of numb. I don't get it." He was one of three children. His father had been extremely brutal with his elder brother. Many nights, Fred reported going to sleep with a pillow over his head, to blank out the anguished screams of his brother. His younger sister was, he said, "adorable and adored, and spoiled." Fred became the "perfect child," always eager to avoid the punishment so generously meted out to his brother. He cried bitterly in one session as he described his anguish and guilt that he could not save his brother, and that he had, in a way, "joined with the enemy, my father," in order to escape his brother's fate.

Fred said he was a "good boy" in many ways. Out of fear, he always sought to please his father. He also sought to please his mother, but for different reasons. He felt that his mother was as much a victim of his father's brutality as was his brother. So, as he said, "the only gifts I could bring my mother were the best grades, the best behavior, the best profession and the best woman to marry." Because he worked so hard in school, he had little time to date or to develop social skills. Following college came dental school. Soon, he found his mother worrying aloud that he didn't seem to be moving towards marriage. It wasn't long after that she introduced him to the daughter of an old college friend. Ariele seemed nice enough, and it wasn't long before they seemed to drift into an understanding that they would marry. Fred reported that he never felt any passion during the courtship. "She was a very bright, sharp-tongued, and demanding girl, he said, and shortly before the wedding, I realized that, unlike me, she had been sexually active. We never talked about it, but I never got over it. The day before the wedding, I knew it was a mistake. But I couldn't back out—I think it would have killed my mother."

Fred functioned in the marriage as he had in school. He was dutiful and extremely successful at his work. But the marriage was loveless and with no sexual passion at all for him. He sustained himself by an occasional one-night stand, once every two or three years. Now, however, his life was in an uproar. Many of his peers and male relatives were in the midst of divorces.

His mother had died several years ago. About a year ago, he had met a lovely women with whom, for the first time in his life, he experienced emotional and sexual intimacy. Although married, she too seemed close to divorce. "With her," he said, "I feel all the things that I didn't know enough to miss when I was a kid. She is kind, attentive, sweet to me. We can just lie in bed for hours, just being with each other. It doesn't even have to be sexual. It's taught me that I can love and be loved." His depression at work, at home, and in his relationships with his now-grown children was so extreme that he had gone to a psychiatrist for medication. But, he knew it wasn't the same as the depression with which he had entered therapy so many years ago, because "Now, when I'm with my woman, I feel better than great." It's when I go back to the spider web of responsibility that I made out of my life, that's when I get depressed. What am I working so hard for?"

Fred continued in the marriage and his new relationship for several years. In therapy, he dealt with his moral responsibility to his wife, to his kids, and to himself. He gradually stiffened himself to accept her rage as he told her he wanted out. He also came to realize that the relationship with his "lady" might or might not work out. Eventually he divorced. Several years later, the new relationship ended. But he had discovered that he could love, and shortly after met and married another woman.

Don Juanism: Compulsive Womanizing

Earlier in this chapter, we examined John's situation. John, as you will remember, felt an entitlement to his frequent one-night stands. The true Don Juan brings still another element to his extramarital adventures—the absolute compulsion to find, seduce, and abandon a woman, usually within the shortest period of time possible. There is nothing accidental or coincidental in his actions. In fact, much of the Don Juan's time is taken up with planning exactly how the mission will be accomplished within the time at his disposal. Nor does sexual attraction appear to play a role. Often a Don Juan will explain that, as the night wore on, he finally picked up this real "dog." Don Juans also often feel compelled to keep a count or a record of their "conquests." Perhaps this is because they are so emotionally numb that, unless the act has been recorded, it will be unmemorable. In Mozart's opera Don Giovanni, the Don announces to his servant, Leporello, that he has a list of his one-thousand-and-three conquests to date, in Spain alone! It is not infrequent that the Don Juan will explain that, even if at first there was some sexual pleasure involved in these encounters, as time goes on, there is little if any sexual pleasure. Often the sex itself is experienced as a tiresome chore.

In describing what they call "sex addiction," Earle and Crowe (1989) list what they see as common attributes of all addicts, sexual or otherwise. These include:

- A tendency to hold low opinions of themselves and to constantly remind themselves of their deficiencies.
- Distorted or unrealistic beliefs about themselves, their behavior, other people, and the events that occur in the world around them.
- A desire to escape from or to suppress unpleasant emotions.
- Difficulty coping with stress.
- At least one powerful memory of an intense high experienced at a crucial time in their lives and an ever-present desire to recapture the euphoric feeling.
- An uncanny ability to deny that they have a problem.

This description is useful in understanding the Don Juan. More characterologically damaged than some womanizers, the Don Juan feels continually compelled to perform his task, often experiences a letdown following it, and then craves still another adventure. It is also helpful to think of Don Juanism as a type of narcissistic personality disorder. Don Juans have a need for excessive admiration, a sense of entitlement, a lack of empathy, and a tendency to be interpersonally exploitative. A Don Juan tends to feel comfortable enough with his own behavior and sees the concern of others as "their problem." Such a person is more like a carrier of a disease than one who suffers from it.

Don Juans are particularly likely to be both highly alexithymic and, in Kuper's term, highly "arrhythmic." They appear to be particularly oblivious to the effects of their behavior on what they often report are, from their standpoint, "perfectly good marriages," except for the fact that their wives seem to want something from them that they can't give—emotional attention. With one exception, the prognosis for change in a Don Juan is very poor. Don Juans are often married, and, for one reason or another, many place a great value on their marriage. Occasionally, the discovery of his behavior by his wife and the subsequent fear of losing her creates sufficient anxiety that the person becomes amenable to therapy.

Don Juans need the almost daily attention of a woman, whom they both want and despise. There is reason to suspect that these people experienced very tenuous and empty relationships with their mothers. It is perhaps because of this that Don Juanism appears to be the most misogynistic type of marital infidelity. While such a person desperately wants womanly attention, he is also angry at the need for this attention. One can look at this repetitive activity as one of seduction and retaliation toward the woman who is its object. Don Juanism, then, is an example of gender role dysfunction, abetted by a male ideology that objectifies women, and probably compounded by early familial history.

Example: Don Richard

Richard was a short, well-built, handsome, and charming man in his early fifties. He always appeared to have a pleasant smile and a kind word. He was a self-made man, who got into the field of computers relatively early, and headed a major consulting firm. He was brought to therapy by Jane, who was so agitated that she could barely contain herself. Shouting and cursing, she accused him of 20 years of marriage in which he had done nothing but "play with his goddamned computers and his goddamned whores." Richard smiled and denied her charges. But there was little doubt in Jane's mind. He had ignored her, she said, and he had constant liaisons with others. Out poured a tale of her endless frustration with his inability to so much as say hello to a woman without attempting to charm her, her constant fights with him about it, and his constant denial that it meant anything.

Eventually, he began to admit a series of what he called brief affairs. At this point, she jumped out of her chair and pulled out a large sheaf of papers which she threw at him. One of them fell at the therapist's feet. It was a computer printout. It contained page after page of women's names, places, and dates, some followed by what looked like a numerical code. "Helga—Gotham Hotel; 8/3/94; 5–7B." His face went white. For the first time, the therapist saw him without a smile on his face. "I've got you now, you bastard," she screamed, "and I did it with your goddamned computer." Little by little the story emerged of his endless compulsion to find and bed women. Richard pleaded with her not to end the marriage. "I really want you and I want the marriage." Eventually, Jane relented a bit and said, "I'll give you a year to find out what the hell is the matter with you. But if you stray once, buddy, you're outta here."

The therapist at first attempted to see Richard alone, but soon realized that it was all but impossible for him to give any history about his family of origin, or to talk about his marriage. It was as if he lived in a world without history and without feeling. It was very hard for the therapist to keep on the subject at hand. It was remarkably easy for Richard to maneuver the session toward areas where he felt quite safe, for example, some wonderful new computer or gadget, some tidbit about world news. The therapist devised a method that involved one weekly meeting with the couple, and two meetings per week with Richard. In the meetings with the two, the therapist was able to remain reasonably certain that Richard was abiding by the contract to have no contact with other women. Jane had become so alert that it would have been all but impossible for him to fool her. She also was an invaluable source of information about his family. "My mother was a perfectly nice lady," he would say." To this, Jane would parry, "I don't think in all the years I knew her, she ever hugged or kissed you, let alone your dad." Or: "My brother is a good guy, even though he's a little low in energy." "Not so low that he couldn't loan you his pad and let you alone to screw Arlette." The therapist was then able to take this information and begin to draw Richard out.

The sessions with Richard alone were at first agonizingly slow. "Jane was saying something about your mother maybe not being such a great lady," the therapist would say. This was followed by perhaps five minutes of silence and the usual charming smile. Finally—"nah, she wasn't a bad lady—Jane is so critical." Over many months, the story of a bleak, emotionless home in which appearance was everything and emotion nothing began to emerge. Richard began to describe how empty his life had been, how alone he felt, what a "wimp" he thought he was—until he discovered his talent with computers. He was also able to describe his marriage as a "way out of having to find women." Up to that point, he'd had a series of "one-nighters," but never a lengthy relationship.

He also felt safe with her because she was about seven years his senior and already had teenage children. He felt he was entering "into an already formed family." In this way, he said, he avoided the "trials and tribulations of raising little kids." The therapist was able to use this to help him to begin to understand how inadequately parented he had felt, and how lacking he was in knowledge about how men and women act toward one another, let alone toward children. He said that earlier in the marriage Jane had been not only an exemplary mother, but also someone who took equally good care of him. He felt "worshipped." But as the marriage went on and she became more sharply critical and more demanding of his interest and involvement, he began to turn off.

It was at that point, when he was feeling like a failure in the marriage, that his old pattern of one-nighters began to seem very appealing. Only at this time it had the quality of a necessity for him, instead of just a kind of "play." Little by little, over the course of over a year of therapy, Richard began to develop the ability to name some of his feelings. He came to see how being worshipped and being masterful over women gave him a temporary charge. He also came to see how, within a few hours, he was filled with the need to do the same again.

Jane's complaints went well beyond the issue of his womanizing. As she became somewhat more convinced that his liaisons had stopped, she focused on how his work and his obsession with his computers and his other gadgets were also kinds of liaisons. If he could not now become intimate with her, she didn't think she could maintain herself in the marriage any longer. At first Richard was incensed. What more could she want of him? Not only had he stopped his liaisons, but he no longer even flirted. It was only at this point that he began to piece together how inadequate he felt about what he called "the task of being intimate." He began to see how he could reduce his stress with his work, his computers, his women, but that he never felt truly comfortable either when alone, or alone with a woman when he didn't have a "job" to do, that is, to seduce her. At that point, the therapy began to focus on helping Richard and Jane to share feelings and time with one another. This combination of individual and couples therapy was helpful in producing what both agreed was positive change.

Conclusion

Theoretical formulations enhance our understanding of various types of marital infidelity. Several examples revealed the impact of masculinity ideology, gender role strain, masculine entitlement, alexithymia, and pathological arrhythmicity on men who cannot maintain monogamous relationships. Pursuit relationships, such as womanizing, one-night stands, and Don Juanism are heavily influenced by a belief system that sees women as objects. Affair behavior is more often based in the ideology that men will achieve high levels of emotional succor in marriage, primarily because they are "good providers."

Men who expect unconditional love or respect in marriage can't find it. Nor can they find power in marriage, which is at its best a relationship of equity and parity. In their affairs, their one night stands and their womanizing, some men seek a kind of surcease, at least for a while, from the pressures of adult relationship. With rare exceptions, even if an affair ends a marriage, it will not become the man's next marriage. If a man doesn't learn what has motivated his affair, he is likely, in the end, to have experienced not one but two failed attempts at monogamy.

References

Bernard, J. (1972). *The future of marriage.* New York: World.

Bernard, J. (1981). The good provider role: Its rise and fall. *American Psychologist, 36,* 1–12.

Brooks, G. R. (1995). *The centerfold syndrome: How men can overcome objectification and achieve intimacy with women.* San Francisco: Jossey-Bass.

Brown, E. M. (1991). *Patterns of infidelity and their treatment.* New York: Brunner/Mazel.

Earle, R., & Crow, G. (1989). *Lonely all the time: Recognizing, understanding and overcoming sex addiction, for addicts and codependents.* New York: Pocketbooks.

Glass, S. P., & Wright, T. L. (1995). Reconstructing marriages after the trauma of infidelity. In K. Halford & H. Markman (Eds.), *Clinical handbook of marriage and couple interventions.* New York: Wiley.

Kinsey, A., Pomeroy, W., & Martin, C. E. (1948). *Sexual behavior in the human male.* Philadelphia: Saunders.

Kupers, T. (1993). *Revisioning men's lives: Gender, intimacy and power.* New York: Guilford Press.

Lawson, A. (1988). *Adultery: An analysis of love and betrayal.* New York: Basic Books.

Levant, R., & Kopecky, G. (1995/1996). *Masculinity reconstructed: Changing the rules of manhood at work, in relationships and in family life.* New York: Dutton.

Lusterman, D.-D. (1989, May/June). Marriage at the turning point. *Family Networker, 13,* 44–51.

Lusterman, D.-D. (1995). Treating marital infidelity. In. R. Mikesell, D.-D. Lusterman & S. McDaniel (Eds.), *Integrating family therapy: Handbook of family psychology and systems theory* (pp. 259–269). Washington, DC: American Psychological Association.

Moultrup, D. (1990). *Husbands, wives and lovers: The emotional system of the extramarital affair.* New York: Guilford Press.

Nordstrom, B. (1986). Why men get married: More and less traditional men compared. In R. A. Lewis & R. E. Salt (Eds.), *Men in families.* Newbury Park, CA: Sage.

Philpot, C., & Brooks, G. (1995). Intergender communication and gender-sensitive therapy. In R. Mikesell, D.-D. Lusterman, & S. McDaniel (Eds.), *Integrating family therapy: Handbook of family psychology and systems theory* (pp. 303–325). Washington, DC: American Psychological Association.

Pittman, F. (1989). *Private lies: Infidelity and the betrayal of intimacy.* New York: Norton.

Pleck, J. (1995). The gender role strain paradigm: An update. In R. Levant & B. Pollack (Eds.), *A new psychology of men* (pp. 11–32). New York: Basic Books.

Smith, T. (1993). *American sexual behavior* (Version 1.2). Chicago: Nation Opinion Research Center, University of Chicago.

Vaughan, P. (1989). *The monogamy myth.* New York: Newmarket Press.

CHAPTER 5

Sex as Commodity: Men and the Sex Industry

WENDY E. STOCK

T HE TERM *sex industry*, including pornography, phone sex, Internet computer sex, interactive compact disc sex, strip shows, and prostitution, is an oxymoron that should alert us that something is amiss in the juxtaposition of these two terms. Were it not for our desensitized tolerance toward the marketing of sex, the very term would shout an alarm to us, revealing the dismembering of sexuality from potentially intimate, mutually vulnerable, human eroticism to a preprogrammed dance of mannequins, interacting as if the only value was the execution of the sex act itself. The sex industry removes sexuality from the interpersonal context into the arena of business and profit, creating and maintaining a market-driven commodity, packaging and selling our eroticism back to us in an almost unrecognizable, decontextualized form, a disembodied product.

What Is the Problem with Nonrelational Sex?

Nonrelational sex is not inherently bad. Indeed, many men and women report positive experiences associated with it. The important distinction is that nonrelational sex can be an option in the repertoire of one's sexuality, and can be engaged in with respect and regard for one's partner. In contrast, traditional male socialization encourages nonrelational sex as the most desirable form of sex, and often as the only option in men's sexual repertoires. Thus, even within a committed relationship, men may be unable to simultaneously engage their emotions and their sexuality with their partners. The commodification of nonrelational sex by the sex industry sells men a limited and often alienating form of sexuality. Males in our culture learn that nonrelational sex gives them permission to deny the humanity of their partners, and to objectify and even violate the partner who is actually treated more as a prop. Men's dysfunctional pursuit of, obsession with, and dependence upon nonrelational sex as a means to confirm manhood undermines their ability to experience relational sex.

Power: Primary Driver of the Male Gender Role and Nonrelational Sex

Gender roles themselves do not appear randomly, but develop within the context of gender inequity and the tendency for social arrangements to reinforce the position of the dominant group. Thus, the male gender role exists within the context of power inequity between men and women, which is fundamental to and etiologic of the construction of gender roles. While the relative importance of power and gender roles has been debated, the notion of gender role and the gender role strain paradigm developed by Pleck (1995) is consistent with a social constructionist approach emphasizing power as an important dynamic in gender. As Pleck (1995) states, the social constructionist approach "does have the strength of making power dynamics between men and women central to the understanding of gender, which they should be" (p. 24). Power dynamics, expressed as the tendency for the dominant group to attempt to maintain advantage over the nondominant group, drives the construction of the male gender role. In a patriarchy, male socialization tends to prepare men as a class to retain their power over women, and social institutions support this. This is not a conscious, planned process. It is logical that the imperative to maintain male power would determine the form that male socialization takes. To put it simply, power is seen as the primary driver shaping the construction of the male role, and gender role socialization provides the mechanisms by which males are trained to maintain power. Men experience gender role strain (Pleck, 1995) when failing to enact gender role behavior that maintains their power, although enacting the traditional male role sometimes carries a cost for men.

For men in our culture, ensuring one-up status in the gender hierarchy relative to women requires *exploitative* rather than *egalitarian* relationships, compromising the potential for true emotional and sexual intimacy. As Brooks (1995) writes, ". . . we need to consider men's reluctance to be intimate not as a fear or as a skill deficit but as a semi-intentional strategy to monitor interpersonal distance . . . emotional stoicism is often taken to represent dispassionate personal control" (p. 105). Individual males maintain gender status over women by disclosing less, avoiding emotional vulnerability, objectifying and depersonalizing members of the nondominant group, having access to resources (sex, for example) without losing advantage (limiting access to one's own emotions and feelings), and using a less vulnerable strategy (money) to procure access to sex, to meet needs for physical contact, and for reconfirmation of masculinity. These methods can often be actualized by means of the sex industry. Patriarchal institutions also tend to preserve male status. Prostitution is an institution within the sex industry that developed to support men's desire for nonrelational sex, yet it is most often the prostitutes who are arrested, less often the pimps, and even more rarely, male customers. The sex industry has developed to serve the need of men to maintain gender advantage over women in the area of sexuality. The price of maintaining power over women is higher than many men realize.

The Gender Role Strain Paradigm and the Sex Industry

The gender role strain paradigm encompasses the specific aspects of the male role that potentiate men's involvement in the various forms of nonrelational sexuality sold by the sex industry. Pleck's (1995) updated gender role strain paradigm identifies three varieties of male gender role strain: trauma-strain, discrepancy-strain, and dysfunction-strain. This paradigm is useful in delineating the paths by which men's potential capacity for relationships is developmentally warped.

TRAUMA-STRAIN

Trauma-strain includes severe forms of trauma related to sexual abuse of males, homophobia, and combat experiences, but has also been applied to male role socialization under traditional masculinity ideology.[1] Levant (1996) has written about gender role socialization of men as "the ordeal of emotion socialization," including it within a discussion of trauma-strain (Pleck, 1995). Levant reviews a number of

---

[1] I am uncomfortable with the characterization of male (or female) role socialization as "traumatic," although I believe that traditional gender role socialization is emotionally and psychologically damaging to both men and women. I prefer to reserve the term "trauma" for extreme experiences that share components of terror or torment, fear for one's own or another's life, severe emotional, physical, or sexual abuse, or witnessing any of the above.

studies showing that although boys start life more emotionally expressive than girls (Haviland & Malatesta, 1981; Weinberg, 1992), they learn to suppress and channel their emotions by adulthood. According to Levant, this "crossover in emotional expression" (Haviland & Malatesta, 1981, p. 16, cited in Levant, 1996) is accomplished by mothers "managing" their more emotional male infants by distracting them from their distress, fathers socializing their toddler children along gender-stereotyped lines, parents discouraging sons' expression of vulnerable emotions, and the influence of all-male peer groups in which stoicism and toughness are valued while empathy and vulnerability are ridiculed. The consequences for men (Levant, 1996) include failure to develop emotional empathy, development of mild alexithymia (lacking words for emotions) leading to inability to access their own emotions, transformation of vulnerable feelings into anger, and overreliance on sexuality for expression of caring emotions.

Socialization leaves men unaware of their own feelings, unable to articulate these to themselves or others, finding the expression of vulnerability unacceptable, translating vulnerable feelings into anger, often without awareness, and dependent upon sexuality for all expression of tenderness and caring. These socialization practices set men up to find nonrelational sex the best solution to meeting their sexual and disowned emotional needs. Nonrelational sex is a means to feel accepted and to feel intimacy in the form of physical contact, without the need to maintain any verbalized or emotional vulnerability. Men's socialized lack of empathy and impaired emotional self-awareness and absence of language for expressing feelings means that men may often be having nonrelational sex even within their long-term, committed relationships. However, women in committed relationships may expect a higher standard of intimacy than do women in casual or anonymous sexual relationships. Hence, men's normative developmental experiences of trauma-strain, which crushes their communication and empathy abilities, prepares men to find nonrelational sex and the products of the sex industry the easiest, most appealing, and most importantly, the emotionally safest form of sex. There is no need for men to establish intimacy when masturbating to a pornography magazine or to a downloaded image from the Internet, engaging in phone sex, sexually manipulating a CD-ROM-produced female image, or having sex with a prostitute.

Several other aspects of normative developmental traumas in male socialization are *separation from mother* (Chodorow, 1978), *defensive autonomy* (Pollack, 1995), and *destructive entitlement* (Boszormenyi-Nagy & Ulrich, 1981).

Separation from Mother

In order for boys to earn male status, they are expected to make an early and sharp separation from their mothers. The cultural imperative for the boy to disidentify with his mother leads inevitably to viewing all females as "the Other." This enforced separation is the single most destructive process in male socialization. The cultural demand to experience the male self as separate from the female caretaker is directly related to maintaining male power (e.g., the need for a dominant group to enculturate an identity as not only different, but superior to the nondominant group). The boy learns that to maintain his higher position in the gender hierarchy, he must, at all costs, avoid exhibiting any femalelike behaviors. Particularly for young boys, being called a girl is deeply insulting and demeaning.

What are the implications of separation from mother for men in their subsequent relationships to women? Emotional and sexual intimacy require viewing one's partner as similar to oneself, as a person whose needs are equally important as one's own, and as a person with whom emotional closeness will not translate to loss of self. The sex industry addresses men's learned aversion to perceiving women as fully human and equal by creating images and services that present women as objects, sexual merchandise—not *real* human beings. The influence of the sex industry goes beyond affecting those men who are direct consumers of its products. The mere existence of the sex industry legitimizes and creates social acceptance for men to objectify, dehumanize, and fetishize all women in their lives, including women with whom men have their most intimate relationships. These internalized images and schemas act as filters through which men learn to view women, preserving a sense of male separateness and higher status, while allowing men sexual contact with women.

Defensive Autonomy

Feelings of yearning for maternal closeness and attachment become equated with loss of separateness and thus, loss of maleness. Such feelings are vigilantly defended against and often denied *(defensive autonomy)*, motivating male distancing in heterosexual relationships. In fact, the breakdown of defensive autonomy may be seen as one cause of discrepancy-strain (discussed later), in which a man has allowed himself to feel too attached to a woman, implying loss of maleness as traditionally defined and generating anxiety and lowered self-esteem. For example, a man may consider himself a "wimp" for seeming to overvalue his monogamous relationship with a female partner and fear that his peers (or an internalized Greek chorus of peers) may accuse him of being "pussy whipped." Such a man might be threatened enough to seek non-relational sex outside his primary relationship by paying for a prostitute, or may utilize pornography to help him reestablish a sense of separateness from his partner. Another example of defensive autonomy is the customary bachelor party the night before a man's wedding ceremony, when he will pledge his love and commitment to one woman. A traditional element of the bachelor party is the hired stripper, the porno film, or a "last night" out with a prostitute, usually done as a group activity. These activities provide the groom with a means to create emotional distance from his future wife by placing her on a level with other women as sex objects. Perhaps this is intended to serve as an emotional prophylactic against attachment for the newly married man.

Destructive Entitlement

The psychic wound resulting in the premature loss of the maternal holding environment can become transmuted into *destructive entitlement*, based on the unconscious belief of the angry, wounded child within the adult man, demanding that other women compensate for his great loss. This dynamic works synergistically with separation from mother, for if a man learns to perceive himself as separate and women as the "Other" (and not a person like oneself), it then becomes easier to enact destructive entitlement upon the female, once reduced to an object. For example, the sheer hostility toward women evident in much pornography; the use of children in place of women in pornography and prostitution; and the high rates of rape, beating, and murder of prostitutes by their customers are instances of destructive entitlement in the sex industry.

Summary of Effects of Trauma-Strain

Levant (Chapter 1) views unconnected lust as "a defensive adaptation to a series of socialization experiences and normative developmental traumas." These aspects of typical male socialization prepare men to avoid identification with their female partners. This disidentification interferes with men's ability to regard women as equals or to consider women's needs and feelings equally important, causes men to disown their own needs for attachment and closeness, and predisposes men to buy or take what they have been so unjustly deprived of in childhood.

Trauma-strain encompasses a range of socialization experiences that lay the blueprint for males to desire nonrelational sex, and to be easy marks for the sex industry that capitalizes on their disidentification with women (separation), imbues with value the sense of distance possible when fantasizing about a pornographic depiction while having sex with one's partner (defensive autonomy), and sexualizes the exploitation and degradation of women, as in pornography and prostitution (destructive entitlement). If unconnected lust is "a defensive adaptation" of individual males to normative developmental traumas, then the sex industry is a culturally defensive adaptation that institutionalizes men's compensatory need for nonrelational sexuality, following the crippling of their ability to value and partake of relational intimacy and sexuality.

DISCREPANCY-STRAIN

Discrepancy-strain is experienced by men when they fail to live up to their internalized ideal of manhood. What are the beliefs males internalize about their sexuality that can cause discrepancy-strain? Zilbergeld (1978), arguably the most prominent sex therapist in treatment of male sexual problems, listed 10 sexual myths believed by most men, in his first edition of *Male Sexuality*. He presented these myths as dysfunctional beliefs, often etiologic of sexual problems among men. As stated in Chapter 1, these were:

Myth 1. Men shouldn't discuss certain feelings.
Myth 2. Sex is a performance.
Myth 3. A man must orchestrate sex.
Myth 4. A man always wants and is always ready to have sex.
Myth 5. All physical contact must lead to sex.
Myth 6. Sex equals intercourse.
Myth 7. Sex requires an erection.
Myth 8. Good sex is increasing excitement terminated only by orgasm.

It is telling that Zilbergeld (1978) originally presented this belief system about male sexuality as damaging "myths" that men should question and reject, and in 1992, framed these beliefs as a neutral description of men's *style* of sex, an essentialist position implying uncritical validation of a nonrelational, mechanistic, and goal-oriented model of male sexuality. (See Chapter 1 for a description of Zilbergeld's position).

The shift in tone between the first and second versions of Zilbergeld's book is consistent with the regressive cultural backlash against the feminist critique of traditional gender roles, as well as the positions of the more defensive and self-serving aspects of the men's movement. Men who criticize traditional ideals of manhood are more often received by other men as traitors to their gender rather than as heroes, and may be less likely to generate enthusiastic book sales among the male audience. Zilbergeld's shift toward uncritical acceptance of traditional male sexuality reveals the depth of cultural resistance to changing gendered power relations in the area of sexuality.

How might discrepancy-strain from failure to live up to these deeply entrenched traditional beliefs about male sexuality make men more reliant on products/services of the sex industry? Imagine the following scenario.

A 50-year-old man who is stressed and exhausted from overwork climbs into bed with his sexually desirous wife and expects that he should be able to respond immediately with an erection, masterfully assume sexual command, and sweep himself and his wife into passionate orgasmic release (Myths 2, 3, and 4). Realistically, this man may be unable to attain or sustain an erection, and he may not be in the mood, in any case, to assume full responsibility for conducting a virtuoso sexual performance (Myths 2, 3, 6, and 7). One way to approach this situation would be for the man to communicate his physical and emotional state to his wife and to offer to snuggle with her, or to sexually pleasure her without intercourse, or to hold her while she sexually pleasures herself. Even more deviant from the traditional male role, this man might ask his wife to hold and reassure him, or ask her for a massage, or ask her for some quality listening time. More typically, this man will follow the traditional male sexual role and not discuss his feelings with his wife, attempt intercourse, fail, turn away from his wife, attempt to go to sleep, and feel like a failure as a man (Myths 1, 5, 6, and 7). Here is an example of discrepancy-strain directly related to the traditional belief system ("myths") about male sexuality. The traditional man will see sex as the only way to experience closeness and acceptance and to bolster his work-battered ego. When he fails, he will feel badly about himself and will likely search for ways to feel better as a sexual performer and hence, as a man. In the absence of alternative conceptualizations of masculinity and sexuality, this man is perfectly primed as a vulnerable and needy consumer for the panoply of products and services sold by the sex industry, by which this man can attempt to restore his deflated ego (and id). The following options are available for this purpose, through the sex industry:

1. Magazine, video, or Internet pornography, presenting women with unrealistically perfect bodies as sexual playthings, devoted to the

sexual pleasure of the male viewer or actor, with whom the consumer can projectively identify.

2. CD-ROM interactive pornography, in which the consumer can experience a sense of control over the electronically-generated fantasy woman, choosing which sexual act to engage her in, including programs with options of bondage, torture, and dismemberment.

3. Phone sex, in which the consumer dictates what type of sexual interaction or fantasy will take place with the paid female operator.

4. Prostitution, in which the consumer can dictate what type of sexual interaction will take place with a real woman, in an anonymous encounter with little emotional risk.

In all of these cases, the consumer can become sexually aroused, develop an erection, and either masturbate or be brought to orgasm, thus reassuring himself of his virility and his male identity. Utilizing pornography or prostitution is a traditional male behavior. These options resolve the anxiety of discrepancy-strain while leaving intact the dysfunctional belief system that originally caused the consumer his distress. This solution also avoids the need to become emotionally vulnerable to his female partner, which could induce more discrepancy-strain. Restoration of a sense of control in a sexual context can alleviate the discrepancy-strain related to sense of failure experienced in the consumer's actual sexual relationship.

DYSFUNCTION-STRAIN

Dysfunction-strain[2] occurs when the successful fulfillment of the requirements of the male role paradoxically have negative side effects for the men themselves, and on those close to them (Levant, 1996). There is much cultural support for dysfunctional behavior as consistent with the male role. For example, Zilbergeld (1992) writes:

As you might expect, men more frequently imagine sex with strangers, sex with more than one person, and forcing a woman to have sex with

---

[2] The concept of dysfunction-strain could be critiqued as unrealistically one-sided. In many cases, men's enactment of their role may result in reward, rather than punishment, given the overwhelming cultural support for traditional male role behavior. For example, sexual coercion and rape are generally not reported or prosecuted, and young men who use sexual coercion may actually receive social recognition from peers for having "scored." It may be useful to consider dysfunction-strain as sometimes dysfunctional for the individual man, or as "functional" for the individual man but dysfunctional in a social/cultural sense.

them . . . *There is no basis for saying that any of these fantasies is abnormal or unhealthy* [italics mine]." (p. 138, pb.)

Although some people have trouble with this one, I also believe it's fine to express anger through sex . . . Some couples report their best sex occurs in the midst of an argument." (p. 87, pb.)

Masculine gender role stress, a form of discrepancy-strain, has been found to indirectly contribute to relationship distress and to sexual aggression (Malamuth, Linz, Heavey, Barnes, & Acker 1995). This finding speaks to dysfunction-strain. Men who are more threatened by discrepancy-strain are more likely to engage in sexual aggression, which may be seen as compensatory behavior. In this prospective study, a sample of 176 men were followed up 10 years later to determine whether their attitudes were predictive of their behavior toward women. The Masculine Gender Role Stress Scale (MGRSS; Eisler & Skidmore, 1987) was used, which primarily measures discrepancy-strain. The MGRSS assesses the degree of stress men associate with situations that challenge traditional sex roles, including physical adequacy, emotional inexpressiveness, subordination to women, intellectual inferiority, and performance failures involving work and sex. Participants indicated how stressful they would rate various situations, such as being unemployed, being around a member of the opposite sex who is much taller than you, letting a member of the opposite sex take control of the situation, and being unable to become sexually aroused. Masculine gender role stress was found to indirectly contribute to both relationship distress and to sexual aggression. Using a confluence model of sexual aggression, two sets of characteristics, labeled hostile masculinity and impersonal sex, were found to predict those men who would be in distressed relationships with women and who would also be sexually aggressive. Masculine role stress contributed directly to the hostile masculinity path. The hostile masculinity path directly predicted sexual aggression. The hostile masculinity path also was related to impersonal sex, which predicted both relationship distress and sexual aggression. Sexually aggressive men reported a greater frequency of becoming aroused by a stranger and a greater number of extramarital affairs. Certainly, if impersonal sex is a central component of the male role, sexual infidelity and sexual aggression represent its successful actualization and at the same time, are often dysfunctional for men themselves in their relationships with women.

Malamuth et al. (1995) suggest that an impersonal orientation permits gratification from coercive sex, in contrast to an orientation toward highly personal or intimate sexual activity, which would be incompatible with sexual coercion. As Malamuth et al. (1995) state:

> An intimate orientation would imply that a person was concerned with his or her partner's reactions, feelings, and pleasure, and particularly concerned that the partner not be injured or his or her feelings hurt. Within such an orientation, much of the gratification from sex may be based on the feedback a person receives from knowing that he or she was worthy enough to have been freely chosen by his or her sexual partner. The impersonal orientation to sex, in contrast, enables a dismissal of concerns about the partner's choice and feelings and sets the stage for the possibility of coercive sex. (p. 367)

According to these authors, a noncommittal orientation to sexuality may contribute to other types of conflict with women in adulthood, in addition to sexual aggression. Men with this orientation may be more likely to be unfaithful in monogamous relationships, which may be a source of conflict that can lead to arguments and physical aggression. It seems likely that a strong predilection for nonrelational sex would also result in greater involvement in the sex industry, regardless of the effect on intimate relationships. Dysfunction-strain has been theorized to result in, among other outcomes, (a) violence, including male violence against women in the family, rape and sexual assault, and sexual harassment; and (b) sexual excess, including promiscuity, involvement with pornography, and sexual addiction (Brooks & Silverstein, 1995).

Men's Nonrelational Orientation to Sex and the Sex Industry

The gender role strain paradigm has provided the overarching framework for the following overview and analysis of several components of the sex industry, and how it helps to create and maintain men's need for nonrelational sex. Although the sex industry markets itself as progressive, unconventional, and iconoclastic, its profits depend on the distress men feel because of the traditional male belief system. The sex industry and traditional masculinity have a symbiotic relationship, with the sex industry supporting myths of male sexuality, while offering a false panacea to males and deriving profit from their pain. A dismantling of traditional male ideology would put the sex industry out of business. The effect of the sex industry on men is less often experienced as direct sexual abuse, sexual coercion, sexual discrimination, and sexual harassment of men, as it is for women.[3] The predominant effect of the sex industry on men is through the alienation from self, an impaired ability to relate intimately to romantic/sexual partners, and an increased likelihood of inflicting emotional and physical harm on female romantic/sexual partners and on children.

ADDICTION TO PRODUCTS OF THE SEX INDUSTRY

Another injurious impact of the sex industry on men, perhaps more insidious than those described so far, is the addictive nature of its products, which provide the most indirect and vicarious forms of nonrelational sex. While application of the addiction paradigm to sexuality has been criticized (Barth & Kinder, 1987; Levine & Troiden, 1988; Moser, 1993), the addictive process does accurately describe a pattern of behavior that has been labeled as sexual impulsivity (Barth & Kinder, 1987), compulsive sexual behavior (Quadland, 1985), sexual addiction (Carnes, 1983; Schwartz & Brasted, 1985), and hypersexuality (Orford, 1978). The cycle of behaviors and subjective experiences attributed to sexual addiction may include craving; disinhibition; dissociative states during use; and remorse, shame, and guilt following use. These elements can characterize the compulsive and dysfunctional use of both sex and substances. While the mechanisms underlying different addictions are assumed to vary, what remains common is the pattern of making poor life choices associated with the addiction, combined with a subjective loss of control over the addictive behavior. The concept of sex addiction has been criticized for repathologizing forms of erotic behavior that became acceptable in the 1960s and 1970s, for "medicalization" of normative departures (Conrad & Schneider, 1980), and for overfocusing on a behavior that may be secondary to other diagnoses (Moser, 1993).

There is agreement, however, that sexually "addictive" behavior exists, although there is controversy as to how to designate it (Moser, 1993). According to Barth and Kinder (1987), the descriptive clinical reports of the presentation of sexual addiction are remarkably consistent. The sexually impulsive individual usually exhibits such behavior in reaction to anxiety, and uses sexual activity as a means of avoiding or escaping from personal problems, social stress, and feeling states of

---

[3] Although all aspects of the sex industry can have seriously damaging and sometimes fatal implications for women, this chapter focuses on the contribution of the sex industry to the problematic aspects of nonrelational sex for men. For an excellent review of the harms of pornography and of sexual objectification to women, the reader is referred to Russell (1993a, 1993b).

loneliness, low self-esteem, boredom, tension, sadness, or anger. These negative feelings are mislabeled as "horniness," and trigger the search for sexual release (Levine & Troiden, 1988). Sexual activity may temporarily reduce these negative feelings, providing relief described as a sexual "fix" or "high" similar to those experienced with use of illegal substances, alcohol, or food. While self-esteem may be increased for a brief time, but may soon be replaced by emptiness, self-disgust, guilt, or remorse over the sexual activity, which rekindles the feelings of anxiety and the cycle of compulsive sexual behavior (Levine & Troiden, 1988). What has been missing from this model, to date, is recognition of the impact of gender role on compulsive sexual behavior. For men, it is likely that gender role strain, specifically discrepancy strain, contributes to many men's anxiety and lowered self-esteem, when they inevitably fail to live up to the beliefs that they have internalized about their sexuality. For this reason, there are many so-called "normative" presentations of sexual addiction that originate from gender role strain and vary in degree of severity. Distinguishing the nonpathologic presentations of sexual addiction from the pathologic is not well-documented, which, according to Moser (1993) is a valid criticism of this concept. Much behavior that would fall short of traditional diagnosis as pathologic sex addiction is nonetheless dysfunctional for men. In relying on video, magazine, Internet, CD pornography, phone sex, strip shows, or prostitution, men become hooked on nonrelational sexual "fixes" that are ephemeral and short-lived, but which carry the promise of satisfaction. Brooks (1995) gives examples from his clients in a men's therapy group who manifest "normative" sex addiction in their compulsively voyeuristic behavior, fixation with new and novel sexual encounters, disappointment with their female partners for their failure to look like the bodies of women in pornography, in a sense of disempowerment and emotional incapacitation in response to attractive women (Brooks, 1995, pp. 38–39).

The rending of relationality and intimacy from physical sexuality has left men with very little of emotional sustenance. Like the well-known experiments in which rats became addicted to non-nutritive drug substances, and continued to press the drug-releasing bar to the point of starvation and death, men use the sex industry to provide them with immediate gratification that leaves them perpetually dissatisfied. Rather than face the inherent emptiness of this pursuit, many men simply increase their consumption of sex industry products, with the hope that "more is better." Ultimately dissatisfied with an exclusive diet of nonrelational sex, but yet unable to achieve connection with the actual women in their relationships, men are kept in a perpetual state of unfulfillment, making them easy marks for spending more money on products of the sex industry. To contextualize the amount of spending this represents, a recent report (*Boston Globe*, 1997) found that the pornography industry alone grosses $10 billion per year, comparable to the commercial film industry ($12.2 billion), and outgrossing by almost 200 percent the music recording industry ($5.8 billion). Were men to invest $10 billion yearly in couple, group, or individual psychotherapy, or the equivalent amount of work time required to earn the money they expend on pornography, this would significantly improve many heterosexual relationships and lower the divorce rate.

It is suggested here that nonrelational sex is by its nature, addictive, in that it provides only temporary relief from the anxiety and alienation created by the sexual expectations of the male gender role. Due to these expectations, many men are unable to experience relational sex even in their intimate relationships. Many men are at the very least, dependent, and frequently compulsive or addictive in their use of, and by, the sex industry.

PORNOGRAPHY

When men hear critiques of pornography, a common reaction is defensiveness and a "don't go there" attitude. John Stoltenberg (1994), when attending a gathering of avowedly antisexist men, urged that some action be organized to protest the movie *Snuff*. As Stoltenberg relates, "I was stunned to hear these men—whose published work I once admired—sputter and spout their rationale for *not* taking action" (1994, p. 11). For many men, criticism of pornography is experienced as criticism of their basic sexuality, and specifically, to an attack on how they attain erections. Since many men's eroticism has been shaped from the beginning by images from pornography, it is impossible for them to envision an alternative. Thus, to criticize pornographized sexuality is perceived by many men as a direct attack on their sexuality with the implied threat of depriving them of erections.

Explicating the content of pornography is crucial to understanding its effects. The most useful typology for describing pornography's content has been developed by Check and Guloien (1989):

1. *Sexually violent pornography*, which includes the overt infliction of pain and use of force, or the threat of either.
2. *Degrading/dehumanizing pornography*, which does not include physical violence, but in which men or women are verbally abused or portrayed as having animal characteristics. In it, women are often shown

as lacking any human character or identity and are depicted as mere sexual playthings, instantly responsive to male sexual demands. They worship male genitals and their own value depends on the quality of their genitals and breasts.

3. *Erotica,* which portrays positive, affectionate human sexual interaction between consenting individuals participating within a balance of power.

It has been estimated that across various media, the content of pornography is approximately 15 percent violent, 70 percent degrading/dehumanizing, and 15 percent erotica. Cowan, Lee, Levy, and Snyder (1988) investigated X-rated videos, finding that dominance and exploitation were major themes in 54 percent of sexually explicit scenes. Smith (1976) in a content analysis of 428 "adults only" paperbacks found that one-fifth of all the sex episodes involved completed rape, and over 97 percent of the rapes portrayed resulted in orgasm for the victims. In 75 percent of these rapes, multiple orgasm occurred. Malamuth and Spinner (1980) found in a content analysis of cartoons and pictorials in *Penthouse* and *Playboy* that about 5 percent of the pictorials and 10 percent of the cartoons were sexually violent.

Much research has been conducted on the effects of men's exposure to violent and degrading pornography, finding increases in acceptance of violence against women, increases in rape supportive beliefs, increases in callous attitudes toward women, increases in rape fantasies, trivialization of rape, increases in blaming the rape victim, decreases in ratings of rape victim trauma, and increased desensitization to violence against women (Malamuth & Donnerstein, 1984; Zillmann & Bryant, 1984). While some researchers have been reluctant to extrapolate from these findings a causal relationship of pornography to rape, Russell (1993a) has developed a theoretical model of pornography as a cause of rape, which is supported by the research cited above. Russell contends that pornography causes rape by predisposing some males to desire rape or by intensifying this desire, and by undermining some males' internal and social inhibitions against acting out rape desires. By normalizing and legitimizing sexual aggression as acceptable male behavior, pornography creates dysfunction-strain for many males. A major attraction of violent and degrading pornography is the pseudo-resolution it offers for trauma-strain, and particularly for men who are affected by destructive entitlement. Unfortunately, pornography is much more pervasive in its influence, beyond its effects on overt forms of sexual violence.

The first cultural representation of sex to which most young males are exposed is pornography (in video, magazine, and computerized formats). Due to their early interpersonal socialization, boys are particularly vulnerable to adopting a sexual belief system emphasizing an instrumental approach, and in particular, sexuality that supports disidentification with females, maintaining male gender status through the objectification, fixation, and conquest of women (Litewka, 1977). The most comfortable form of sexuality for men becomes one in which control of self and other is maintained, vulnerability is minimized, and in which the other is not engaged emotionally, but instead is used as an object, as found in most pornography.

Young males frequently report that their first experience of orgasm, usually through masturbation, was accompanied by the use of pornography. The pairing of a powerful sexual experience (orgasm) with exposure to positive portrayals of nonrelational sex has a strong conditioning effect. In addition to the simple behavioral conditioning of sexual arousal, it is well-known that initial and early experiences of orgasm can have a formative influence on "sexual scripts" (Gagnon & Simon, 1973), and on what is later considered erotic. Given the positive interpersonal outcomes portrayed by male actors in pornography, it is likely that young, sexually inexperienced males, often in the absence of realistic, accurate information about sexuality or relationships with women, might conclude that the scripts of males in pornography represent the successful enactment of the male role in sex, consistent with Zilbergeld's (1978) myths of male sexuality. This may be the most common way that the male consumer audience for products of the sex industry and for nonrelational sex is developed. It is through this bidirectional influence process that male sexual socialization potentiates men's desire for commodified forms of sex. This socialization creates and sustains a consumer market for products which in turn, strengthens this preference among current and newly-initiated male consumers.

Research has documented the pervasive exposure of children and adolescents to pornography. Anderson summarizes Check's (1995) findings:

> Pornography is often the first exposure children have to sexually explicit subject matter, so it can set the standard for normal or appropriate sexual behavior. Teenage boys are the biggest consumers of pornography. Teenagers don't just look; they learn from pornography. Twenty-nine percent of boys rated pornography over parents, teachers, books, school, and peers, as their source for the most useful information about sex. And what do they learn? Forty-three percent of boys and 16 percent of girls

think it is okay or are not sure if it's okay for a boy to hold down a girl and force her to have sex if she sexually excites him. (1995, p. 126)

Bryant (1985) conducted 600 telephone interviews with male and female students, evenly divided into junior high school, high school, and adults aged 19 to 39 years. For males, exposure to pornography occurred generally before age 13. High school males reported having seen an average of 16.1 issues of soft-core magazines, and junior high males said they had seen an average of 2.5 issues. Although they were legally under age, junior high students reported having seen an average of 16.3 "unedited sexy R-rated films" (p. 135). The average age of first exposure to sexually oriented R-rated films for all respondents was 12.5 years (p. 135). Among junior high school students, 72 percent of the males reported that "they wanted to try some sexual experiment or sexual behavior that they had seen in their initial exposure to X-rated material" (p. 140). Male high school students were the most likely (31%) to report trying the behaviors portrayed (Bryant, 1985, p. 141, cited in Russell, 1993a). Stock (1993) reported on the specific behaviors imitated from pornography among a sample of 160 heterosexual male undergraduates, their average age 21. Sixty-nine percent reported that pornography had significantly influenced their early sexual fantasies, and 81 percent, their current sexual fantasies. Sixty-four percent reported that they had initiated sexual behaviors with female partners that they had seen in pornography. Among these behaviors were ejaculation on the face/body of partner, 37 percent; anal intercourse, 19 percent; bondage/discipline, 13 percent; golden showers (urinating on partner) 8 percent; and sadomasochism, 5 percent. Thirty-seven percent of these men had described sex acts they had seen in pornography and asked their partners to do them, including "her giving you oral sex," 41 percent; "her giving you 'deep throat' oral sex," 32 percent; "making her talk dirty," 24 percent; anal intercourse, 15 percent; and "making her do acts she felt ashamed of," 12 percent. It should be noted that the behaviors described above are not often cited by women as sexually arousing or emotionally pleasing. As a more dramatic example of dysfunction-strain, 27 percent reported having ignored their partner's request to stop sexual activity, based on the depictions of women in pornography who enjoyed being coerced, and male actors who were rewarded for sexual coercion.

Pornography could also be said to be both a cause and a reflection of discrepancy-strain. Relatively large percentages of these males reported disappointment with their own appearance relative to male actors in pornography (60%), specifically with their height (22%), muscularity

(48%), and penis size (29%) (Stock, 1993). Men also reported disappointment with their partner's body in comparison to women in pornography (51%), specifically with their partner's breasts (27%), rear end (35%), legs (27%), and weight (23%). These males further reported that pornography made them feel sexually inadequate (16%), pressured to perform (20%), and makes sex feel like a performance (26%). However, pornography packs in considerable sexual arousal value in combination with destructive messages, as 79 percent of the men indicated that "porn turns me on."

The weekly television program, *20/20* (January 29, 1993), interviewed a group of Duke University students, members of Men Acting for Change. This group developed out of their concern for the difficulties they and their peers were experiencing in relationships with women, and their concern regarding the level of sexual coercion directed against the women that they knew. Anecdotal comments of these young men speaking about the effects of pornography on their sexuality and relationships further illustrate research findings cited above:

- My first masturbatory experience (and first orgasm) involved pornography.
- The standards of beauty I developed for women were based on images I saw in porn (modelesque features, large breasts).
- I kept waiting for my penis to grow as large as those portrayed in pornography. It was depressing when I realized that it never would.
- A magazine picture of a woman never says "no," doesn't talk, doesn't have needs, and when you're done, you just shut the magazine and put it back on the shelf.
- In order to reach climax, I had to fantasize about a body part of my sexual partner, or to an image from pornography; I couldn't relate to the person who I was with.

These comments suggest that the use of pornography led these men to feel dependent upon it for their sexual fantasies and arousal, and caused them to experience alienation from their sexual partners during their most intimate moments of lovemaking. These men also learned, through pornography, to objectify their female partners as a collection of body parts. Objectification is a well-known strategy historically, used by Nazis against Jews in anti-Semitic propaganda, by the Ku Klux Klan against Blacks, and by the United States against the Vietnamese people, as a means to dehumanize the "enemy" and to reduce internal or social inhibitions against harming them. It is easier to harm an object than a human being seen as like oneself.

Pornography produces dysfunction-strain in men by helping to create a compulsive, arguably addictive relationship to attractive female bodies. Brooks (1995) provides examples from his clients in a men's therapy group of how the Centerfold Syndrome can manifest in compulsively voyeuristic behavior, a fixation with new and novel sexual encounters, and in a sense of disempowerment and emotional incapacitation in response to attractive women (Brooks, 1995, pp. 38–39). According to one group member, "Women were put on this earth to tantalize men, to make their lives miserable. They were created to be gorgeous and irresistible, with those fantastic tits and asses, looking totally incredible. But it's a fuckin' trap. Whenever they want something, or just want to control some poor bastard, they just . . . flash some thigh, and a guy is totally fuckin' helpless, man" (p. 41). This adversarial belief system, based on the objectification of women leads to anger, and to men's use of exploitative strategies in their relationships with women, "The only defense is to outsmart them . . . Pretend to care, but be cold and heartless . . . Just get what you want . . . getting your rocks off—then get the fuck outta Dodge" (p. 41).

In clinical practice, I have seen a number of men who are dependent on masturbation to magazine pornography, which they often preferred to actual sexual partners. Roy B., a male in his late thirties, had used pornography as his main stimulus for masturbation during adolescence, and heavily for five years following the end of his marriage. Although he was able to develop an erection, he was unable to reach orgasm easily with his dating partners. He began to wait until his partners went to sleep after sex, and then retired to the bathroom in order to masturbate alone there to pornography. In an attempt to deal with his orgasmic difficulty, he also asked his sexual partners to wear more provocative (exhibitionistic) clothing, to act more seductive, and to undress slowly as if doing a striptease. Although some of his dating partners had complied, others had taken offense. Roy saw this as a problem of his female partners, and wished that they weren't "so prudish."

Other couples encounter conflict over the male partner's viewing of pornographic magazines or videos, and/or his requesting/insisting that his female partner view pornographic materials with him and/or engage in the sexual behaviors depicted in pornography. Quite often couples presenting for therapy with these issues are counseled that use of pornography is normative and acceptable, that it is often helpful as a sexual stimulus in relationships, and that the female partner should not be so "uptight." Rarely is the issue of the man's desire for introducing a form of sex experienced as aversive, non-intimate, and nonrelational into the couple's relationship, and rarely is his need for additional sexual stimulation of a novel type examined as a potential failure to engage with his female partner as a person, rather than as a body.

The sexual arousal patterns of a large proportion of American boys, adolescents, and men, according to Brooks (1995), meet the DSM-IV diagnostic criteria for sexual fetishism. Through classical conditioning of males' sexual responses through masturbation to "glossy, two-dimensional replications of naked female strangers," men meet all three criteria for fetishism, which include (a)"recurrent, intense sexually arousing fantasies, sexual urges, or behaviors involving the use of nonliving objects"; (b) "the fantasies, sexual urges, or behaviors can cause clinically significant distress or impairment in social, occupational, or other areas of functioning"; and (c) "the fetish objects are not limited to articles of female clothing used in cross-dressing or devices designed for the purpose of tactile genital stimulation" (American Psychiatric Association, 1994, p. 526). As Brooks (1995) notes, males are conditioned by pornography and similarly objectifying, sexually explicit materials to "make their sexual arousal more dependent upon use of sexualized images of nonliving objects than on real women with whom they are in relationships" (p. 114). The ultimate outcome of the normative paraphiliac use of pornography is desensitization to less novel stimuli, or a sexual deadening. Hugh Hefner, the founding publisher of *Playboy* magazine, has been quoted as saying he couldn't make love without drugs. Hefner admitted feeling little or nothing during sex (Mellum, 1994).

The degree of violence and hostility directed toward women in pornography serves the compensatory function of bolstering men's defenses against trauma-strain, evidencing the dynamic of destructive entitlement. Eroticized violence against a nonrelational "object" permits the fantasy of retribution against women as a class for an earlier loss of attachment, and for affronting male status, since she/they continue to exist. This function is articulated clearly by Bill Margold, a veteran actor-writer-director in pornographic movies:

> My whole reason for being in the [pornography] Industry is to satisfy the desire of the men in the world who basically don't much care for women and want to see the men in my Industry getting even with the women they couldn't have when they were growing up. . . . So we come on a woman's face or somewhat brutalize her sexually: we're getting even for their lost dreams. I believe this. I've heard audiences cheer me when I do something foul on screen. When I've strangled a person or sodomized a person or brutalized a person, the audience is cheering my action, and then when I've fulfilled my warped desire, the audience applauds. (quoted in Stoller, 1991, p. 31)

The deadening of male sexual sensibility and the eroticizing of sexual violence against women through the use of pornography both exemplify the extremes of dysfunction-strain. In the case of both Margold and Hefner, these men are producers as well as ultimate products of the sex industry.

HIGH-TECH DEVELOPMENTS IN PORNOGRAPHIC MEDIA

Pornography has continued to expand as a major player among the entertainment industries, with over $10 billion in gross revenues (*Boston Globe*, 1997). However, the media that contribute to this sum have shifted rapidly to keep pace with advances in technology that make even more degrading, violent, and explicit pornography more readily available to consumers. In the mid-1980s, magazine readership of the major pornography magazines (*Playboy, Penthouse, Hustler*, and *Oui*) began to sharply decline (Leerhsen, Greenberg, Malone, & Michael, 1986, p. 51). From an all-time high of 7.2 million in 1972, *Playboy* magazine's circulation had plunged to 3.4 million in 1986. In 1984, the Eckerd Drug Company removed *Playboy* and *Penthouse* from the racks in its 1,410 stores in 16 Southern states (Galloway & Thornton, 1984). In 1986, the removal of *Playboy* and *Penthouse* from 7-Eleven and other drug-and-convenience stores was the first visible effect of the Attorney General's Commission on Pornography (Leerhsen et al., 1986). However, although circulation for *Playboy* has dropped over time, the magazine remains in the top 15 in circulation (Action Agenda, 1995).

Although the *Playboy* Channel has not been profitable recently, *Playboy's* pay-per-view operation has quadrupled in users since 1989. *Playboy* plans to market internationally, and currently has 16 foreign editions, with *Playboy* TV available in 97 countries and home videos available in 38 countries. Christie Hefner said, "As we look at the year 2000, this company will be electronically driven and not print driven, and it will be far more international than it has been" (Action Agenda, 1995).

Video Pornography

The advent of the videocassette player seemed perfectly timed to coincide with the crackdown on magazine pornography. Consumers could purchase or rent hard-core pornographic movies (more explicit than cable television offerings such as the *Playboy* Channel), and view these within the privacy of their homes. As pornography magazine sales dropped in the early 1980s, hardcore videocassette sales doubled from

$220 million in 1983 to $450 million in 1986 (Leerhsen et al., 1986, p. 54). In 1994, more than 2,400 new pornography videos were produced (*Minneapolis Star Tribune,* 1994). Pornographic films now outnumber other films three to one (Anderson, 1995). The content of X-rated videos, often sold by mail, included a range of more violent, degrading, and fetishistic behaviors than previously available to a mass market. A listing of the top 50 adult renters and 25 sellers videos posted in a Minneapolis "family friendly" video store chain included these titles: "Bend Over Brazilian Babes," "Gang Bang Fury," "Nurse Tails," "Sorority Sex Kittens," "Butt Slammers," and "Anal Rampage" (Action Agenda, 1995). In addition, a strong market has grown for amateur pornographic videos of "every sexual act imaginable with people who could be your neighbors" (*Mail Order Central,* catalogue, 1994). At present, photo releases are no longer mandatory when publishing or televising images. Thus, men who photograph or videotape their sexual partners in what many women are led to believe are private sex acts or images also hold the legal right to sell and distribute those images without the consent of the woman featured in those images.

Telephone Sex

Dial-a-porn is a telephone service in which users call a number to hear a sexually explicit message. Phone sex has been highly profitable and is found in every major city. *High Society* magazine set up a dial-a-porn bank that immediately began earning $8,000 a day (Galloway & Thornton, 1984). Porn lines have recently found new ways around the deterring 1–900 pay numbers, which can be blocked electronically. "Porn operators have discovered loopholes that allow charging on 800 lines as long as they enter into a contractual agreement with callers. . . . The illusion of toll-free means that callers are racking up huge charges that businesses like hotels, hospitals, and universities, as well as residential phone owners are responsible for paying" (Action Agenda, 1994).

An article by a female phone sex operator describes the logistics and feelings associated with her work (Dawson, 1996). When she is next in line on the rotating roster of phone sex operators in her agency, she is contacted by a dispatcher who calls with the customer's telephone number, the amount of time he's purchased (10, 12, 15, or 20 minutes), and the category he's requested ("naughty nurse," "bitch," "hot and sexy," "bisexual," "dominance," or "kinky" are typical menu items). The majority of her customers tend to be in their 20s, although the age ranges up to 70. Motivations seem to include being physically handicapped and unable to find a sexual partner, suffering from painful shyness, fear of contracting AIDS, men who want variety in their sex lives without being unfaithful to their partners, use as an educational resource, as a lark, and having fantasies they're afraid to share with their partners. The author admits that she was surprised at the feelings of arousal and empathy she had for her callers, and writes, ". . . there's a lot to be said for sharing your orgasm with another human being, even if you can't see or touch them. . . . Even now that I do share my life with a partner, I still get excited and still feel kindly toward my customers." During her first call, in which she began describing a "kinky" scene as requested:

> There was silence on the other end for three minutes, then the line went dead. Convinced that I'd been a flop, I called the agency and apologetically told the dispatcher what had happened. She burst into laughter and said, "Honey, you did your job!" It turns out that hanging up as soon as they've been satisfied is not an uncommon practice on the part of phone sex customers. But even though it makes my job quicker and easier, a click following an intimate moan causes me to feel subhuman. After all, I've just shared some very intimate words with my caller— sometimes he's even shared his personal problems with me. So when he hangs up without so much as a thank-you or goodbye, I feel the way most people think sex workers feel all the time—exploited.

A variation of telephone sex is the "peep show," in which men pay to watch a woman behind a glass window undress, touch herself, and talk to him on a telephone. Sabrina, a university student working in the sex industry to support her studies, finds that most men don't talk much:

> The majority of them really just go in there and look at my body parts and masturbate. . . . Most of them, when they come in there, they just want to get off. Most of them are really impatient. . . . That has left me with a bad feeling lately, and I wonder what these men are like in real life. . . . Sometimes I do feel as though I am contributing to some of the sexual problems that we have in our society because I will lie to the men about the fact that I'm enjoying it. There's that whole distinction between the Whore and the Madonna, because when I do that, that's when I really feel like I'm the Whore, you know. . . . One thing that I do that has probably affected me the most is when I will do, like, simulated oral sex. . . . Most of these men will cum all over the glass as though they're cumming all over my face, and I'm always like, "Ah, Ah that's so wonderful," and most of the time thinking to myself . . . it is pretty disgusting. I don't think it's operating on the same level as a relationship—the

fact that they really get off on thinking that they're cumming all over my face. For some reason, I just have this feeling that it's not really that healthy. (Guidroz, 1996)

It is unfortunate that most accounts of the interpersonal transactions, as such, in phone sex, as well as in much of the sex industry, are from the women who provide services rather than the male consumer. Although some brief but genuine moments of contact do occur on occasion, many transactions proceed with a minimum of communication, and conclude when the man has ejaculated, with the woman disposed of like a used tissue. Women who provide these services know that any warmth or connection they feel may not be reciprocated by the male consumer. Perhaps the men who utilize these services alleviate discrepancy-strain, as they are proving their masculinity by having a sexual experience with (in the presence of) a woman, with none of the concomitant expectations inherent in relational sexuality.

Interactive CD-Roms

Although some CD pornography currently sold as interactive is actually only a selection of *Playboy*-style video clips, the viewer's only input is to choose from a menu of women the one he wants to watch. However, producers are increasingly developing genuinely interactive games. Mike Saenz, a leader of the new sexware merchants, developed *Virtual Valerie 2*, which has a new "cybercock" option. When selected, a computer graphic of a penis appears at the bottom of the screen, as if, in effect, it were the player's own. In addition to stimulating Valerie with a dildo, the player can appear to have intercourse with her himself. According to a spokesperson representing Saenz' company, "What the industry is now crying out for is a crucial piece of technology: an electronic penis sheath, equipped with tactile feedback so that the player would feel as if he were actually engaging in sex with the virtual woman" (Wertheim, 1993). As Wertheim points out,

Valerie is the quintessential realization of woman as sex object. . . . What is to stop anyone from making games in which virtual women are hurt, tortured or even killed as part of the erotic thrill? . . . With virtual reality, logic takes a backseat to sensual perception. My guess is that it would be a shorter step from violent virtual porn to actual violence than it is from violent magazine porn to actual violence—particularly for a viewer who might already be a little off-kilter. (1993, p. 243)

One of the first pornographic interactive CDs that became available, also designed by Mike Saenz, is called *MacPlaymate*. Although this CD was available through a mail-order catalogue for $50, it was also possible to download this program from an electronic bulletin board for free. This software was initially aimed at corporate offices where it won a cult following among male workers. With MacPlaymate the user is both passive voyeur and actively participating pornographer, taking pornography beyond the passivity of X-rated videos and peep shows. The female model, "Maxie," can be manipulated with the use of a mouse. The user may remove her clothes until she's lying spread-eagled and naked, and may then select gloves, corset, stocking, and spike heels. MacPlaymate offers a box of "toys" such as "deep plunger" and "helping hands." For the sadomasochist, there's a bondage option in which Maxie lies gagged, wrists tied, legs chained. Printouts—electronic pinups—can be made at any point. Prudence Baird, a Los Angeles-based public relations executive and a foe of MacPlaymate, said the disturbing thing about MacPlaymate is that it enables the user to act out on screen the ultimate rapist's fantasy. Maxie asks to be stripped—asks to be tied up and gagged—asks to be violated and sodomized and moans with orgasmic pleasure when it happens. According to Dr. Marilyn Walker, psychology professor, "Your civilized man is not going to enjoy [MacPlaymate]. The question then becomes: How many civilized men are there?"

Internet Pornography

The Internet can be used anonymously to obtain private, often free, and unregulated access to a wide variety of pornographic materials. The two primary areas where Internet computer technology has been adapted by the pornography industry are adult commercial bulletin board services accessible via modem for a fee (BBSs), and through the Internet itself, through which discussion lists can be accessed (Usenet), and web sites, usually containing advertising for sex-related businesses, or cyberspace versions of pornography magazines. A furious debate following the release of a study of Internet-driven pornography has concerned the prevalence of Internet pornography. Rimm (1995) concluded that 83.5 percent of Internet transmissions are pornographic, while Post (1995) and Hoffman and Novak (1995) estimated less than one-half of 1 percent. Legislative steps have subsequently been taken in the United States and internationally to control the accessibility of pornography on the Net.

Typical pornographic offerings of files that may be downloaded from a bulletin board service include:

Candid Local Amateur #7! Sexy pregnant brunette housewife gets nasty!
Girls shitting! Drink piss! Fuck dogs! Masturbation! Enema!
Horny girls suck and fuck big dog! And gag on big loads of dog sperm!
Cute brunette coed shits and pisses!
Petite slut gets her asshole fisted to the ELBOW! Also sexy slut shits!
Rape, torture, pussy nailed to a table!
Kidnapping and rape! Amputee fucks a girl with her leg stump!

A listing of usenet groups under the alt.sex heading includes the following suffixes: movies, necrophilia, pedophile, pictures, spanking, voyeurism, wanted.escorts, watersports.

Also popular on the Internet are chat groups where people can engage in real time conversations, and may use pseudonyms facilitating self-presentation as any chosen gender, age, or physical appearance.

Some typical advertisements offered at "11 Top Sex Sites by Mr. Porn," (http://www.greendoor.com/mr.porn/mrporn.htm) included a Mr. Porn's Slut of the Week graphic.

Russell (in press) has critiqued the Rimm (1995) study for failing in coding of data to distinguish violent from nonviolent imagery, for its use of largely genderless categories, and for failing to distinguish between paraphilias involving harmless deviations from the norm, such as transvestitism, from violent and abusive sex acts including rape and incest. However, Russell does consider the Rimm study (1995) "rigorous" and "important," and cites among its most important findings the following:

1. The consumption and distribution of pornography is "one of the largest (if not the largest) recreational applications of users of computer networks" (p. 1861).
2. The market for computer pornography is driven by a strong demand for pedophilic imagery (p. 1914).
3. Computer technology is saturating the market with an endless variety of atypical sexual practices, including coprophilia, bestiality, sadomasochism, and so on.
4. Identification of three powerful marketing techniques used by Robert Thomas, the market leader among adult BBS (p. 1896). One of these is "portraying a 'power imbalance' between the sexes, including a disproportionate representation of women in acts which may be considered degrading" (p. 1898). Rimm provides an example of how Thomas transforms a relatively unpopular image of fellatio into a more popular one by using language that highlights the subordination of the woman (Russell, in press):

> When Thomas describes an image as "Horny sexy blonde sucks cock! She is rubbing her wet pussy!" he generates an unusually low number of downloads. Whenever he uses the word "choke" in his fellatio descriptions, however, he doubles his downloads. (Rimm, 1995, p. 189)

The expansion of the sex industry to the electronic media provides a plethora of new opportunities for men to experience nonrelational sex. Larry Flynt (1996), the publisher of *Hustler* magazine, noted that while circulation rates for all pornographic magazines have declined significantly over the past decade, *Hustler Online* grew at a rate of 500 percent last year. As Flynt adds:

> I think it could be the convenience and privacy that the Internet offers. . . . Guys don't want their wives to know they read magazines like *Hustler*. They're really scared, so they keep the magazine at the office or hide it at home. Now you have a guy sitting in his den at his computer. He doesn't have to go to the newsstand to buy the material; he doesn't have to worry that his kids will find it; there's nothing for his wife to nag him about. It's a very private moment for him, which is why the Internet's become popular.

This description of an Internet pornography user's " very private moment" in front of the computer can be metaphoric for the new high-tech nonrelational sex. Is masturbating in front of a computer screen any more alienating than masturbating to an image in a magazine? Somehow the image seems even more autistic, and hence, sadder. What effects does use of these nonrelational outlets have on men and on their relationships with women? Some men clearly develop an addictive pattern of use of Internet pornography that can end up dominating free time and creating distance in the primary relationship if one exists. In preparation for this chapter, I interviewed a mother of two in her mid-30s about her husband's Internet pornography use which had become problematic.

Kate (a pseudonym) blamed herself for not putting the pieces together sooner. Her husband had gradually grown more distant, exuding low-level hostility, when he began to share the sexual fantasy of having her go out and become sexually involved with other people (swinging) while he watched. This fantasy was so ego-dystonic for Kate that she just blocked his voice out during their sexual interactions. Her husband had become increasingly dependent on the use of shared fantasy during foreplay in order to become aroused. Kate reported feeling as if somebody was there between them. Her husband seemed to desire intercourse rarely, but instead preferred to watch her while she masturbated. He was spending most evenings at his computer, staying up long after Kate went to sleep, sometimes all night. Her husband, continuing to be interested in setting up a swinging situation, uploaded some tasteful nude photographs that Kate had given to him for his birthday. These private portraits were uploaded to a sex usenet discussion list, which means that they can be downloaded and then re-uploaded at any time in the future, that is, that they will not necessarily fall out of usage. Kate had discussed her concerns and strong feelings about this with two different couples therapists, but neither one seemed to understand her level of distress. In addition, Kate's husband insisted that she go to a bar, where he introduced her to a couple, whom, as she discovered later, he had met on the Internet through a chat room for swingers. Kate resisted becoming sexually involved with them once she realized her husband's plan. She soon found out that her images had been posted globally without her consent. Kate described this as "the ultimate betrayal . . . like a rape . . ." feeling that her husband had acted in total disregard of her self. Her experience of having a therapist trivialize her feelings about the posting of her nude photographs, as well as her concerns about his excessive time online, had also been experienced as a betrayal. Kate demanded that her husband move out at the time of this interview (conducted during Spring, 1996).

Anecdotal accounts similar to that above have appeared with increasing frequency in newspaper and magazine advice columns (Landers, 1996), on call-in radio and television talk shows, and in clinicians' offices. A typical presentation is that of a husband who becomes increasingly involved in Internet use, on sex bulletin boards and/or sex chat rooms. At some point, the amount of time spent online becomes an issue in the relationship, or the man becomes involved in a "relationship" with someone he has met online, and may or may not ever meet this person face-to-face. In some cases, the online contact does lead to an extra-relationship sexual involvement. In many others, the emotional involvement and intense focus on another party is nevertheless experienced as a major betrayal by the female partner.

Conclusion

The sex industry has embraced new technologies that have made its products available to male consumers to use with more privacy and ease of accessibility than ever before. The types of material now available have also proliferated and reflect a wider range of brutal, pedophilic, degrading, and paraphiliac themes, which can both satisfy an existing audience and create new markets simultaneously. As MacKinnon (1995) states:

> Like a Trojan horse, each new communication technology—the printing press, the camera, the moving picture, the tape recorder, the telephone, the television, the video recorder, the VCR, cable, and now, the computer—has brought pornography with it. Pornography has proliferated with each new tool, democratizing what had been a more elite possession and obsession, spreading the sexual abuse required for its making and promoted through its use. Ever more women and children have had to be used ever more abusively in ever more social sites and human relationships to feed the appetite that each development stimulates and profits from filling. More women have had to live out more of their lives in environments pornography has made. As pornography saturates social life, it also becomes more visible and legitimate, hence less visible as pornography. . . . Pornography on computer networks is the latest wave in this tide. Pornography in cyberspace is pornography in society—just broader, deeper, worse, and more of it. Pornography is a technologically sophisticated traffic in women. . . . (p. 1959)

Many pedophiles trade thousands of pictures of illegal child pornography on the Internet, film and broadcast live sexual interactions with minors, and solicit children or abuse by using chat lines that are heavily populated by minors.

To the extent that men in our culture continue to use nonrelational sex to bolster themselves against gender role-strain, there will most likely be a menu of new products to address these preferences. The male sex industry consumer of the future will most likely be found garbed in a full-body suit of virtual reality suiting, complete with the electronic penis sheath, all equipped with tactile feedback and interactive programming with cybersex partners. A full head covering with sensory input from the computer will shut out all external stimuli. The cybersex partner could be preprogrammed in keeping with the consumer's sexual preferences.

With such technological toys available, it seems unlikely that male consumers will notice that they are missing something. Although the need for nonrelational sex, theoretically, can never be completely fulfilled, and is inherently addictive, as long as new "fixes" continue to be produced, the impetus for change will lie with only those who feel emotional pain most acutely. This is generally not true of most men in our current culture. As Dworkin (1976, p. 108) writes, "It is necessary to understand that what is experienced by the male as authentic pleasure is the affirmation of his own identity as a male. Each time he survives the peril of entering the female void, his masculinity is rei-fied. He has proven both that he is not her and that he is like other hims. No pleasure on earth matches the pleasure of having proven himself real, . . . a man and not a woman, a bona fide member of the group which holds dominion over all other living things." In our his-torical context, women in heterosexual relationships report more dissatisfaction and distress in their relationships, due to their subor-dinate position in the patriarchal power structure. It is likely that for men and women to experience fully intimate and relational sexual connection, that men need to see women as equals in every way, so that sexuality is not used to maintain the status quo. As Dworkin (1976, p. 62) writes, "As we are destroying the structure of culture, we will have to build a new culture—nonhierarchical, nonsexist, nonco-ercive, nonexploitative—in other words, a culture which is not based on dominance and submission in any way. As we are destroying the phallic identities of men and the masochistic identities of women, we will have to create, out of our own ashes, new erotic identities. These new erotic identities will have to repudiate at their core the male sex-ual model: that is, they will have to repudiate . . . genital sexuality as the primary focus and value of erotic identity; they will have to repu-diate and obviate all of the forms of erotic objectification and alien-ation which inhere in the male model." Dworkin (1976) holds that transformation of the male sexual system will require a congruence of feeling and erotic interest, rather than a separation (p. 13). Dworkin (1983, p. 53) speaks of the concept of sexual intelligence, de-fined as "a human capacity for discerning, manifesting, and con-structing sexual integrity. Sexual intelligence could not be measured in numbers of orgasms, erections, or partners; nor could it show itself by posing painted clitoral lips in front of a camera; . . . nor would it manifest as an addiction." I concur with Dworkin's (1976) analysis of how this change will occur: "I believe that freedom for women must begin in the repudiation of our own masochism . . . it is the first deadly blow that we can strike against systematized male dominance. In effect, when we succeed in excising masochism from our own per-sonalities and constitutions, we will be cutting the male life line to power over and against us, to male worth in contradistinction to fe-male degradation." Ultimately, I believe that women will have to ini-tiate change by refusing to tolerate economic cultural institutions that enforce male dominance, including the sex industry itself. For those men who no longer take pleasure in nonrelational sex or domi-nant status, your voices may be heard, where women's voices are not, by your brothers.

References

Action Agenda. (1995). Pornography and abuse industry: Title wave. *Action Agenda, 1*(4), 16.

Action Agenda: Media action alliance and media watch. (1994). Pornography briefs. *Action Agenda, 1*(3), 19.

American Psychiatric Association. (1994). *Diagnostic and statistical manual of mental disorders* (4th ed.). New York: Author.

Anderson, M. (1995). Silencing women's speech. In L. Lederer & R. Delgado (Eds.), *The price we pay: The case against racist speech, hate propaganda, and pornography* (pp. 122–130). New York: Hill and Wang.

Barth, R., & Kinder, B. (1987). The mislabeling of sexual compulsion. *Journal of Sex and Marital Therapy, 13*(1) 15–23.

Boszormenyi-Nagy, I., & Ulrich, D. N. (1981). Contextual family therapy. In A. S. Gurman & D. P. Kniskern (Eds.), *Handbook of family therapy* (pp. 159–186). New York: Brunner/Mazel.

Brooks, G. R. (1995). *The centerfold syndrome: How men can overcome objectification and achieve intimacy with women.* San Francisco: Jossey-Bass.

Brooks, G. R., & Silverstein, L. S. (1995). Understanding the dark side of masculinity: An interactive systems model. In R. F. Levant & W. S. Pollack (Eds.), *A new psychology of men* (pp. 280–333). New York: Basic Books.

Bryant, J. (1985, March). *Frequency of exposure, age of initial exposure, and reactions to initial exposure to pornography.* Report presented to the Attorney General's Commission on Pornography, Houston, TX.

Carnes, P. (1983). *Out of the shadows: Understanding sexual addiction.* Minneapolis, MN: CompCare.

Check, J. (1995). Teenage training: The effects of pornography on adolescent males. In L. Lederer & R. Delgado (Eds.), *The price we pay: The case against racist speech, hate propaganda, and pornography* (pp. 89–91). New York: Hill and Wang.

Check, J., & Guloien, T. (1989). Reported proclivity for coercive sex following repeated exposure to sexually violent pornography, nonviolent dehumanizing pornography, and erotica. In D. Zillman & J. Bryant (Eds.), *Pornography: Research advances and policy considerations* (pp. 159–184). Hillsdale, NJ: Erlbaum.

Chodorow, N. (1978). *The reproduction of mothering: Psychoanalysis and the sociology of gender.* Berkeley: University of California Press.

Conrad, P., & Schneider, J. (1980) *Deviance and medicalization: From badness to sickness.* St. Louis, MO: Mosby.

Cowan, G., Lee, D., Levy, D., & Snyder, D. (1988). Dominance and inequality in X-rated videocassettes. *Psychology of Women Quarterly, 12,* 299–311.

Dawson, M. (1996). Talking dirty: True confessions of a phone sex operator: It's a menial job, but somebody's gotta do it. *East Bay Monthly, 26*(5), 19–21.

Duke University students in Men Acting for Change. (1993, January 29). Television interview on pornography, *20/20.* New York: ABC.

Dworkin, A. (1976). *Our blood: Prophecies and discourses on sexual politics.* New York: Harper & Row.

Dworkin, A. (1983). *Right-wing women.* New York: Wideview/Perigee.

Eisler, R. M., & Skidmore, J. R. (1987). Masculine gender role stress: Scale development and component factors in the appraisal of stressful situations. *Behavior Modification, 11,* 123–136.

Gagnon, J. H., & Simon, W. (1973). *Sexual conduct: The social sources of human sexuality.* Chicago: Aldine.

Galloway, J., & Thornton, J. (1984, June 4). Crackdown on pornography—A no-win battle. *U.S. News & World Report,* 84–85.

Guidroz, K. (1996). I'm more than my body parts: An erotic performer's experiences. *Off Our Backs, 26*(6), 8–11.

Haviland, J. J., & Malatesta, C. Z. (1981). The development of sex differences in nonverbal signals: Fallacies, facts, and fantasies. In C. Mayo & N. M. Henly (Eds.), *Gender and non-verbal behavior* (pp. 183–208). New York: Springer-Verlag.

Hoffman, D., & Novak, T. (1995, July 2). Posted on the Internet. A detailed analysis of the conceptual, logical, and methodological flaws in the article: "Marketing pornography on the information superhighway" (version 1.01).

Landers, A. (1996, May 26). On-line flirting spells trouble for many marriages. *San Francisco Chronicle,* Sec. C-12.

Leerhsen, C., Greenberg, N., Malone, M., & Michael, R. (1986, August 4). Aging playboy. *Newsweek,* 50–56.

Levant, R. F. (1996). The new psychology of men. *Professional Psychology: Research and Practice, 27*(3), 259–265.

Levine, M., & Troiden, R. (1988). The myth of sexual compulsivity. *Journal of Sex Research, 25*(3), 347–363.

Litewka, J. (1977). The socialized penis. In J. Snodgrass (Ed.), *For men against sexism.* Albion, CA: Times Change Press.

MacKinnon, C. (1995). Vindication and resistance: A response to the Carnegie Mellon study of pornography in cyberspace. *Georgetown Law Review, 83*(5), 1959–1968.

Mail Order Central. (1994, December 1). Catalogue.

Malamuth, N., & Donnerstein, E. (1984). *Pornography and sexual aggression.* New York: Academic Press.

Malamuth, N., & Spinner, B. (1980). Longitudinal content analysis of sexual violence in the best selling erotica magazines. *Journal of Sex Research, 16,* 226–237.

Malamuth, N. M., Linz, D., Heavey, C. L., Barnes, G., & Acker, M. (1995). Using the confluence model of sexual aggression to predict men's conflict with women: A 10-year follow-up study. *Journal of Personality and Social Psychology, 69*(2), 353–369.

Mellum, J. (1994). The five most disturbing facts about *Playboy. Action Agenda: Media Action Alliance and Media Watch, 1*(3), 28.

More hustler than hero in the real man. (1997, January 10). *Boston Globe,* C1.

Moser, C. (1993). A response to Aviel Goodman's "Sexual addiction: Designation and treatment." *Journal of Sex and Marital Therapy, 19*(3), 220–224.

Orford, J. (1978). Hypersexuality: Implications for a theory of dependence. *British Journal of Addictions, 73,* 299–310.

Pleck, J. H. (1995). The gender role strain paradigm: An update. In R. F. Levant & W. S. Pollack (Eds.), *A new psychology of men* (pp. 33–67). New York: Basic Books.

Pollack, W. S. (1995). No man is an island: Toward a new psychoanalytic psychology of men. In R. F. Levant & W. S. Pollack (Eds.), *A new psychology of men* (pp. 33–67). New York: Basic Books.

Pornography film industry. (1994, November 17). *Minneapolis Star Tribune.*

Post, D. (1995, June 28). Posted on the Internet. A preliminary discussion of methodological peculiarities in the Rimm Study of pornography on the information superhighway.

Quadland, M. (1985). Compulsive sexual behavior: Definition of a problem, approach to treatment. *Journal of Sex and Marital Therapy, 11*(2), 121–132.

Rimm, M. (1995). Marketing pornography on the information superhighway: A survey of 917,410 images, descriptions, short stories, and animations downloaded 8.5 million times by consumers in over 2000 cities in forty counties, provinces, and territories. *Georgetown Law Review, 83*(5), 1849–1934.

Russell, D. (1993a). *Making violence sexy: Feminist views on pornography.* New York: Teachers College Press.

Russell, D. (1993b). *Against pornography: The evidence of harm.* Berkeley, CA: Russell.

Russell, D. (in press). Pornography in cyberspace. In *Child pornography.* Newbury Park, CA: Sage Press.

Schwartz, M., & Brasted, W. (1985). Sexual addiction. *Medical Aspects of Human Sexuality, 19,* 103–107.

Smith, D. (1976). The social content of pornography. *Journal of Communication, 26*(1), 16–33.

Stock, W. (1993, August 20). *Pornography and gender alienation.* Paper presented in the symposium, "Centerfold or person? Clinical implications of men's images of women's bodies," at the 101st annual convention of the American Psychological Association at Toronto, Canada.

Stoller, R. (1991). *Porn: Myths for the twentieth century.* New Haven, CT: Yale University Press.

Stoltenberg, J. (1994). *What makes pornography "sexy?"* Minneapolis, MN: Milkweed Press.

Weinberg, M. K. (1992). *Sex differences in 6-month-old infants' affect and behavior: Impact on maternal caregiving.* Unpublished doctoral dissertation, University of Massachusetts, Amherst.

Wertheim, M. (1993, March). The electronic orgasm. *Glamour,* 242–243.

Zilbergeld, B. (1978). *Male sexuality.* New York: Bantam Books.

Zilbergeld, B. (1992). *The new male sexuality.* New York: Bantam Books.

Zillmann, D., & Bryant, J. (1984). Effects of massive exposure to pornography. In N. Malamuth & E. Donnerstein (Eds.), *Pornography and sexual aggression* (pp. 115–138). New York: Academic Press.

CHAPTER 6

Sexual Harassment and Rape: A View from Higher Education

EARL L. BACKMAN AND LINDA R. BACKMAN

MEN'S SEXUALITY IS well represented in the current literature on the new psychology of men (Betcher & Pollack, 1993; Brooks, 1995; Farrell, 1993; Goldberg, 1987; Hudson & Jacot, 1991; Kipnis, 1991; Levant & Pollack, 1995; Osherson, 1992; Zilbergeld, 1992). Scholars have vigorously debated male sexual behavior and its ramifications from both a feminist perspective and a men's movement orientation. Although such discussions can be useful and, at times, entertaining, they frequently fail to address the salient issues. A clearer understanding of men and their sexual behavior is critical in ameliorating maladaptive behavior and its negative consequences.

Previous chapters in this book have addressed less severe forms of nonrelational sexuality. In this chapter, we focus on behaviors that Brooks and Silverstein (1995) refer to as the "dark side of masculinity." These extreme behaviors cannot be viewed simply in terms of men's inability to relate in a sexually appropriate manner. Sexual harassment, date rape, acquaintance rape, and stranger rape not only represent dysfunctional sexual communication but also are violent and harmful to others, usually women. When these forms of male nonrelational sexuality mix with anger, misogyny, or psychopathology, both men and women often pay tragic costs.

Our purpose in this chapter is to shed additional light on these negative male sexual behaviors. Our goal is not the condemnation of men; nor is it useful to see such sexual behavior as the activity of a few deviant men who cannot conform to our cultural norms. Rather, our objective is to demonstrate how these behaviors are consistent with traditional male socialization and to suggest gender-informed measures to eliminate them.

Harassers and rapists are not born; they are made. Such behavior is not simply the end result of being male and having the need to prove one's sexuality. If this were so, the problem, as big as it now is, would be even larger. Likewise, the notion that men who commit these acts are but a few of the most deviant males in our culture camouflages the severity of the problem and its causes. Instead, male socialization patterns in our culture, the stresses involved in attempting to live up to a traditional masculinity ideology, the shame attached to being perceived as not "male enough," and the patriarchal power dynamics underlying our social and political institutions all contribute to creating men who sexually harass and rape.

Before proceeding with analysis of these behaviors, a brief description of the phenomena is in order. What some men and women see as sexual harassment, others may define merely as inappropriate behavior or indeed as acceptable. Furthermore, attempting to define date rape (an increasingly frequent occurrence on university and college campuses) meets with even greater objections. Mindful of these challenges, we suggest the following definitions as a point of departure.

Defining Sexual Harassment

Sexual harassment is a form of discrimination prohibited by Section 703 of Title VII of the Civil Rights Act of 1964, as amended, Title IX of the Education Amendments Act of 1972, the Civil Rights Act of 1991, and Executive Order 11246. The behavior must be unwelcomed by the recipient, and the victim must be unable to stop the behavior. Unwelcome sexual advances, requests for sexual favors, and other verbal or physical conduct of a sexual nature constitute sexual harassment when:

- Submission to such conduct is made either explicitly or implicitly as a term or condition of an individual's employment.
- Submission to or rejection of such conduct by an individual is the basis for employment decisions affecting such individual.
- Such conduct has the purpose or effect of unreasonably interfering with an individual's work performance or creating an intimidating, hostile, or offensive work environment.

The most extreme form of sexual harassment is an attempt to coerce an unwilling person into a sexual relationship by misusing an employment or educational relationship. Sexual harassment occurs frequently in the business world, but for reasons to be described, our analysis focuses particularly on sexual harassment in an academic setting. Sexual harassment differs from voluntary sexual relations because it involves *coercion, threat,* or *unwanted sexual attention:* It is abusive and violent.

Defining Sexual Assault and Rape

Sexual assault and rape are not motivated solely by sexual passion or lust: They are violent crimes that are designed to hurt and humiliate—sex is only the weapon. Rapists are mostly men, and although many victims are also men (particularly in prison settings), the vast majority of victims are women.

Rape is most frequently defined as intentionally or knowingly engaging in sexual intercourse or oral/anal sexual contact with another person without that person's consent. In many states, it also includes nonconsensual penetration of any part of another person's body by any part of the perpetrator's body or with other objects. Sexual assault is the touching or feeling of the body of another person without consent. Lack of consent can take many forms including coercion of the victim by immediate or threatened use of force, and/or the victim's inability to consent because of mental disorder, drugs, alcohol, sleep deprivation, or advanced age.

Stranger rape—a fear of many women—accounts for only 20 percent to 40 percent of reported rapes in this country (Koss et al., 1994; Michael et al., 1994). Date rape and acquaintance rape, accounting for between 60 percent and 80 percent of all rapes, refer to sexual assault by a perpetrator who is known to the rape victim. For substantial reasons, date and acquaintance rape are highly prevalent on this nation's campuses, as will be discussed. Our experience in higher education convinces us that date rape is vastly underreported either because the victim is afraid to do so or assumes it was her fault, or because the victim and the rapist fail to see the sexual assault as rape.

The breadth and depth of the phenomena being discussed require delimiting our analysis. First, this is not an in-depth treatise; rather, it is a brief examination of sexual harassment and rape from the perspective of the new psychology of men. We will consider: (a) the way men are socialized; (b) the traditional masculinity ideology that men strive to meet; and (c) the corresponding traumas that result from a "failure to measure up," which affect how men relate sexually. When a man, as a result of these socially constructed norms, fails in his perceived ability to relate in a sexually effective manner, the resulting behaviors can be highly dysfunctional, or even violent.

Second, our discussion of sexual harassment and date rape as a consequence of male socialization will be from a higher education perspective, where these behaviors are acted out by both university employees and students. We have chosen higher education, rather than the corporate world, because of our experience, and the need to delimit our analysis, and because sexual harassment and date rape have been addressed more aggressively by colleges and universities than by other sectors of our society.

Finally, this analysis does not include a critique of the theories put forth over the past few decades that purport to explain male sexual behavior and the problems of men and their relationships. The literature available offering explanations is varied and replete with theoretical models. For our purposes, we join with other chapter authors and use Joseph Pleck's gender role strain paradigm (1981, 1995) as the theoretical framework for a better understanding of why men harass and rape women.

Gender Role Strain and Socialization: The Roots of Dysfunction

Why do men sexually harass their female coworkers? Why do young fraternity men find it acceptable to sexually assault and rape their dates? Why do some men express their anger and hatred toward women through the abusive behavior of sexual assault and rape? The answers to these and related questions are the primary focus of this chapter. Although theories abound explaining these highly dysfunctional and abusive behaviors primarily toward women, this knowledge and awareness has not led to a reduction in violence. The following list states our views, based on more than 18 years of experience working with men in both the institutional setting of a university and in private practice:

- Most men are not sexual harassers, nor are they rapists.
- Men receive mixed messages about sex and male sexual behavior.
- Sexual harassment and rape are the extreme on a continuum of dysfunctional sexual behaviors and are a result of the need to dominate, control, and abuse women.
- The dominant masculinity ideologies in this country convey to men a sense of entitlement, reward aggression, and support patriarchal power dynamics.
- When charged with sexual harassment, many offenders "just don't get it."
- Only recently have the major social institutions in this country accepted sexual harassment as a major problem in the workplace.

- Myths surrounding sexual harassment continue to be accepted by many men in the workplace.
- Sexual harassment tends to take place in settings dominated by men, including institutions of higher education.
- Date rape, described mostly in college settings, is greatly exacerbated by alcohol abuse, and is more prevalent where fraternities are influential in campus life.
- Men who were abused as children are more likely to display their anger toward women through sexual harassment and rape.

Based on present knowledge, what is it about being raised male in this society that leads some men to act out their behavior in such negative, harmful, and abusive ways? Pleck's gender role strain paradigm offers a partial explanation. Pleck argues convincingly that negative male behaviors are a result of internally inconsistent and constantly changing gender roles (Pleck, 1995). Attempting to conform to socially constructed gender role norms inherently creates psychological dysfunction in many men, who feel inferior, "less manly," ostracized, powerless, and angry when they violate these role norms. If such feelings are combined with a desire to "prove one's self," to control one's environment, and to be in power, inappropriate acting-out behavior, including sexual harassment and rape, becomes likely.

Three aspects of Pleck's (1981) model are of particular importance in examining negative aspects of men's nonrelational sexual behavior. First, we examine the notion of gender role discrepancy or the failure of males to fit the expectations and norms defined within the traditional masculinity ideology. Seeing oneself as not measuring up to idealized role norms lessens self-esteem. One highly regarded male role characteristic is athletic success. Studies of sexual harassers who teach in universities indicate that most male professors were nonathletes, and, in fact, many have been "socially put down" for past athletic failures (Zalk, 1996). Furthermore, such harassers are found to have been unpopular in high school, more academically oriented, and possessing low self-esteem; a discrepancy exists between the ideal masculine norm and their own achievements. The academic setting, with its patriarchal orientation, offers men an environment in which they can act out their frustration and find ways to be in control, to be powerful, and to be aggressive. In short, to compensate for not measuring up to idealized role norms (i.e., athleticism).

A second aspect of gender role strain model deserving attention is the trauma men experience fulfilling the expectations of traditional masculinity ideology. The process of being raised to be a man is inherently traumatic and has severe consequences for one's psychological well-being (Krugman, 1995; Levant, 1995; Osherson, 1992). Shame, fear of intimacy, aggression, violence, and rage—all result from the trauma of undergoing male socialization in our society. This does not mean that growing up male is entirely negative; nor does it suggest the entire male socialization process be altered. Rather, certain socialized role norms do contribute substantially to a variety of dysfunctional behaviors.

According to Pleck (1981), the third component of this model is male gender role dysfunction, which suggests that as men fulfill male role norms, negative outcomes may and often do occur. Being a successful breadwinner can lead to minimal family involvement, less intimacy with one's spouse, a high degree of loneliness, and feelings of abandonment. Again, studies of sexual harassers in higher education (Dziech & Weiner, 1990; Zalk, 1996) have found that many professors fit this stereotype. Bathrick and Kaufman (1990) and Koss et al. (1994) argue that the very norms we stress as desirable for men contribute to male violence and male abuse of power. Furthermore, to view controlling and dominating women as permissible—that men are entitled to do so—directly contributes and leads to sexual harassment. The widely held notion that husbands cannot be guilty of raping their spouse further supports the idea of male entitlement to sex (Koss et al., 1994).

Prior to analyzing sexual harassment and rape, it is important to explain several contributors to the dysfunctional aspects of nonrelational sex. Discrepancy, trauma, and dysfunction strain result in a range of fears—shame, inadequacy, and intimacy; and a range of needs—power, control, entitlement, and success. Furthermore, societal reinforcement of male aggression can lead to violence being viewed as an appropriate outlet for anger and rage. Finally, family-of-origin issues, particularly childhood abuse, frequently contribute to a man's likelihood to harass and rape (Hunter, 1990). Consistent with the "aberrant male hypothesis" identified by Brooks and Silverstein (1995), individual acts of sexual harassment and rape cannot be understood as random acts of individual psychopathology. Harassment and rape must be viewed in a sociocultural context where gender role norms and expectations, hierarchical and patriarchal institutions, and changing traditional masculinity ideology are all recognized as contributing factors (Brooks & Silverstein, 1995; Koss et al., 1994; Krugman, 1995; Osherson, 1992).

MEN AND THEIR FEARS

If men's relational behavior is not merely an inevitable by-product of being biologically male, but instead is a result of socially constructed masculinity ideology, then we must closely examine what men learn during the socialization process. What norms, values, attitudes, and behaviors form the ideology to which men are encouraged to adhere (Brooks & Silverstein, 1995)? To comprehend why some men harass and rape, we must look at their fears and the dysfunctional, harmful, and abusive behaviors they adopt to compensate.

Osherson (1992) and Krugman (1995) document the impact on male behavior of shame and fear arising from the failure to live up to internal values and beliefs. These values, which are a part of traditional masculinity ideology, are often unattainable—leading to feelings of inadequacy, withdrawal behavior, loneliness, fear of intimacy, and anger (Osherson, 1992). As a result of shame, men frequently feel they have "failed"—failed to be manly, to achieve success, to gain respect. As Pleck (1981, 1995) argues, failing to live up to a set of expectations for the masculine gender creates gender role strain, a normal occurrence for most men. When they fail to deal appropriately with feelings of shame, however, dysfunctional behavior is likely to occur. Failing to adapt creatively to gender role strain often leads men to socially and psychologically withdraw (fear of intimacy), to develop compulsive work or social habits, to abuse drugs and alcohol, and to adopt aggressive behavior to gain control or establish power (Krugman, 1995). At its extreme, shame becomes intolerable, and these coping mechanisms are integrated into the sense of self, a mode of compensation that becomes destructive for men and for the women in their lives. At the extreme, it can lead to rageful behavior against others, the projection of contempt for one's own self into contempt for others, and aggressive, violent, or abusive behavior toward women. Sexual harassment and rape are often the result. As Krugman (1995) asserts, shame not well-socialized into the male sense of self frequently leads to aggressive responses.

In our work with male sexual harassers in a university setting, we have found men frequently exhibit narcissistic personality traits to mask shame. By attempting to maintain control of all matters, including people, men protect themselves from their vulnerability and fear. This need to exert power and control (to avoid intimacy) leads to unhealthy behaviors that are sexually harassing to women.

Surrounding and augmenting men's fear of shame is the fear of inadequacy—or of not measuring up. When they cannot address failure with a healthy response, men may act out in a harmful manner. Men who feel internally inadequate often attempt to prove their manliness in sexually inappropriate behaviors. Rapists who feel inferior engage in sexual assault to overpower, dominate, and humiliate, affirming to themselves that they are men.

Much has been written (Abbott, 1990; Goldberg, 1987; Kipnis, 1991; Nelson, 1988; Osherson, 1992) about men's fear of intimacy, the fear of connection by expressing emotions. Anger is the singular emotion men do express liberally. Many years of work with couples have convinced us that most men want to be intimate and emotionally connected, yet, they simply do not know how to achieve intimacy. Forced early separation from mothers, coupled with emotionally unavailable fathers and strong socialized messages such as "be strong," "don't cry," "don't be a sissy," and "defend yourself," lead men to fear intimacy and vulnerability (Pollack, 1995). Furthermore, messages such as "be aggressive," "be competitive," and "win at any cost" inhibit establishment of intimacy. As long as intimacy is viewed as weakness, and nurturance is still needed, how can men resolve their dilemma?

Men tend to struggle with fears, expectations, and relationship issues for most of their lives. Our clinical experience illustrates that this struggle is further complicated by the seemingly contradictory expectations women have for men. As a group, males are expected to be assertive, protective, successful, and manly, while simultaneously being tender, nurturing, empathetic, emotional, and connected. Men struggle to balance women's expectations with their own expectations, needs, and values. Failure to integrate these roles in a healthy and constructive manner may lead to anger expressed in dominating, controlling, abusive, and violent behavior. As Kipnis (1991) argues, the answer lies in understanding the wounds—the pain, hurt, suffering, anger, and changing expectations—not in projecting these wounds onto women through abuse and violence.

MEN'S DESIRES FOR POWER AND CONTROL

To conform to male gender role expectations in this society, men strive to meet competing needs. In addition to fulfilling their needs to be accepted, loved, and nurtured, men also need to aggressively seek power and control. These attributes, an integral aspect of our patriarchal society, in turn generate notions of entitlement, the desire to control women, and legitimization of aggression. Koss et al. (1994) noted that for many men, expression of their masculinity comes through the subordination of women by gender inequality. Sexual harassment and rape are direct outcomes of male behavior stemming from both a need to dominate and a sense of entitlement. Male students often insist that it was not date rape because "I paid for a wonderful evening, and I was *entitled* to sex for my effort."

As previously noted, these power needs are not biologically based. They are part of a socially defined male gender role that sanctions the expression of aggressiveness, power, and control needs through entitlement, abuse, dominance, and violence. Our focus is on maladaptive behavior that stems from men's failure to adequately respond to gender role strain. Although sexual harassment and rape can be individual manifestations of male trauma, these behaviors are embedded within our social structure and must be addressed at both the individual and institutional levels (Koss et al., 1994).

SOCIALIZED SEXUAL VIOLENCE

Violent sexual behavior toward women is best understood in the context of a history of family violence (Koss, 1994). Because violence begets violence, boys raised in an environment of parental violence and sexual abuse are more likely to develop violent and abusive behaviors toward women. Koss et al. (1994) references repeated studies illustrating the long-term impact of growing up male in a violent household. According to Koss and Dinero (1989), sexually aggressive behavior among college males is much more likely if they experienced abuse as a child.

Sexually abused boys frequently grow up to be fearful and mistrustful. They tend to be highly guilt- and shame-laden, and prone to experience intense anger (Hunter, 1990). For many, this results not only in inappropriate sexual behavior, but in wide-ranging relationship problems as well. Rapists frequently describe their need during rape to hurt someone as they were hurt. Repressed anger and rage felt as a child can be later manifested in dysfunctional sexual behavior as a way of exerting control and power. If the perpetrator of boyhood sexual abuse was a female, as the victim grows into manhood, he must struggle with his own shame, rage, and aggressiveness while processing his feelings toward women. Failure to deal adequately with violence from a trusted female is another precursor to misogyny. Hatred of women, when combined with a socialized need for control and power, fear of intimacy, and a view that violence is acceptable, contributes to extreme nonrelational sexual behavior.

Sexual Harassment and Rape

Most sexual harassers are not rapists, and most rapists do not sexually harass. Men who commit date rape usually do not commit stranger rape. What accounts for these variations?

SEXUAL HARASSMENT

As with rape, our society has been slow in recognizing sexual harassment as a form of victimization of women (Brooks & Silverstein, 1995). Unlike rape, this abuse has been institutionally sanctioned and, in fact, the patriarchal structure of higher education, as well as the business world, has approved its existence. As Koss et al. (1994) point out, sexual harassment can be seen as an effective instrument of social control designed to maintain male dominance.

Extensive and rigorous longitudinal studies of sexual harassment are nonexistent. For those studies that have been conducted, the controversy over definition has raised many questions about validity, methodology, and accuracy. Because sexual harassment is not treated as a crime, but rather as a civil rights violation, accurate reporting statistics are not available (Koss et al., 1994). In contrast to rape, most sexual harassment does not involve physical violence. However, like rape, sexual harassment serves as a means of maintaining male power and patriarchy. Hence, we join many researchers in viewing sexual harassment as a form of violence against women (Brooks & Silverstein, 1995; Fitzgerald, 1993; Koss et al., 1994).

Research on sexual harassment including its causes, the motivation of men who harass, and the role of societal variables is in its infancy. However, examination of this phenomenon in higher education has provided important insights (Dziech & Weiner, 1990; Koss et al., 1994; Paludi, 1996). The following summary is based both on research findings and on our clinical experience:

- Because of disparities of power, the academic setting allows control and domination by male faculty and administrators (Paludi, 1996).
- Perpetrators are almost always male and victims, female (Koss et al., 1994).
- University men most likely to harass utilize sex to exhibit dominance, power, and misogyny (Koss et al., 1994).
- There is a vast difference between the perceptions of men and women on what constitutes sexual harassment (Dziech & Weiner, 1990).
- The status and influence accorded male professors provides a ripe environment for harassing female students (Paludi, 1996).
- Men in supervisory positions who lack high self-esteem view their work as the domain of males and fear (and/or hate) women; such men use sexual harassment to control, dominate, and abuse.
- Sexual harassment has more to do with power, control, and dominance than with sex (i.e., sex is the instrument; Koss et al., 1994).

• Men who harass are drawn to those they can dominate (e.g., female students and employees). In this context, they can exert their need for power and domination as compensation for their own vulnerability (Zalk, 1996).

Sexual harassment is a problem for higher education; yet, most male faculty and administrators do not sexually harass students and employees. More research must be conducted to understand the relationship between higher education, men drawn to academia, and the differences between the profiles of harassers and nonharassers. Falk (1996) and Dziech and Wiener (1990) found faculty harassers possess a fear and hatred of women, doubt their own masculinity, and are highly confused about their self-worth. Additional research must be conducted to understand fully the multifaceted interaction of the variables that account for why some men sexually harass. It is incumbent on academic institutions to take the necessary responsibility to prevent sexual harassment and to create a safe working and learning environment. Such an environment protects all employees from exploitation and abuse. Men need to play a major role in this transition; sexual harassment is damaging to them and to their relationships with women.

DATE RAPE

Date and acquaintance rape are similar and yet different. Acquaintance rape, that is, rape by someone known to the victim, is the most prevalent category (Warshaw, 1988). Date rape, a subcategory of acquaintance rape, is being discussed separately here for the following reasons:

1. It is primarily an individual behavior that has been identified in and around academic institutions.
2. It is often not defined as rape by either the victim or the perpetrator.
3. It is highly sanctioned male behavior by some college sectors (e.g., fraternities).
4. It illustrates the great disparity between female and male perspectives on sexual behavior.

The considerable controversy that has surfaced about date rape includes these basic questions: What is it? Who should accept responsibility? What constitutes a "no" response?

MacKinnon (1987) presented a radical feminist perspective in her argument that date rape needs to be considered an integral aspect of male domination, that is, sex "being done to" women. From this perspective, a "yes" is meaningless when the woman does not feel free to say "no" (i.e., is coerced).

Warshaw (1988) offered support for the idea that date rape is part of male dominance socialization. To be a "real man," you must push a woman to engage in sex, even when she expresses neither interest or desire. In her *Ms Report* (1988), Warshaw noted that men believe date rape is not really rape when they pay for the date—an issue of entitlement.

Two alternative, and highly controversial, perspectives have been presented by persons representing what Paludi (1993) called "the neo-conservative backlash." Farrell (1993) and Roiphe (1993) argued that men have been assigned disproportionate responsibility for date rape. Roiphe, in fact, argues that the extreme male-responsible views are destructive to women, since they enhance the notion of "female weakness."

These perspectives confuse the issue of research into date rape, since they so dramatically differ about the phenomenon. Though definitive research must await greater conceptual clarity, certain statements seem to have great consensual support:

- Men frequently misread friendly female behavior as an invitation to have sex.
- Male socialization contributes to the notion that aggressive sexual behavior is appropriate, and even expected in living up to gender role norms.
- Men often have difficulty discussing sexual behavior with women, and misinterpret their desires and needs (Michael et al., 1994).
- Date rape is perpetrated by men who are insensitive to others, see their role as one of initiation and domination of sexual behavior, and equate manliness with a high level of sexual activity.
- Alcohol and drug use are highly correlated with incidences of date rape (Warshaw, 1988).
- Men who rape dates are much more likely to believe in rape-supportive myths than are men who do not rape (Koss et al., 1994).
- Men who rape dates are more likely to objectify women—seeing them as objects to be conquered, dominated, and controlled.

Date rape will not disappear from our nation's campuses until (a) male sexual socialization stops emphasizing domination and sexual coercion; (b) men become unwilling to pursue sexual activity with anything less than a clear and continuous expression of interest from women; (c) men cease to channel their anger and rage into dysfunctional sexual behavior; (d) men stop viewing sex in terms of entitlement;

(e) men stop using sex as a way of responding to their own fears of intimacy and inadequacy; (f) academia views this phenomenon as both an institutional problem and an individual one; and (g) men are able to integrate, in a healthy manner, mixed messages they receive about women with the normative expectations derived from a masculine ideology.

Date rape is an extreme form of nonrelational sexuality and is an expression of men's demands for power and control over women.

ACQUAINTANCE RAPE

Although much of what is true of date rape also applies to acquaintance rape, there are important differences. Acquaintance rape occurs outside an ongoing relationship, is more overt, and is experienced in radically differing ways by men and women. It is more nonrelational than date rape and is usually more violent. Men who rape female acquaintances are typically so filled with fear and rage that they take action against innocent parties. Acquaintance rapists tend to view sex as part of a male-female seduction-conquest scenario and tend to endorse the most negative features of male sexual socialization. These negative extremes call for (a) men to be sexually self-centered, (b) men to always seek sexual activity and be the principal sexual initiators, (c) sexual objectification of women's bodies, (d) the belief that sexual conquest is a sign of manliness, (e) endorsement of the rape myth that women secretly wish to be "taken," and (f) the belief that sex is the best method to achieve intimacy.

Although sexual behavior is the vehicle, date rape and acquaintance rape are both really about power and domination.

STRANGER RAPE

Men who rape women they do not know epitomize nonrelational sexual behavior. It is a way of avoiding relational intimacy and emotional attachment. Camouflaging the fear of intimacy is a mask preventing acceptance of a need for control and dominance, and the feeling of misogyny. This mask allows men to rationalize their behavior—to justify rape.

Rape does not primarily represent sexual frustration. Rapists are influenced by their need for power, their feelings of anger, their hatred toward women, and their inability to integrate their fears into a positive self-concept. At the extreme on the continuum of nonrelational sexuality are men dominated and controlled by the most negative aspects of their socialization process. These men feel powerless in the face of trying to meet the norms of their gender role. In conjunction with the strain of growing up male is the prevalence of family violence, particularly sexual abuse. Failing to come to grips with abusive and violent pain leads directly to a projection of this wound onto others, especially women.

Kokopeli and Lakey (1990) view rape as a natural extension of patriarchy. Patriarchy allows for the domination of women by men; it allows for the power imbalance. It also shapes male sexuality within traditional masculinity ideology. Out of patriarchy evolves men's acquisition of love, respect, and value through being powerful, masculine, and aggressive. This can naturally lead to violent behavior, hence defining the relationship between sexuality and violence. Rape then, according to Kokopeli and Lakey (1990), is for many men the logical end point of masculine sexuality. Rape becomes an act of violence expressed sexually—a highly dysfunctional by-product of our patriarchal society.

As long as violence by men remains acceptable and a core component of our notion of masculinity, rape will be a natural outcome. If angry men fail to address their hatred of women; sense of inadequacy; need to express their masculinity through power, control, and dominance; and acceptance of aggression and violence as legitimate, they will continue to rape. Rape is an act by an individual, but the source of such behavior is cultural. To appropriately address rape, our society must curb male aggression. Intervention and prevention programs must be instituted.

Prevention and Intervention

Healthy sexuality calls for the most intimate connection between persons. Sexual harassment includes power tactics that create deep and insidious harm to victims and to the potential for intimacy. To eliminate coercive sexuality and to promote positive intimate relationships between women and men, our society must challenge the aspects of male sexual socialization that associate sex and power.

Both prevention and intervention programs are necessary, because each design addresses the problem of sexual coercion from a different direction. Prevention is the ultimate objective, but intervention programs to ease the distress of victims and curb the pathology of perpetrators will be necessary as long as sexual harassment and acquaintance rape continue. In the following section, we examine existing programs and suggest others for the prevention and treatment of sexual harassment and acquaintance rape. Although our focus is on ways to change men's behavior, we recognize the critical importance of programs to ameliorate the anguish of victims.

SEXUAL HARASSMENT

In treatment programs, it is not uncommon to hear the following: "It wasn't harassment . . . I was only teasing. These secretaries invite me to pinch them and make (suggestive) comments. I'm sure they feel flattered." Men with such beliefs must be educated to recognize that it is inappropriate to boost their self-esteem by using women this way. Swecker (1985) notes that because some women and men view physical attraction as innate, they are prone to view men's pursuit of women as "natural," and, in turn, are likely to downplay harassing behavior. To prevent this type of thinking, we join with Landis-Schiff (1995) to suggest groups or classes for young men to elevate their consciousness about male sexual socialization and about the appropriate treatment of women. A critical element of this consciousness-raising effort is to increase awareness about how men are taught to prize power and control and to inordinately fear any sign of powerlessness, weakness, or lack of control.

Society teaches men that emotional expression is aversive, since it connotes being out of control and unmanly. This aversion creates special problems when a man is strongly attracted to a specific woman and experiences feelings he may have great difficulty controlling. To cope with his discomfort, he may turn away from his desire for emotional and physical connection and focus instead on the socialized need for control and conquest. Men must be socialized (or resocialized) to realize that this process is self-defeating because attempts to exercise power and control do not attract women, but typically repel them. To alter the thinking underlying sexual harassment and acquaintance rape, men must come to appreciate the value of meeting a partner on common ground and discovering shared connections.

LEGAL AVENUES OF PREVENTION

Although broad-brush societal reeducation is critical, it cannot resolve the problem by itself; legal and legislative reform are also necessary. Over the past several years, legal strategies have been developed to achieve harassment-free workplaces (National Council for Research on Women, 1991; Webb, 1991). The Civil Rights Act of 1991 and the Supreme Court decision in *Franklin v. Gwinnett County* (1992) have established corporate and institutional liability. As a result, organizations have developed prevention and intervention strategies for work environments in the attempt to reeducate and to avoid expensive litigious procedures.

The higher education environment has been more active than the business community in developing programmatic responses to sexual harassment legislation. The programs developed by Biaggio, Watts, and Brownell, (1990), Fitzgerald (1992), Paludi and Barickman (1991), and Northern Arizona University's Safe Working and Learning Environment Project (*Safe Working and Learning*, 1995) emphasize the need to include the following components:

1. A clear behavioral definition of sexual harassment.
2. A clear definitive policy statement of no tolerance for sexual harassment.
3. Clear and effective access for filing of grievances.
4. Availability of informal and formal resolution.
5. Easily available information and education for all employees regarding sexual harassment.
6. Strong, overt support from management or institutional administration.

Because current state and federal laws identify sexual harassment as illegal, but not a criminal offense, an employer or offender is subject to civil (financial penalties) rather than criminal penalties (imprisonment). Employers have been held institutionally liable even when an antiharassment program has been established, attempts have been made to stop known harassment, or there was ignorance of a harassing event. The court has held employers accountable for a reasonable degree of awareness of employee conduct and for control of employee behaviors. Additionally, when sexual harassment has been detected, employers must handle matters in a fashion that respects the dignity and privacy of all employees. The legal status of sexual harassment will continue to be modified as district courts rule on what constitutes "a hostile environment," what constitutes an appropriate awareness program, and what constitutes appropriate disciplinary action.

PREVENTION AND INTERVENTION

In their examination of the dark side of masculinity, Brooks and Silverstein (1995) described men as being so heavily influenced by normative demands that they circumvent any needs or feelings they consider feminine. Empathy is disparaged, whether for their own vulnerabilities or for the emotional needs of their loved ones. More than 25 years ago, Broverman, Broverman, Clarkson, Rosenkrantz, and Vogel (1970) illustrated this with their survey of 69 mental health professionals who described the characteristics of a healthy male. They found that healthy males are very independent, not at all emotional, very fond of math and science, very worldly, and leaderlike. The socially defined ideal man thus is an independent leader without emotional needs and feelings. Consequently, power and control are perceived as necessary, to ensure that needs and feelings do not get in the way. At a minimum, this prescription sets the stage for nonrelational sexuality. At its worst, it can lead to date rape and acquaintance rape. To combat these destructive behaviors, intervention, treatment, and prevention programs must address the roots of the problem in the socioemotional socialization of men.

Because so many men have minimal understanding of their emotional needs, intervention programs must include components designed to reeducate men about power, dominance, and social control. Men's sexual expectations can be viewed as hopes crystallized by silence. Rape is more likely in situations where sexual desires are unspoken, a woman's consent is assumed from ambiguous behavior, and a man does not work openly to clarify his confusion about a woman's messages. Because honest talk about sex is a cultural taboo, men have frequently made assumptions about a woman's sexual desires. When she is not forthright about these desires, men are more prone to accept the "no means yes" position and initiate coercive behavior. This exacerbates the traditional situation whereby women are expected to be the sexual "gatekeepers" (Gross, 1978). Men continue as sexual "pushers," while women continue to be laden with the duty to act as sexual "police." This problematic situation cannot be changed unless heterosexual couples honestly and respectfully discuss their differing sexual expectations, beliefs, and feelings. Such communication is often tedious and painful, but it can ultimately lead to more mutually satisfying interactions.

Because men have been taught to distrust a woman's overt statements about sexuality, they have been susceptible to dismissing a "no" response to their sexual overtures. Men must learn to abandon their past habits of reading into a woman's answer to decipher her "true" interests. "No" must be seen at face value, not as a statement of seduction, such as "maybe" or "yes." Without clear consent where sexuality is concerned, seduction becomes rape. Choices about sexual behavior are critical to anyone's identity. Men must allow women to have the same power and control they seem to require. All people must control the sexual activity of their own bodies. Even if a woman has already given consent, she has the right to change her mind.

Emotional maturity requires personal insight as well as empathy for others. Although nearly all women and men are capable of a wide range of emotions, they have been constrained by a culture that labels some emotions as appropriate for only one gender. When a man feels restricted from experiencing certain emotions in himself, he is subject to emotional stoicism and emotional intolerance of others. He comes to dismiss the emotional needs of others as unimportant or unreal. This lack of interpersonal empathy makes it more likely that a man will reject a woman's "no," or decide that she doesn't really mean it.

Men are capable of sexual activity even when they are not feeling emotionally close or intimate. At times, they expect women to adopt the same stance, by suppressing or denying their emotional signals and continuing with a sexual encounter. When women don't continue, men may become angered or punitive and feel entitled. Rather than projecting blame, men need to learn to become more emotionally attuned to themselves, more integrating of their sexual and emotional selves, more respectful of women's sexual reservations, and more compassionate for emotional needs of both women and themselves. Men who allow themselves to examine their own emotional needs will ultimately experience greater control of their affective lives and not be as likely to run from emotion. This greater affective awareness and communication skill will likewise lead to more satisfying emotional and sexual relationships. Levant (Levant & Kopecky, 1996) has developed programs for helping men learn emotional skills, such as emotional empathy and emotional self-awareness.

In the realm of emotional education, anger has a special place. It is a particularly troubling emotion for genders. Many women are likely to suppress it, producing passivity, self-denigration, and depression. Many men, on the other hand, are likely to channel all their emotions into anger. When they are fearful of expressing their anger, men adopt suppressive techniques and become subject to intellectualization, emotional withdrawal, tension, and terse communication. Eventually suppression may give way to violent emotional explosions. Interventions for this pattern include programs of exercise, diversionary activities, and effective strategies for appropriate time-out. At a minimum level, men must become far more insightful about their emotional lives if there is to be hope of eliminating nonrelational or violent sexuality.

As they become more involved in consciousness-raising activities, men can overcome their fears of emotional openness and can recognize the empowerment inherent in self-knowledge. Women who speak of empowering themselves are referring to extremely useful, personal change. Men can learn that personal power and control do not require denial of their needs and feelings. Once they understand this, they can begin to overcome their nonrelational sexual behavior. Men must understand that their behavior is a product of normative masculine socialization, and their notion of power and control is one of weakness, not strength. By learning to be accountable for self-behavior and becoming aware of their own needs and feelings, men can avoid violence within the context of sexuality.

Conclusion

Sexual harassment, date rape, and acquaintance rape are among the most violent and abusive manifestations of men's nonrelational sexuality. Utilizing Pleck's (1981, 1995) gender role strain model, we have attempted to show why some men engage in sexual harassment and rape. Trauma, discrepancy strain, and role dysfunction strain lead men to experience fear, shame, feelings of inadequacy, and discomfort with intimacy. When men fail to cope with these negative feelings, they sometimes try to compensate through exercises of power, control, and dominance over women, actions that are extolled and reinforced in patriarchal and misogynistic cultures. Parental violence and harsh socialization of young boys create an environment conducive to the perpetuation of interpersonal violence and sexual coercion. Consumption of alcohol, a socially sanctioned coping strategy for men, leads to its abuse and further contributes to the problems of nonrelational sexuality.

Sexual harassment and acquaintance rape must not be viewed exclusively as isolated manifestations of individual psychopathology, but must be seen in a sociocultural context that incorporates awareness of male role norms and patriarchal institutions.

As a society, we must do much more to ameliorate sexual harassment and rape behavior. Not to do so constitutes a major disservice to men, women, and their relationships. Social, political, and economic institutions must enforce laws that prohibit sexual harassment and rape. Equally important, however, is the need for organizations and institutions to implement orientation programs to explain why such behavior is not only inappropriate in a work setting, but harmful and destructive to male/female relationships. Ultimately, much of the solution for reducing rape and harassment lies in reducing male role trauma strain. Men must learn to accept all their emotions, communicate their needs and feelings, and realize the negative impact of power and control. To accomplish this feat, men will need to take full responsibility for their sexual behavior, while women and men work cooperatively to eliminate the environments that are conducive to nonrelational sexuality. Failure to do so will condemn us all to suffer the impact of violence and abuse.

References

Abbott, F. (Ed.). (1990). *Men and intimacy: Personal accounts exploring the dilemmas of modern male sexuality.* Freedom, CA: Crossing Press.

Bathrick, D., & Kauffman, G., Jr. (1990). Male privilege and male violence: Patriarchy's root and branch. In F. Abbott (Ed.), *Men and intimacy: Personal accounts exploring the dilemmas of modern male sexuality* (pp. 111–118). Freedom, CA: Crossing Press.

Betcher, W., & Pollack, W. (1993). *In a time of fallen heroes: The re-creation of masculinity.* New York: Atheneum.

Biaggio, M., Watts, D., & Brownell, A. (1990). Addressing sexual harassment: Strategies for prevention and change. In M. Paludi (Ed.), *Ivory power: Sexual harassment on campus* (pp. 213–230). Albany: State University of New York Press.

Brooks, G. (1995). *The centerfold syndrome: How men can overcome objectification and achieve intimacy with women.* San Francisco: Jossey-Bass.

Brooks, G. R., & Silverstein, L. B. (1995). Understanding the dark side of masculinity: An interactive systems model. In R. F. Levant & W. S. Pollack (Eds.), *A new psychology of men* (pp. 280–336). New York: Basic Books.

Broverman, I. K., Broverman, D. M., Clarkson, F., Rosenkrantz, P. S., & Vogel, S. (1970). Sex role stereotypes and clinical judgments of mental health. *Journal of Consulting and Clinical Psychology, 34,* 107.

Dziech, B. W., & Weiner, L. (1990). *The lecherous professor: Sexual harassment on campuses.* Urbana: University of Illinois Press.

Farrell, W. (1993). *The myth of male power.* New York: Simon & Schuster.

Fitzgerald, L. (1993). Sexual harassment: Violence against women in the workplace. *American Psychologist, 48,* 1070–1076.

Fitzgerald, L. F. (1992). *Sexual harassment in higher education: Concepts and issues.* Washington, DC: National Education Association.

Goldberg, H. (1987). *The inner male: Overcoming roadblocks to intimacy.* New York: New American Library.

Gross, A. (1978). The male role and heterosexual behavior. *Journal of Social Issues, 34,* 87–107.

Hudson, L., & Jacot, B. (1991). *The way men think: Intellect, intimacy and the erotic imagination.* New Haven, CT: Yale University Press.

Hunter, M. (1990). *Abused boys: The neglected victims of sexual abuse.* New York: Fawcett Columbine.

Kipnis, A. R. (1991). *Knights without armor: A practical guide for men in quest of masculine soul.* Los Angeles: Jeremy P. Tarcher.

Kokopeli, B., & Lakey, G. (1990). More power than we want: Masculine sexuality and violence. In F. Abbott (Ed.), *Men and intimacy: Personal accounts exploring the dilemmas of modern male sexuality* (pp. 8–15). Freedom, CA: Crossing Press.

Koss, M., & Dinero, T. E. (1989). Predictors of sexual aggression among a national sample of male college students. Human sexual aggression: Current perspectives. *Annals of the New York Academy of Sciences, 528,* 133–146.

Koss, M. P., Goodman, L. A., Browne, A., Fitzgerald, L. F., Keita, G. P., & Russo, N. F. (1994). *No safe haven: Male violence against women at home, at work, and in the community.* Washington, DC: American Psychological Association.

Krugman, S. (1995). Male development and the transformation of shame. In R. F. Levant & W. S. Pollack (Eds.), *A new psychology of men* (pp. 91–126). New York: Basic Books.

Landis-Schiff, T. (1995). Sexual harassment: Why men don't understand it. *Initiatives, 57*(2), 15–26.

Levant, R. F. (1995). Toward the reconstruction of masculinity. In R. F. Levant & W. S. Pollack (Eds.), *A new psychology of men* (pp. 229–251). New York: Basic Books.

Levant, R. F., & Kopecky, G. (1996). *Masculinity reconstructed: Changing the rules of manhood—at work, in relationships, and in family life.* New York: Plume/ Penguin Books.

Levant, R. F., & Pollack, W. S. (Eds.). (1995). *A new psychology of men.* New York: Basic Books.

MacKinnon, C. (1987). *Feminism unmodified.* Cambridge, MA: Harvard University Press.

Michael, R. T., Gagnon, J. H., Lauman, E. O., & Kolata, G. (1994). *Sex in America: A definitive survey.* New York: Warner Books.

National Council for Research on Women. (1991). *Sexual harassment: Research and resources.* New York: Author.

Nelson, J. B. (1988). *The intimate connection: Male sexuality, masculine spirituality.* Philadelphia: Westminster Press.

Osherson, S. (1992). *Wrestling with love: How men struggle with intimacy with women, children, parents, and each other.* New York: Fawcett Columbine.

Paludi, M. (Ed.). (1996). *Sexual harassment on college campuses: Abusing the ivory power.* Albany: State University of New York Press.

Paludi, M. A., & Barickman, R. B. (1991). *Academic and workplace sexual harassment: A manual of resources.* Albany: State University of New York Press.

Pleck, J. H. (1981). *The myth of masculinity.* Cambridge, MA: MIT Press.

Pleck, J. H. (1995). The gender role strain paradigm: An update. In R. F. Levant & W. S. Pollack (Eds.), *A new psychology of men* (pp. 11–32). New York: Basic Books.

Pollack, W. S. (1995). No man is an island: Toward a new psychoanalytic psychology of men. In R. F. Levant & W. S. Pollack (Eds.), *A new psychology of men* (pp. 33–67). New York: Basic Books.

Roiphe, K. (1993). *The morning after: Sex, fear, and feminism.* Boston: Back Bay Books/Little, Brown.

Swecker, J. (1985). *Straightening out the power curve: Eliminating sexual harassment in institutions.* Paper presented at the meetings of the American Psychological Association, Los Angeles.

Warshaw, R. (1988). *I never called it rape: The Ms report on recognizing, fighting, and surviving date and acquaintance rape.* New York: Harper & Row.

Webb, S. L. (1991). *Sexual harassment: Shades of gray. Guidelines for managers, supervisors and employees.* Seattle: Premiere.

Zalk, S. R. (1996). Men in the academy: A psychological profile of harassers. In M. Paludi (Ed.), *Sexual harassment on college campuses: Abusing the ivory power* (pp. 81–113). Albany: State University of New York Press.

Zilbergeld, B. (1992). *The new male sexuality: The truth about men, sex, and pleasure.* New York: Bantam Books.

Bibliography

Ackerman, R. (1993). *Silent sons: A book for and about men.* New York: Simon & Schuster.

Allen, M. (with Robinson, J.). (1993). *In the company of men: A new approach to healing for husbands, fathers, and friends.* New York: Random House.

Astrachan, A. (1986). *How men feel: Their response to women's demands for equality and power.* Garden City, NY: Anchor Press/Doubleday.

Balswick, J. O. (1988). *The inexpressive male.* Lexington, MA: Lexington Books.

Bem, S. L. (1993). *The lenses of gender: Transforming the debate on sexual inequality.* New Haven, CT: Yale University Press.

Biaggio, M., & Brownell, A. (1996). Addressing sexual harassment: Strategies for prevention and change. In M. Paludi (Ed.), *Sexual harassment on college campuses: Abusing the ivory power* (pp. 216–234). Albany: State University of New York Press.

Bly, R. (1990). *Iron John: A book about men.* New York: Addison-Wesley.

Brownmiller, S. (1975). *Against our will: Men, women, and rape.* New York: Simon & Schuster.

Chan, A. A. (1994). *Women and sexual harassment: A practical guide to the legal protections of Title VII and the hostile environment claim.* New York: Harrington Park Press.

Chodorow, N. (1989). *Feminism and psychoanalytic theory.* New Haven, CT: Yale University Press.

Corneau, G. (1991). *Absent fathers, lost sons: The search for masculine identity.* Boston: Shambhala.

Estrich, S. (1987). *Real rape: How the legal system victimizes women who say no.* Cambridge, MA: Harvard University Press.

Fairstein, L. A. (1993). *Sexual violence: Our war against rape.* New York: Morrow.

Finkelhor, D., & Yillo, K. (1985). *License to rape: Sexual abuse of wives.* New York: Holt.

Gilmore, D. D. (1990). *Manhood in the making: Cultural concepts of masculinity.* New Haven, CT: Yale University Press.

Gurian, M. (1994). *Mothers, sons and lovers: How a man's relationship with his mother affects the rest of his life.* Boston: Shambhala.

Keen, S. (1991). *Fire in the belly: On being a man.* New York: Bantam Books.

Kipnis, A., & Herron, E. (1994). *Gender peace: The quest for love and justice between women and men.* New York: Morrow.

Koss, M. P. (1993). Rape: Scope, impact, interventions, and public policy responses. *American Psychologist, 48,* 1062–1069.

Lewis, M. (1992). *Shame: The exposed self.* New York: Free Press.

Lundy, M., & Younger, M. (Eds.). (1994). *Empowering women in the workplace: Perspectives, innovations, and techniques for helping professionals.* Binghamton, NY: Harrington Park Press.

Miedzian, M. (1992). *Boys will be boys: Breaking the link between masculinity and violence.* New York: Doubleday.

Morrison, A. P. (1989). *Shame: The underside of narcissism.* Hillsdale, NJ: Analytic Press.

Nowinski, J. (1990). *Men, love, and sex: A couple's guide to male sexual fulfillment.* New York: Thorsons.

Osherson, S. (1986). *Finding our fathers: The unfinished business of manhood.* New York: Free Press.

Pasick, R. (1992). *Awakening from the deep sleep: A powerful guide for courageous men.* San Francisco: Harper.

Pirog-Good, M. A. (1989). *Violence in dating relationships: Emerging issues.* New York: Praeger.

Pittman, F. (1993). *Man enough: Fathers, sons, and the search for masculinity.* New York: Putnam.

Quina, K. (1996). Sexual harassment and rape: A continuum of exploitation. In M. Paludi (Ed.), *Sexual harassment on college campuses: Abusing the ivory power* (pp. 183-197). Albany: State University of New York Press.

Richardson, L., & Taylor, V. (Eds.). (1993). *Feminist frontiers iii.* New York: McGraw-Hill.

Riggs, R., Murrell, P. H., & Cutting, J. C. (1993). *Sexual harassment in higher education: From conflict to community* (ASHE-ERIC Higher Education Report No. 2). Washington, DC: George Washington School.

Ross, J. M. (1992). *The male paradox.* New York: Simon & Schuster.

Rue, N. M. (1989). *Coping with dating violence.* New York: Rosen.

Safe working and learning environment policy. (1995). A policy of Northern Arizona University, Flagstaff.

Sanday, P. R. (1990). *Fraternity gang rape: Sex, brotherhood and privilege on campus.* New York: New York University Press.

Sandler, B. (1981). Sexual harassment: A hidden problem. *Educational Record, 62,* 52-57.

Sanford, J. A., & Lough, G. (1988). *What men are like: The psychology of men, for men and the women who live with them.* New York: Paulist Press.

Silverstein, O., & Rashbaum, B. (1994). *The courage to raise good men.* New York: Viking.

Tangri, S., Burt, M., & Johnson, L. (1982). Sexual harassment at work: Three explanatory models. *Journal of Social Issues, 38,* 33–54.

Thompson, K. (Ed.). (1991). *To be a man: In search of the deep masculine.* Los Angeles: Jeremy P. Tarcher.

Tingley, J. C. (1993). *Genderflex: Ending the workplace war between the sexes.* Phoenix, AZ: Performance Improvement Pros.

CHAPTER 7

Male Gender Socialization and the Perpetration of Sexual Abuse

DAVID LISAK

FEW PEOPLE WOULD consider male gender socialization to be a public health issue. Certainly, the Centers for Disease Control have not made such a pronouncement. Yet there is considerable evidence to support such a pronouncement, evidence that links sexual abuse and a vast array of interpersonally abusive and violent behavior to the process by which male children, male adolescents, and young men are socialized into masculinity.

Consider the prima facie evidence. U.S. prisons are overflowing with a shocking percentage of our population, and prisons are bastions of masculinity. Interpersonal violence, including sexual abuse, similarly remains a stronghold of male domination (FBI, 1992). The past two decades have seen an explosion of research on child abuse and other violations of trust and, with only a few exceptions, these forms of violence are found to be disproportionately perpetrated by men (e.g., Berliner & Elliot, 1996; Kilmartin, 1994).

Some argue that biology plays an important role in the male propensity for sexual abuse and violence (e.g., Barash, 1979). However, as yet, there is little direct evidence. Indeed, it has been argued that even relatively strong genetic influences are so mediated by environmental (e.g., socialization) conditions, that it is mistaken to conceive of biology and environment as separable influences (Fausto-Sterling, 1985). Recent research demonstrating the profound impact of psychological trauma on neurophysiology and even neuroanatomy underscores how inextricably intertwined are biology and environment (e.g., McEwan & Mendelson, 1993).

Different forms of sexual victimization—for example, child sexual abuse and sexual exploitation of patients—each have unique motivational components. Further, individual perpetrators of sexual victimization vary in their motivational make-up. However, the disproportionate role of males in perpetrating these offenses suggests that, despite these variations, there is something about being male—or growing up male—that predisposes some men to sexually victimize others.

There is actually considerable evidence indicating a link between various forms of sexual and interpersonal violence and male gender socialization. This link has been established by numerous researchers who have investigated a diverse sampling of male populations. While the evidence thus far obtained pertains disproportionately to sexual violence against women, there is both theoretical and empirical evidence indicating that the link between male gender socialization and various forms of sexual abuse and exploitation is equally salient. The evidence implicates particular behavioral and attitudinal legacies of the masculine gender socialization process—stereotyped sex role beliefs, particular attitudes toward women, hostility toward women, and hypermasculine beliefs—as part of the motivational substructure of violence against women and also of sexual abuse of children (Briere & Runtz, 1988; Crossman, Stith, & Bender, 1990; Fromuth, Burkhart, & Jones, 1991; Gold, Fultz, Burke, Prisco, & Willett, 1992; Koss, Leonard, Beezley, & Oros, 1985; Lisak & Ivan, 1995; Lisak & Roth, 1988; Lisak & Roth, 1990; Malamuth, 1986; Malamuth, Sockloskie, Koss, & Tanaka, 1991; Mosher & Anderson, 1986; Muehlenhard & Falcon, 1990; Rapaport & Burkhart, 1984; Stith & Farley, 1993).

The most rigorous test of the hypothesis that masculine socialization is implicated causally in the genesis of sexual victimization was reported by Malamuth et al. (1991). Through structural equation modeling, they tested a causal model in which masculine socialization was implicated both distally and proximally to the perpetration of sexual victimization. Distally, the factor "involvement in delinquency" consisted in part of an assessment of the subject's involvement with other delinquent youths. Delinquent peer groups have long been identified as intensive training grounds for hypermasculine behavior and attitudes (Kanin, 1984; McCord, McCord, & Thurber, 1962; Munroe, Munroe, & Whiting, 1981). Proximally, the factor "hostile masculinity" was associated with both sexual and nonsexual coerciveness.

The preponderance of this evidence relates to attitudes and beliefs because such more-or-less conscious attributes are relatively accessible to the methodologies currently in use in the social sciences, particularly psychology. However, a substantial body of work, primarily theoretical but which includes some empirical findings, has examined other, less conscious legacies of the male gender socialization process (Chodorow, 1978; Pollack, 1995). This work has focused much more on the emotional legacies of being socialized into masculinity, and it is here that this chapter will focus: pathways by which the emotional socialization of males potentiates the perpetration of sexual abuse and violence.

Theoretical Framework

An examination of any aspect of the male gender socialization process requires some clarification about language and underlying assumptions. If there *is* a "male gender socialization process"—and here the evidence from decades of social science research is overwhelming—then its endpoint, masculinity, must be a created entity; what is often now called a "cultural construction." Indeed, the evidence from recent cross-disciplinary scholarship suggests that it would be more accurate to refer to *masculinities,* because it would appear that cultures and cultures-within-cultures construct numerous forms of masculinity (Brod, 1994; Gilmore, 1990). If masculinities are constructed, then it is important to distinguish them from the biological sex category—male—with which they are typically associated. That is, while a human being may be identified at birth as male by virtue of his genitalia, this identification does not tell us anything about the nature and form of his masculinity. This will be determined by a myriad of factors, ranging from personal choice and unique psychodynamic influences, to the shaping influences of his culture, the economic constraints of his environment, and the historical epoch in which he is raised (e.g., Kimmel, 1996).

Thus, in the ensuing discussion, it is presumed that "male" is not synonymous with "masculine," and that when we speak of the legacies of masculine socialization we are not speaking of intrinsic male attributes, or of the natural unfolding of a "natural" or "normal" male personality. Rather, we are speaking of the legacies of socialization processes that are generally applied to male children, legacies that produce roughly predictable outcomes.

One of the most salient features of masculinity, a commonality that seems to characterize many of its different instantiations around the world, is its precariousness. It appears not only to be a culturally created entity, but one that is not easily created or sustained. Anthropologists have provided numerous examples of the great lengths to which many cultures go to transform male children into masculine beings;

and the great lengths that these newly created masculine beings then go to preserve this state of masculinity (Gilmore, 1990; Webster, 1908). Thus, in some cultures, dramatic and even traumatic initiations are deemed necessary to create new masculine beings. In other cultures, constant proving is necessary—displays of courage, demonstrations of honor—to sustain the masculine state. In still others, the focus may be on preventing dishonor, the dreaded state of shame.

The very presence of these cultural codes and institutions further underscores the cultural origins of masculinities. One would have to wonder why, if masculinity were an innate unfolding of inherent male attributes, cultures would have evolved such dramatic and pervasive means for its creation and maintenance.

"WARRIOR MASCULINITY"

One attempt to explain the transcultural ubiquity of relatively severe forms of masculinity focuses on the survival advantages that accrue to cultures that create rigid masculine norms to which males must aspire. According to this theory (e.g., Gilmore, 1990), the underlying purpose of this type of masculine socialization is the creation of a class (gender) of people within the society who are well-conditioned to perform certain tasks for the preservation of that society. Although the most dramatic of these tasks is warfare, they also include other forms of work that require similar psychological conditioning, such as hunting.

What is the nature of the necessary psychological conditioning? Perhaps the clearest insight into this is provided by military training practices. These practices have often been compared to male initiation rituals, and the commonalities are numerous. In basic training, the new recruit is subjected to intense physical hardship and is frequently terrorized both physically and emotionally. Simultaneously, the recruit's normal, human emotional responses to such treatment—terror, vulnerability, for example—are vigorously, sometimes violently, suppressed. This process, reinforced by intense group pressure and physical isolation from family, tends to deintegrate the recruit's pretraining identity. The recruit is offered a single path toward reintegration: the identity offered by the military, that of a soldier. This "warrior identity" becomes internalized in the intense conditions of basic training just like any other identity. To the extent that the process is successful, the new recruit will now autonomously suppress those "vulnerable" emotions and convert them into anger and aggression.

The cauldron of basic training offers a clear view into the process of creating "warrior masculinity," a process that can be applied to either men or women (remember: sex does not equal gender). The clarity stems from the very focused purpose of this training—the creation of soldiers who will suppress their fears in the face of danger and function effectively within a military unit. However, the process of basic training is simply a crystalline form of the less focused process of masculine gender socialization that is generally applied to almost every male in the United States, with variations attributable to varying cultural and economic conditions.

Further, it would be mistaken to presume that the process of gender socialization that most men are subjected to is necessarily a "kinder and gentler" version of military training. If the methods appear less extreme, remember that the "men" are typically preschoolers when they first enter "masculine socialization training"; it doesn't take as much to terrorize a 4-year-old.

That masculine socialization is often, if not typically, a traumatic process was underscored in the course of an interview study conducted by the author several years ago (Lisak, 1994). The interviews were completely unstructured and autobiographical. In the course of these interviews, nearly every man described at least one—often several—intensely traumatic experiences having to do with their gender socialization. They described incidents in which they were so traumatically humiliated for displaying gender inappropriate emotions that the experiences were forever etched into memory, in just the way that traumatic experiences are.

One need not conduct an interview study to see the traumatic nature of the masculine socialization process. Witness the following scene, observed by the author in a community playground—a living laboratory in which the process of gender socialization is vividly on display:

A 3-year-old boy and his father are standing before a spiral slide. The boy is looking up at the slide with a mixture of fear and excitement, but it is clear that the fear is winning out. The father also sees this and begins to urge, then nudge, then goad, then taunt the boy: "Come on Eric, don't be scared. It's just a slide." In response, Eric shies away more visibly. This incites the father. "Don't be a sissy, Eric. Just get on up there and do it." Now Eric is truly frightened and the corners of his mouth begin to curl downward as his face moves to the threshold of tears. At the sight of this, the father becomes angry. "Don't be such a crybaby. If you're going to cry I'm not going to hang around with you." And with that the father walks off. And of course as the father walks off, Eric begins to weep, and then to sob, because his fear is now compounded by this abandonment, and on top of it he feels the intense humiliation of being shunned by his father, and the shame of his fear. The scene ends with Eric slumping to the ground and sobbing.

Such scenes are played out millions of times every day across the country. Scenes of little boys learning to conform their behavior, and most importantly their emotions and their emotional experience, to the dictates of masculinity. Long before they have the slightest inkling of the meaning of that word—masculinity—they are well on their way to shaping themselves according to its dictates. Eric will learn very quickly that to avoid the humiliation, the terror of abandonment, and the scorn of his father, he must suppress the very human fears that he innocently expressed.

MASCULINITY AS REGULATOR OF EMOTIONAL EXPERIENCE

Although there are many aspects to any particular form of masculinity, including attitudes and beliefs, styles of dress, physical mannerisms, and so on, it is arguable that the core—particularly of "warrior masculinity"—is the regulation of emotional experience (see e.g., Levant, 1995). Warrior masculinity is predicated on denial, suppression, and repression. Fear and other emotional states associated with vulnerability are suppressed, then their very presence is denied, and ultimately they are repressed; there remains no conscious awareness of them. Although men vary greatly in the degree to which they reach this endpoint, there is considerable evidence that this endpoint is indeed the goal of masculine socialization. To be disconnected from one's own fears and vulnerabilities, and disconnected from those of others, renders one a formidable soldier in any theater of combat, be it on the battlefield or in the "corporate jungle."

The differential emotional socialization of male and female children has by now been well-documented. It is a process carried out by virtually all of the major categories of caretakers commonly found in children's lives, from parents to daycare workers to teachers (e.g., Brody, 1985; Fivush, 1989; Kuebli & Fivush, 1992; Malatesta & Haviland, 1985). Relative to female children, male children receive far less training and reinforcement for the process of learning about their emotional experience, and are often subject to punishing humiliation for expressing "counter-gender" emotions. The product of this differential emotional socialization has also been well-documented: men experience emotions less intensely; they are less capable than women of identifying and expressing their emotions; and they are less capable of empathically responding to the emotions expressed by others (Diener, Sandvik, & Larsen, 1985; Eisenberg & Lennon, 1983; Kilmartin, 1994).

THE MASCULINIZATION OF SEXUALITY

Sexuality, like almost every facet of human experience, is almost defined by its plasticity. Sexuality is experienced both intrapersonally and interpersonally. It can be experienced as a preponderantly physical act, or its physicality can be secondary to the intense emotions to which it is so easily connected. It can be experienced as the ultimate form of human connection, or as the most painful condition of alienation and disconnection. Thus, even a behavior and experience so clearly rooted in the biological imperatives of species survival is subject to enormous cultural channeling and modification. It is little wonder then that sexuality, too, is subject to the powerful forces of gender socialization; all the more because sexuality and gender are so culturally interwoven.

While there are many ways in which masculine socialization can and does influence the development and experience of men's sexuality, and while there are many individual and cultural differences, there are also certain basic directional biases. The process of emotional socialization that so commonly accompanies men's indoctrination into masculinity has certain predictable consequences. To the extent that intense emotions—other than anger—are experienced as threatening to masculine identity, and to the extent that vulnerability, dependency, and the helplessness of being out-of-control are also so experienced, to that extent will a man's capacity to experience sexuality as an intensely emotional connection be dramatically curtailed. Normative masculine socialization, by its constrictive influence on emotional experience, inhibits the relatively natural confluence of sexuality and intense emotionality. The very intensity of sexual experience, which by its nature at least potentially can evoke intense emotions, is likely to thereby evoke the constrictive influences that most men have internalized through the process of their masculinization.

The consequences of this masculinization of sexual experience are varied. For many men, it is simply another aspect of the human condition which they experience in a somewhat disconnected form; a flattening or deadening of a potentially enlivening human experience. However, there are other, potentially more dangerous consequences. Sexuality is, by its very nature, an experience of great potential intensity. It consists of intense physical sensations; it is typically associated with enormous social meanings and taboos and is therefore easily connected to shame; it often includes the penetration of actual physical boundaries. For all of these reasons, a sexual encounter is likely to be experienced intensely. These inherent qualities of sexuality make it uniquely vulnerable to exploitation and abuse. When two people enter a sexual encounter, if one is disconnected from his capacity to experience the intense emotional component of the encounter, while the other is not disconnected, then the potential for harm and exploitation is enormously heightened. This is dramatically heightened further when the encounter itself is not mutual, but rather the result of manipulation, control, coercion, or actual physical force.

Indeed, it can be argued that the very fact of being disconnected from emotional experience dramatically increases the likelihood that someone would be able and willing to exploit and abuse the sexuality of another person. Separated from its emotional associations, unlinked from its relationship to human connection, sexuality is more likely to be experienced as simply another physical sensation; a physical need to be gratified. With the thread of human (emotional) connectedness severed, the "other" can be experienced as pure object; as a source of sexual gratification whose experience of the encounter has no reality. What this describes is a profound disruption of the human capacity for empathy.

The evidence suggests that the normative process of male gender socialization, in which males develop relatively constricted emotional lives, leads to impaired empathic capacity. Simultaneously, this normative socialization process tends to accentuate males' experience of, and access to anger, the emotion that is most sanctioned by male gender norms. Indeed, it has been argued that men who rigidly adhere to gender norms for emotional expression are likely to convert a variety of "nonmasculine" emotional states into anger (Mosher & Tomkins, 1988). This combination of impaired empathy and anger accentuation may well have something to do with the disproportionate male involvement in sexual abuse.

Pathways from Emotional Socialization to Perpetration

EMPATHY DEFICITS

Empathy has often been thought of as a critical inhibitor of interpersonal aggression, and this view is supported by considerable empirical evidence that deficits in empathy are associated with aggressive behavior (Miller & Eisenberg, 1988). Unfortunately, the concept of empathy has proven to be somewhat illusive, particularly when attempts have been made to operationalize it. However, research and theorizing during the past decade has led to significant refinements in the concept. Empathy is now thought to have a cognitive component—perspective-taking—and an emotional component—vicarious emotional responding. Further, vicarious emotional responding has itself been analyzed into at least two distinct components: "sympathy" and "personal distress."

Batson, Fultz, and Schoenrade (1987) contended that witnessing another person's distress—a situation that typically evokes some form of vicarious emotional response—can induce either a sympathetic emotional response, such as compassion and tenderness, or it can induce distressful emotions, such as alarm and "upset." They argued, citing supportive experimental evidence, that a sympathetic response may lead to helpful behavior, whereas a distressed response is more likely to lead to behavior aimed at terminating the negative internal state generated by witnessing the other person's distress. This formulation has been supported by research by Eisenberg, Fabes, Schaller, Carlo, and Miller (1991a) that has linked differential physiological responses to these alternative vicarious emotional reactions. Individuals who react sympathetically tend to manifest a decrease in heart rate, while individuals who react with distress tend to manifest an increase in heart rate.

If we extrapolate these findings to the domain of male gender socialization, we might well predict that, in general, males might be more prone to experiencing distress in reaction to witnessing another person's distress. The other person's distress, be it fear or emotional pain or some other expression of vulnerability, is likely to evoke the male's own reservoir of such vulnerable emotional states. Once evoked, these states are in turn likely to create distress, since they are precisely the emotions that the male has had to suppress in the service of achieving and maintaining his masculine identity. To the "masculinized" male, the evocation of these emotional states is a direct assault on a cornerstone of his identity. To the extent that the male begins to vicariously experience the other person's vulnerable emotions, he will begin to feel anxious ("distress" in empathy terminology), with, presumably, a concomitant increase in his heart rate.

A state of heightened anxiety tends to decrease the likelihood of prosocial behavior, and increase the likelihood of a variety of unhelpful behaviors. Anxious, "distressed" individuals tend to focus their attention on their own aversive internal state, not on the originally distressed person who evoked their anxiety. They tend to seek ways to relieve their anxiety. This can be accomplished in several ways. They may disconnect their conscious awareness of their emotional reactions.

That is, they disconnect their ability to resonate with the other person's distress, thereby also disconnecting themselves from their anxiety reactions. They may also attempt to relieve their anxiety through the emotional conversion process described by Mosher and Tomkins (1988). The sequence of this process would be as follows: (a) they experience some resonance with the emotional state of the distressed person; (b) these resonant emotions quickly induce an anxiety state; (c) their anxiety is quickly transformed into anger, and/or aggressive action; (d) the expression of anger and/or aggressive action relieves the anxiety state.

The conversion of "personal distress" reactions to anger and aggression may be responsible for the observed tendency among abused children to respond aggressively toward peers who display overt distress (Klimes-Dougan & Kistner, 1990; Main & George, 1985). Such aggressive reactions in a context that would ordinarily evoke sympathy are almost never seen in children who have not been maltreated. These reactions are consistent with the hypothesis that the maltreated children experience intense anxiety when confronted with other children's distress, and need to relieve the anxiety by turning it into aggressive action.

A similar process may have been responsible for the finding in the Gold et al. study (1992), in which the high "macho" males responded to a crying baby not only with less empathy, but also with more anger. The baby's cries may have evoked resonant emotions in these "hypermasculine" men, emotions that conflict markedly with the gender norms that these men try to adhere to. By converting the emotions quickly into anger, the men are relieved of the conflict.

The link between such anxiety or "personal distress" reactions and empathy deficits is also supported by the observation that the abuse of infants and children is often triggered by the child's expression of distress (Zeskind & Shingler, 1991). Frodi and Lamb (1980) have demonstrated experimentally that child abusers are more physiologically reactive (increased heart rate and skin conductance) and experience greater aversion to the sound of a crying infant. This increased aversive arousal can be interpreted as a physiological manifestation of the evocation of distress in the abuser. The heightened distress experienced by abusers would motivate them to seek to terminate this aversive state rather than to sympathize with the distressed child.

THE RELATIONSHIP BETWEEN EMPATHY FOR THE SELF AND EMPATHY FOR OTHERS

In dramatically—and traumatically—constricting the male's capacity to experience the full range of his emotions, masculine socialization does more than obstruct the male's ability to respond sympathetically to other people's distress. It also obstructs his ability to respond sympathetically to his own distress. As he learns that vulnerable emotional states are "unmasculine," and that they must be expunged from his experience lest he be forced to label himself "unmasculine," the male is forced to respond as aggressively to his own internal displays of vulnerability as he would to those of others. The harsh and denigrating words inflicted on him in the course of his socialization into masculinity are internalized. If he shows himself his fear or his hurt, he is likely to respond spontaneously with the vocabulary of masculine epithets: "you're a girl," "a sissy," "weak," "a crybaby."

Thus, the normative socialization process for males is likely to leave them quite intolerant of their own innate, human tendency to experience vulnerable emotional states in response to the inevitable stresses of life. This intolerance is then very likely to transfer to other people's vulnerable emotions. Barnett and McCoy (1989) demonstrated this relationship in a study that has since been replicated by Ivan (1996). College students were asked to identify a range of distressing experiences they had experienced during childhood, and to then rate how distressing each of those experiences was for them. They were also given a measure of empathy for others. There was no relationship between the number of distressing experiences a person had and their current empathy level. However, their rating of how distressing their experiences were for them was related to current empathy. Those who rated their experiences as relatively *more* distressing displayed higher levels of current empathy. In other words, if they were able to acknowledge their own distress, they were more able to resonate with distress felt by others.

A number of other studies lend support to the link between people's capacity to tolerate their own distressful emotions and their capacity to empathize with distress in others. Lenrow (1965) demonstrated experimentally that children who openly expressed their own distress in stressful situations were more responsive to the expression of distress in others. A study reported by Bryant (1987) provides a clue to the origins of these differences among children. He found that children whose mothers were more positively responsive to them when they experienced stress at age 10 were significantly more empathic at age 14 than children whose mothers had been less responsive. By responding in such positive ways, these mothers may have been teaching their children to be tolerant of their distressful emotional states, a tolerance that later transferred to a tolerance and sympathy for distress in others. In a similar finding, Eisenberg et al. (1991b) reported a significant correlation between the sympathy levels of fathers and their male children. Further, parents who strongly discouraged their male children from expressing sadness and anxiety had sons who were low in sympathy. The authors concluded that "children who receive negative reactions when they respond emotionally may learn to deny or suppress their emotional reactions and to experience anxiety internally" (Eisenberg et al., 1991a, p. 1405). They further noted that this process was more evident in boys than in girls, a finding that is consistent with "cultural norms regarding the importance of males' inhibition of emotion."

These findings suggest that there is a relationship between a person's capacity to experience and express their own painful emotions and the capacity to respond sympathetically to the emotional pain of another person. To the extent that the masculine-socialized male has internalized stereotypical gender norms that dictate a suppressive attitude to those painful emotions, he will be less likely to respond sympathetically to his own distress, and therefore to the emotional distress of another person.

THE INTERACTION OF CHILDHOOD ABUSE, MASCULINE SOCIALIZATION, AND PERPETRATION

In the search for the causes of sexual victimization, one of the most consistent findings is a history of childhood abuse among its perpetrators. These findings have led to the "cycle of violence" hypothesis, which posits that childhood abuse is a predisposing factor for the later perpetration of violence. It is clear that the relationship between early abuse and later perpetration is far from direct (Widom, 1989). In a series of studies from our own laboratory at the University of Massachusetts-Boston, in which more than 1,000 men were assessed, two-thirds of abused men never perpetrated either sexual or nonsexual forms of interpersonal violence (Lisak, Hopper, & Song, 1996; Lisak, Miller, & Conklin, 1996). However, a strong majority of the men who perpetrated had themselves been victimized as children; the data suggest that the proportion is at least two-thirds. The strongest relationship holds for men who perpetrate sexual violence against children. Of these men, more than 80 percent had themselves been abused as children.

There are good reasons to suspect that masculine gender socialization may be partly responsible for this link between early abuse and later perpetration; and once again, emotional experience may play an important role. The interaction between early abuse and the process of masculine socialization can create an intense conflict for male victims. To be abused as a child is to experience fear, helplessness, powerlessness, shame, and humiliation, and at an intensity that is overwhelming.

Herein lies the core of the conflict that will plague the male abuse victim. He is plunged by the abuse into a sea of emotions that have already been identified as inherently non-masculine; emotions that in fact define nonmasculinity. Yet he is experiencing them and they become indelible parts of him, because they are traumatically etched into his memory and therefore his experience of himself; of who he is.

As intense as this conflict is, it is based on an illusion, the illusion of masculinity. In reality, the male victim is simply a human being who is responding to traumatic injury precisely the way humans are endowed to respond. But his gender socialization prevents him from ever seeing the utter normalcy and simplicity of his response; the humanness of his fear, his pain, and his vulnerability. His gender socialization ensures that he will war against these basic human responses. He will try to excise them; he will beg them to go away; he will pretend they don't exist; he will seal up vast chambers of his humanity in a futile effort to believe they have disappeared. All because he has already internalized his culture's dictates about which parts of himself are appropriate and acceptable, and which are emblems of nonmasculinity.

How does the male victim live with such a conflict? Our research and clinical findings suggest that it is not easy. It appears that the majority of men who struggle with the interacting legacies of abuse and gender socialization suffer the predictable consequences of the conflict. Many feel inadequate. They feel like failures; they feel alienated from other men; they feel they must hide the telltale signs of that inner brand that marks them forever as nonmen. They struggle and suffer with intrapersonal and interpersonal consequences of the conflict (Lisak, 1994).

Faced with such an unrelenting conflict, and an unrelenting assault on their deep-felt need for a masculine identity, some men "choose" to psychologically banish one side of the conflict—the abuse, and/or the psychological legacies of the abuse. For these men, this "choice" actually becomes more of a drive; a driven need to expunge the evidence of their vulnerability, of their nonmasculinity. To accomplish this, they must banish their fear, their helplessness, their powerlessness, and their shame, because now they are all dangerous nodal points that can draw them back into that expunged nonmasculine state.

These men monitor their world, both inside and out, for any sign or gesture that might link back to that repressed but vibrating core of pain and vulnerability that they have entombed within themselves. These are the men whom you learn not to tease about certain things; the men you are careful not to shame. These are the fathers in the playground who cannot tolerate to see the childlike fear in their sons' eyes because that fear has the power to resonate through the circuits of their memory and open the door to their own fear that they are desperate to hold shut.

The role of masculine socialization, and in particular gender rigidity and emotional constriction, in mediating the link between childhood abuse and the perpetration of sexual abuse has received some empirical support (Lisak, Hopper, & Song, 1996). In this sample of nearly 600 men, abused men who perpetrated scored higher on measures of gender rigidity and of emotional constriction than abused men who did not perpetrate. Interestingly, the abused men who did not perpetrate actually scored *lower* on these measures than the non-abused "control" subjects. Together, these results point to divergent adaptations to the conflict created by the interacting legacies of abuse and of masculine socialization. One group—the nonperpetrators—appear to have evolved a less rigid gender identity than is the norm, perhaps in response to their abuse experiences. The other group—the perpetrators—appear to have evolved a rigid, hypergendered masculine identity.

Two recent follow-up studies have added credence to this interpretation. In one sample, abused perpetrators scored significantly lower on measures of psychological distress than did abused non-perpetrators, including a measure of Posttraumatic Stress Disorder (Lisak, Miller, & Conklin, 1996). These results are consistent with the hypothesized hypergendered adaptation of abused perpetrators—men who deny and suppress their emotional distress, but who are more likely to act out violently against other people. In the second study, abused perpetrators scored significantly lower than abused non-perpetrators on a measure of empathy (Hopper, 1996).

Together, these results paint the picture of an identifiable adaptation to the conflict between abuse and masculine socialization. It is an adaptation in which the abused male is driven to suppress the emotional legacy of his abuse in the service of adhering to male gender norms, norms that prohibit the experience or expression of such intense and vulnerable emotional states. The fact that those emotional states are nevertheless indelible parts of his experience necessitates a rigid, hypergendered masculinity, with a concomitant increase in emotional constriction, a denial or suppression of emotional distress, and a decrease in the capacity for empathy.

These findings are consistent with the research cited earlier that points to a relationship between a person's capacity to experience and express their own painful emotions, and their capacity to respond sympathetically to the emotional pain of another person. To the extent that the abused male has internalized stereotypical gender norms that dictate a suppressive attitude to those painful emotions, he will be less likely respond sympathetically to his own distress, and therefore to the emotional distress of another person.

Two studies that compared the consequences of alternative responses to childhood abuse experiences provide support for this relationship. Hunter and Kilstrom (1979) compared abused mothers who did and did not abuse their own children. They found the non-abusing mothers were able to describe in more detail their own abuse experiences and were more expressive of their anger. In contrast, the abusing mothers were more vague in their recollections, less willing to talk, and less expressive of anger.

Very similar differences were noted by Burgess, Hartman, McCausland, and Powers (1984) in their study of children and adolescents abused in sex and pornography rings. Those victims who had integrated the event were more able to talk openly about their experiences and manifested less anxiety when doing so. Other victims manifested an avoidant strategy, in which their anxiety lingered but was "sealed off." These children were considerably more symptomatic and were more likely to have engaged in antisocial acts. Another group of children appeared to have identified with their perpetrators. These children minimized the negative nature of their experiences and were also more likely to be engaging in antisocial acts.

Support for the relationship between suppression of abuse-related emotions and increased propensities for aggression can also be found in the literature on clinical interventions with abused males. Friedrich, Berliner, Urquiza, and Beilke (1988) reported that the abused boys they treated were generally unable to verbalize their feelings about their abuse, typically denied their existence, and instead manifested them in various forms of acting out, including sexualized aggressiveness. They noted that in treatment groups for abused girls there was typically far less denial and sexual aggressiveness, a finding that suggests the importance of gender socialization in channeling children's response to abuse.

Freeman-Longo (1986) concluded that most incarcerated sex offenders have never dealt with the emotional legacies of their own abuse experiences and do not consider that their victims must experience the same emotions. Schact, Kerlinsky, and Carlson (1990) argued, on the basis of their experience leading groups for abused boys, that the boys were unable to consciously experience their feelings of fear and vulnerability and so they induced them in other people, where they could experience them vicariously and therefore more safely.

The evidence cited above suggests that there may be two, perhaps interrelated, ways in which intolerance of distressful emotions leads to inhibited empathy. To the extent that such intolerance leads to a constriction of the experience of such distressful emotions, the constricted individual will be less likely to be able to vicariously experience the distressful emotions experienced by others. They may in fact recognize that the other person is experiencing distressing emotions, but there will be no emotional resonance within them; their disconnection from their own distressful emotions impairs their capacity to vicariously experience those emotions in others.

The second apparent pathway to inhibited empathy is through the evocation of a "personal distress" reaction in response to witnessing distress in another person. Such a reaction has been shown to decrease the individual's tendency to respond sympathetically, and increase their need to find a way to terminate their aversive state. This may be accomplished by active avoidance of the stimulus, or possibly by converting the distressful emotions that have been evoked into one that may be experienced as less distressful, such as anger. Once evoked, this anger may well be channeled as aggression against the "other" who is perceived to be in distress. The aggression may be purely instrumental, designed to terminate the state of inner distress by "getting rid" of the perceived external source of it (the other person). Or, the aggression may be rooted in a similar, but somewhat more complex dynamic. In this case, the distress and vulnerability expressed by the other person triggers resonant, unconscious emotions in the perpetrator. The perpetrator then turns on these despised emblems of his vulnerability by crushing them in the other person through an act of aggression. In such a case, what the perpetrator actually perceives in the other person is largely irrelevant, since the dynamic is essentially one of projection, followed by an unconscious reaction to the projection.

Case Study: From Abuse to Perpetration to the Recovery of Empathy on Death Row

Death row is hardly what most people would think of as a therapeutic environment. Condemned prisoners spend most of their days alone in tiny cells, waiting out the legal process that for many of them ends in execution. Yet for some of these men (there are only a handful of women on the nation's death rows), death row represents the first environment in which they are free of the unrelenting violence, poverty, and degradation of their lives. In this environment, some prisoners embark on a reevaluation of their lives, a process that for some leads to significant psychological transformation.

Don G. was sentenced to death for the murder of a woman with whom he had had a brief, stormy relationship mostly centered on the consumption of drugs and alcohol. While this murder was the only crime for which

Don had been convicted, during the course of the evaluation he disclosed other offenses he had committed, including sexually exploitative and abusive acts. As a young adolescent, Don had sexually abused slightly younger children on two occasions. These acts, it became evident, mirrored the abuses he had himself suffered as child.

After 10 years on death row, Don was undergoing the first comprehensive psychological evaluation organized by his attorneys, an evaluation intended to provide mitigating evidence to support an appeal of his death sentence. The evaluation involved many hours of interviews covering Don's entire developmental history; it also included the examination of virtually every school, medical, and psychiatric record that could be recovered; and it included interviews with numerous family members, friends of the family, former teachers, and treating professionals. Such an evaluation, rarely even attempted in the routine of normal psychological assessments, can provide a remarkably thorough delineation of the developmental factors that lead a man to death row.

Don was born into a chaotic, poverty-stricken family. His parents, both alcoholics and drug abusers, beat each of the five children and subjected them to an array of sadistic punishments. When Don was not being beaten—with fists, shoes, telephones, and whatever was within reach—he was neglected to the point of hunger and malnutrition. His teachers recalled him as emaciated, skittish, forlorn, and depressed. Although Don was at first loath to acknowledge it, interviews with his brothers and others who knew the family revealed that he had also been sexually abused. Eventually, Don began to disclose these victimizations: an uncle and an older cousin orally raped him before he was 10; a middle-aged woman friend of his father seduced him into intercourse when he was 11; between the ages of 12 and 15, he was anally raped on three separate occasions by men who picked him up off the streets where he had sought refuge from the violence and neglect of his home.

As Don matured into adolescence, the terror, humiliation, and degradations of his childhood were sealed away as memories that were unreachable but yet tormented him and drove his behavior. He became what he called a "survivor," which to him also meant a perpetrator. In his world, there were only predators and prey; to him, growing into manhood meant the opportunity to finally turn predator. Which he did, committing numerous assaults and at least several rapes before he was arrested and convicted of the murder of his girlfriend.

As the years on death row tolled onward, the seals that secured the bottomless pain of his childhood became frayed. By the time the evaluation began, 10 years into his incarceration, they were ready to be broken. As the interviews progressed, Don began having nightmares that were repetitive reexperiences of the rapes he had suffered. Soon he was tormented both day and night by the sounds, the smells, and the physical sensations of being orally and anally raped. He stopped sleeping entirely, could not eat, had constant headaches, and his muscles were tensed like drawstrings. Finally, midway through one of the interviews, be broke down, sobbing uncontrollably for 45 minutes, until an alarmed prison guard had him escorted back to his cell.

Don's breakdown initiated a whole new series of disclosures. There were other abuses he had suffered, but most importantly, he disclosed and reexperienced the details, the actual pain of the multiple traumas of his childhood and adolescence. Then, at the conclusion of one of the final interviews, as he collected himself and prepared for the strip search that followed each meeting, he suddenly began sobbing again. After 15 minutes, he pulled himself together enough to say that he could now not bear the pain of knowing what he had done to the women he had raped. He forced out those words through shame and guilt and physical pain that were literally contorting his body. His last statement at the end of the final interview was, "My lawyers may save my life, but I don't know if I can live with myself." In the ensuing months, Don experienced similar levels of excruciating remorse over the sexual abuses he had committed when he was a young teenager, and over the rapes he had committed later during his adolescence and young adulthood.

The transformation that Don underwent was essentially the recovery of his humanity; a reconnection to his human capacity to feel. It began with a reconnection to the pain of his childhood, and resulted in a restoration of his ability to connect to the pain of other human beings—his capacity to empathize. The transformation represented an unraveling of Don's lifelong adaptation to his traumatic childhood, an adaptation that was organized and facilitated by a masculine ideology that was provided to him by his culture.

The extremity of the abuse that Don had suffered, and the environment in which he grew up, foreclosed most positive outcomes for him. Adolescence produced an option for Don that could not be turned down: a masculine identity that validated his rage, validated his repression of his enormous reservoir of pain and vulnerability, and offered him "valid" targets for his vengeance—children, women, anyone more vulnerable than he was. As social science research has demonstrated, Don's adaptation to the pain of his childhood exemplified a masculine ideology that is endorsed by a large proportion of males. For some men, those whose endorsement is driven by such profound levels of pain and rage, such a masculine ideology clears the path to the sexual exploitation of others, and to the perpetration of interpersonal violence.

Conclusion

Sexual abuse and sexually exploitative behavior are interpersonally violent and damaging acts committed disproportionately by men. Among the many factors contributing to this violence, male gender socialization is one of the most prominent. Stereotyped masculine attitudes and behaviors have been linked to the perpetration of sexually exploitative acts by both clinical and experimental research.

At the core of the male gender socialization process is the often traumatic constricting of the male's capacity to experience and express his emotions. In particular, emotions associated with vulnerability—such as fear and shame—are excised and often supplanted by the acceptably male emotion of anger. The result often is a relatively disconnected experience of sexuality, in which intense emotions are suppressed, and an impaired capacity for empathy. Both of these impairments increase the male's capacity for sexually exploitative or sexually violent behavior.

References

Barash, D. (1979). *The whisperings within.* New York: Harper & Row.

Barnett, M. A., & McCoy, S. J. (1989). The relation of distressful childhood experiences and empathy in college undergraduates. *Journal of Genetic Psychology, 150,* 417–426.

Batson, C. D., Fultz, J., & Schoenrade, P. A. (1987). Distress and empathy: Two qualitatively distinct vicarious emotions with different motivational consequences. *Journal of Personality, 55,* 19–39.

Berliner, L., & Elliot, D. M. (1996). Sexual abuse of children. In L. Briere, L. Berliner, J. A. Bulkley, C. Jenny, & T. Reid (Eds.), *The APSAC handbook on child maltreatment* (pp. 51–71). Thousand Oaks, CA: Sage.

Briere, J., & Runtz, M. (1988). Symptomology associated with childhood sexual victimization in a nonclinical adult sample. *Child Abuse and Neglect, 12,* 51–59.

Brod, H. (1994). Some thoughts on some histories of some masculinities. In H. Brod & M. Kaufman (Eds.), *Theorizing masculinities* (pp. 82–96). Thousand Oaks, CA: Sage.

Brody, L. R. (1985). Gender differences in emotional development: A review of theories and research. *Journal of Personality, 53,* 102–149.

Bryant, B. K. (1987). Critique of comparable questionnaire methods in use to assess empathy in children and adults. In N. Eisenberg & J. Strayer (Eds.), *Empathy and its development* (pp. 361–373). Cambridge, England: Cambridge University Press.

Burgess, A. W., Hartman, C. R., McCausland, M. P., & Powers, C. (1984). Response patterns in children and adolescents exploited through sex rings and pornography. *American Journal of Psychiatry, 141,* 656–662.

Chodorow, N. (1978). *The reproduction of mothering.* Berkeley: University of California Press.

Crossman, R. K., Stith, S. M., & Bender, M. M. (1990). Sex role egalitarianism and marital violence. *Sex Roles, 22,* 293–304.

Diener, E., Sandvik, E., & Larsen, J. (1985). Age and sex effects for affect intensity. *Developmental Psychology, 21,* 542–546.

Eisenberg, N., Fabes, R. A., Schaller, M., Carlo, G., & Miller, P. A. (1991). The relations of parental characteristics and practices to children's vicarious emotional responding. *Child Development, 62,* 1393–1408.

Eisenberg, N., Fabes, R. A., Schaller, M., Miller, P., Carlo, G., Poulin, R., Shea, C., & Shell, R. (1991). Personality and socialization correlates of vicarious emotional responding. *Journal of Personality and Social Psychology, 61,* 459–470.

Eisenberg, N., & Lennon, R. (1983). Sex differences in empathy and related capacities. *Psychological Bulletin, 94,* 100–131.

Fausto-Sterling, A. (1985). *Myths of gender.* New York: Basic Books.

Federal Bureau of Investigation. (1992). *Uniform crime reports of the United States.* Washington, DC: U.S. Government Printing Office.

Fivush, R. (1989). Exploring sex differences in the emotional content of mother-child conversations about the past. *Sex Roles, 20,* 675–691.

Freeman-Longo, R. E. (1986). The impact of sexual victimization on males. *Child Abuse and Neglect, 10,* 411–414.

Friedrich, W. N., Berliner, L., Urquiza, A. J., & Beilke, R. L. (1988). Brief diagnostic group treatment of sexually abused boys. *Journal of Interpersonal Violence, 3,* 331–343.

Frodi, A. M., & Lamb, M. E. (1980). Child abusers' responses to infant smiles and cries. *Child Development, 51,* 238–241.

Fromuth, M. E., Burkhart, B., & Jones, C. W. (1991). Hidden child molestation. *Journal of Interpersonal Violence, 6,* 376–384.

Gilmore, D. D. (1990). *Manhood in the making.* New Haven, CT: Yale University Press.

Gold, S. R., Fultz, J., Burke, C. H., Prisco, A. G., & Willett, J. A. (1992). Vicarious emotional responses of macho college males. *Journal of Interpersonal Violence, 7,* 165–174.

Hopper, J. (1996). *The relationship between childhood abuse, male gender socialization, and perpetration.* Doctoral dissertation, University of Massachusetts, Boston.

Hunter, R. S., & Kilstrom, N. (1979). Breaking the cycle in abusive families. *American Journal of Psychiatry, 136,* 1320–1322.

Ivan, C. (1996). *Big boys don't cry: Socialization of emotional displays and emotional empathy in males.* Doctoral dissertation, University of Massachusetts, Boston.

Kanin, E. (1984). Date rape: Unofficial criminals and victims. *Victimology, 9,* 95–108.

Kilmartin, C. T. (1994). *The masculine self.* New York: Macmillan.

Kimmel, M. (1996). *Manhood in America.* New York: Free Press.

Klimes-Dougan, B., & Kistner, J. (1990). Physically abused preschoolers' responses to peers' distress. *Developmental Psychology, 26,* 599–602.

Koss, M. P., Leonard, K. E., Beezley, D. A., & Oros, C. J. (1985). Nonstranger sexual aggression: A discriminant analysis of the psychological characteristics of undetected offenders. *Sex Roles, 12,* 981–992.

Kuebli, J., & Fivush, R. (1992). Gender differences in parent-child conversations about past events. *Sex Roles, 27,* 683–698.

Lenrow, P. B. (1965). Studies of sympathy. In S. L. Tomkins & C. E. Izard (Eds.), *Affect, cognition, and personality* (pp. 264–294). New York: Springer.

Levant, R. F. (1995). Toward the reconstruction of masculinity. In R. F. Levant & W. S. Pollack (Eds.), *A new psychology of men* (pp. 229–251). New York: Basic Books.

Lisak, D. (1994). The psychological consequences of childhood abuse: Content analysis of interviews with male survivors. *Journal of Traumatic Stress, 7,* 525–548.

Lisak, D., Hopper, J., & Song, P. (1996). Factors in the cycle of violence: Gender rigidity and emotional constriction. *Journal of Traumatic Stress, 9,* 721–743.

Lisak, D., & Ivan, C. (1995). Deficits in intimacy and empathy in sexually aggressive men. *Journal of Interpersonal Violence, 10,* 296–308.

Lisak, D., Miller, P., & Conklin, A., (1996). *The relationship between abuse, perpetration, and the experience of emotional distress.* Manuscript submitted for publication.

Lisak, D., & Roth, S. (1988). Motivational factors in nonincarcerated sexually aggressive men. *Journal of Personality and Social Psychology, 55,* 795–802.

Lisak, D., & Roth, S. (1990). Motives and psychodynamics of self-reported, unincarcerated rapists. *American Journal of Orthopsychiatry, 60,* 268–280.

Main, M., & George, C. (1985). Responses of abused and disadvantaged toddlers to distress in agemates: The day care setting. *Developmental Psychology, 21,* 407–412.

Malamuth, N. M. (1986). Predictors of naturalistic sexual aggression. *Journal of Personality and Social Psychology, 50,* 953–962.

Malamuth, N. M., Sockloskie, R. J., Koss, M. P., & Tanaka, J. S. (1991). Characteristics of aggressors against women: Testing a model using a national sample of college students. *Journal of Consulting and Clinical Psychology, 59,* 670–681.

Malatesta, C., & Haviland, J. M. (1985). Signals, symbols and socialization: The modification of emotional expression in human development. In M. Lewis & C. Saarni (Eds.), *The socialization of emotions* (pp. 89–115). New York: Plenum Press.

McCord, J., McCord, W., & Thurber, E. (1962). Some effects of paternal absence on male children. *Journal of Abnormal and Social Psychology, 64,* 361–369.

McEwan, B. S., & Mendelson, S. (1993). Effects of stress on the neurochemistry and morphology of the brain: Counterregulation versus damage. In L. Goldberger & S. Breznitz (Eds.), *Handbook of stress: Theoretical and clinical aspects* (pp. 101–126). New York: Free Press.

Miller, P. A., & Eisenberg, N. (1988). The relation of empathy to aggressive and externalizing/antisocial behavior. *Psychological Bulletin, 103,* 324–344.

Mosher, D. L., & Anderson, R. (1986). Macho personality, sexual aggression, and reactions to guided imagery of realistic rape. *Journal of Research in Personality, 20,* 77–94.

Mosher, D. L., & Tomkins, S. S. (1988). Scripting the macho man: Hypermasculine socialization and enculturation. *Journal of Sex Research, 25,* 60–84.

Muehlenhard, C. L., & Falcon, P. L. (1990). Men's heterosocial skill and attitudes toward women as predictors of verbal sexual coercion and forceful rape. *Sex Roles, 23,* 241–259.

Munroe, R., Munroe, R., & Whiting, J. (1981). Male sex-role resolutions. In R. Munroe, R. Munroe, & B. Whiting (Eds.), *Handbook of cross-cultural human development* (pp. 611–632). New York: STM Press.

Pollack, W. S. (1995). No man is an island: Toward a new psychoanalytic psychology of men. In R. F. Levant & W. S. Pollack (Eds.), *A new psychology of men* (pp. 33–67). New York: Basic Books.

Rapaport, K., & Burkhart, B. (1984). Personality and attitudinal characteristics of sexually coercive college males. *Journal of Abnormal Psychology, 93,* 216–221.

Schacht, A. J., Kerlinsky, D., & Carlson, C. (1990). Group therapy with sexually abused boys: Leadership, projective identification, and countertransference issues. *International Journal of Group Psychotherapy, 40,* 401–417.

Stith, S. M., & Farley, S. C. (1993). A predictive model of male spousal violence. *Journal of Family Violence, 8,* 183–201.

Webster, H. (1908). *Primitive secret societies.* New York: Macmillan.

Widom, C. S. (1989). Does violence beget violence? A critical examination of the literature. *Psychological Bulletin, 106,* 3–28.

Zeskind, P. S., & Shingler, E. A. (1991). Child abusers' perceptual responses to newborn infant cries varying in pitch. *Infant Behavior and Development, 14,* 335–347.

PART III

VARIATIONS

CHAPTER 8

Men's Resolution of Nonrelational Sex across the Lifespan

GLENN E. GOOD AND NANCY B. SHERROD

I T IS COMMON for American boys to learn to distance themselves from girls, women, and "feminine" qualities within themselves early in their development. Boys learn this with the first women that most encounter—their mothers. Early experiences typically force boys to disidentify with their mothers (Pollack, 1995). Subsequent gender socialization processes often foster development of defensive autonomy and sexual conquest. Thus, many men learn to value independence (as contrasted with dependence, a "feminine" quality) to such an extreme that they become disconnected from others, both men and women. Further, they learn to value sex as an achievement, a goal in itself. As a result, it is surprising that an even greater percentage of men do not have lasting, serious problems with nonrelational sex (NS). This chapter examines men's nonrelational and objectification-based view of sex as a culturally prescribed psychosocial developmental stage, which most men in North America enter and some successfully resolve. As with other stages of psychosocial development, we can examine the relations of the NS stage to preceding life stages, and the implications of successful and unsuccessful resolution on subsequent development. While perhaps understandable among adolescents or young adults who are experimenting with sexuality, intimacy, and identity issues, unsuccessful resolution of issues associated with NS frequently becomes problematic for men in later life stages.

In NS—the tendency to experience sex primarily as lust without any requirements for relational intimacy or emotional attachment—targets

The authors would like to express their appreciation to Ann Fischer, Noboru Komiya, Laurie Mintz, and Monica Smith for providing suggestions for this chapter.

of sexual desire are often objectified. Indeed, at times they are not even people in one's life, for example, women or parts of women in pornographic books or videos. These targets of desire are pursued in an agentic fashion to meet needs, which, in addition to the release of sexual tension, include nurturance and affirmation of one's adequacy as a man (Levant, 1997). NS is encouraged by the media (in rock and rap songs, MTV, TV, movies, and magazines) and reinforced in most men's peer groups. NS has many variations and can exist to various degrees. NS includes men's behavior, but also men's attitudes, and the consequences for men and women, which occur within the context of gender socialization and patriarchy (see concept of "rape domain"; Stevens, 1985). Nonrelational sexual behavior can be viewed as occurring along a continuum. One pole of this continuum is reflected by consensual casual sex with a likewise NS-oriented partner, the middle by casual sex with an intimate-sexual-relations (ISR)-oriented partner, and the opposite pole by forced sex (Figure 8.1). This chapter examines global NS through a developmental lens.

Similar to the psychosocial developmental theory of Erikson (1968), in which stages are named for their successful and unsuccessful resolutions (e.g., trust vs. mistrust; autonomy vs. shame and doubt), the corresponding name for this stage would be intimate sexual relations versus nonrelational sex (ISR/NS). Successful resolution of this stage results in an ISR stance, while unsuccessful resolution of the stage results in a continued NS orientation.

In examining ISR/NS as a developmental stage, it is important to make the distinction between attitudes and behaviors associated with NS, and the life stage of ISR/NS. The ISR/NS life stage is the time period in which boys or men endorse the belief system that having nonrelational sex is the goal to be accomplished and that women are sexual objects to conquer. How men meet this conquest/accomplishment wish may vary: some men have NS with women they know, others use prostitutes, some use pornographic magazines, videos, and Internet images, while still others endorse these views without behaviorally acting upon them (i.e., they view sexual relations and

FIGURE 8.1
Nonrelational Sexual Behavior Continuum

Casual sex with a likewise NS-oriented partner	- - - - - - -	Casual sex with an ISR-oriented partner	- - - - - - -	Forced sex (rape)

Source: Redrawn from Ann R. Fischer, 1996.

women in this way, hence are cognitively in the NS stage though they are not behaviorally engaging in NS).

Developmental forces encourage entrance into the NS stage for men (Figure 8.2). These forces include male childhood experiences and cultural messages that shape individual's conception of masculinity

FIGURE 8.2
Developmental Factors Associated with Nonrelational Sex

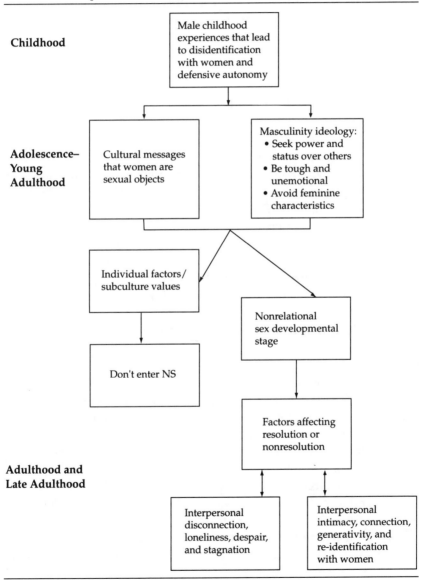

ideology and attitudes toward women. In this chapter, we explore these childhood and adolescent forces and discuss reasons why some men do not enter the NS stage. We then discuss the developmental tasks associated with resolution of this stage; here we mention how tasks proposed by well-known developmental theorists such as Chickering relate to and overlap with the ISR/NS tasks. Importantly, we also discuss factors associated with resolution and nonresolution of the ISR/NS stage. We then discuss the impact of resolution or nonresolution of the ISR/NS stage on later life; again the relation of our schema to existing theory on the development of later years (e.g., Levinson et al., 1978; Jung, 1971) will be noted. Finally, suggestions for therapists and recommendations for further research are discussed.

Developmental Forces Leading to the ISR/NS Stage

Prior to entering the NS stage, men have already experienced important developmental tasks that set the stage for their resolution—or nonresolution—of the NS stage. Traditional theories of male development (Freudian, Neo-Freudian [e.g., Erikson, 1968], object relations [e.g., Kernberg, 1976; Mahler, 1975], and self-psychologists [e.g., Kohut, 1977]) stress the process of separating and individuating (Bergman, 1995). More recently, Bergman (1995) and Pollack (1995) offered reanalyses of issues associated with gender-linked, normative, developmental traumas and losses occurring in early childhood. According to these theorists, it is the male child's forced disidentification and separation from the mother that results in his early identification with males. It has also been theorized that men's fear of femininity is a core aspect of their subsequent gender role conflict (O'Neal, 1981, 1982; O'Neal, Good, & Holmes, 1995). Men's ambivalent feelings about femininity may be a critical component in their subsequent failure to move beyond NS. Concurrently, a boy's identification with his father (if he is present in the household) may arise through competition, fear, and renunciation of interest in his mother. This process leaves men vulnerable to difficulties with dependence and "defended against the very intimate merger that they seek" (Pollack, 1995, p. 34). Further, this process sets the stage for a patriarchal hierarchy, based in dominance, entitlement, power over women, and fear of other men. Hence, male children learn to adopt a defensively autonomous stance to life; they seek to become an island unto themselves, needing and emotionally vulnerable to no one.

Kaschak (1992) offers a similar conceptualization in which contemporary U.S. mainstream culture is viewed as being stuck in a societal-level (redefined) Oedipal phase. More specifically, as Oedipus used others, subsumed them (especially women) under his overextended boundaries, so does our patriarchal society teach boys/men that they are entitled to use and subsume women. Boys/men learn that women are "[theirs] to possess and to evaluate according to [their] desires and needs" (p. 67). Similarly, boys/men in our patriarchal society are extended "the right to view and evaluate, to sexualize any woman who falls within range of their sight" (p. 62). Hence, Kaschak (1992) notes that the typical man in the United States "is an eternal adolescent in an adolescent culture" (p. 73).

This defensive autonomy begins in childhood and continues into adolescence. Adolescent boys learn to become the agents of disconnection—indeed experts at disconnecting from attachments. Additionally, the view that "I am not enough" becomes the impetus for further striving, which creates a cycle of disengagement and achievement (Bergman, 1995, p. 75). For many boys and men, the fantasy arises that by achieving more they can win love and acceptance. The intimacy disconnection may be further exacerbated during experiences in which internal states of high anxiety and sexual tension are released through activities of an impersonal or aggressive nature. For example, violent sexual fantasies may involve individuals (or symbolic representations of individuals) with whom one has experienced perceived rejection. When the pleasure associated with release of sexual tension becomes paired with violent fantasies and masturbation, the connection between sex and violence, pleasure and devaluation may be strengthened. Thus, when men develop views associated with what has been termed "the whore-madonna complex," they split off partners whom they will value and care about from devalued objects with whom they engage in sex. A similar phenomenon probably exists for some gay men who split off partners whom they value and care about from those with whom they have sex and devalue. Hence, men frequently learn to split off caring and connection from sex and devaluation.

A related set of adolescent development forces involves what "being a man" means in our culture. Brannon's (1976) "blueprint for manhood" recently revised as "traditional masculinity ideology" has emerged as a concise and empirically supported model. More specifically, masculinity ideology has been defined as the "endorsement and internalization of cultural belief systems about masculinity and male gender, rooted in the structural relationship between the two sexes" (Pleck, Sonenstein, & Ku, 1993, p. 88). The main components of traditional masculinity ideology as derived through factor analysis of one instrument are status, toughness, and antifemininity.

Hence, the complex interaction of traditional masculinity ideology, related societal messages that endorse viewing women as sexual objects for men's pleasure (see *Dreamworlds*, 1990), and biological factors associated with puberty direct most men into the NS stage of development.

Why Some Men Never Enter the NS Stage

Some males may never enter the NS stage. These males may avoid NS because of their strong ties to a particular subculture. For example, many religious groups teach values directly opposed to NS, such as the view that sexual activity should be practiced exclusively in a consecrated marriage between husband and wife. Additionally, some individuals are raised in profeminist, gender-aware environments in which factors associated with problematic masculinity ideologies and NS are actively and effectively discussed and countered. Similarly, some ethnic/racial/cultural groups may hold beliefs that allow male adolescents to address sexuality without entering into NS.

A variety of individual psychological factors are also potentially associated with males who do not enter the NS stage. For example, some males do not risk attempting to initiate sexual relations due to fears of humiliation, shame, or rejection associated with their lack of sexual knowledge or experience. Although such fears are common during adolescence, these concerns may be especially damaging for men who missed a period of sexual experimentation during adolescence and who subsequently perceive themselves as being "out-of-phase" with their more sexually experienced cohorts. Other males are frightened by their feelings of attraction to other males (i.e., internalized homonegativity), and subsequently attempt to repress exploration of their sexuality due to their fear of becoming a homosexual. Other men may have particularly low libido and consequently little interest in sexual matters. Another group are those who, for various reasons, have experienced so little social acceptance and had so little exposure to mainstream socializing influences that they have developed their own idiosyncratic developmental processes that do not include NS. A final group may consist of men who realized that NS could be damaging and who therefore do not engage in it. Although worthy of further study, the developmental paths of these men are beyond the scope of this chapter.

Developmental Tasks in Resolving the ISR/NS Stage

Most psychosocial theories of development delineate tasks to be accomplished for successful resolution of a developmental stage, and our model is no exception. There are four tasks which must be accomplished for successful resolution of the ISR/NS stage:

1. Gaining experience as a sexual being.
2. Gaining experience with interpersonal aspects of sexuality.
3. Developing identity.
4. Developing comfort with interpersonal intimacy.

Task 1: Gaining Experience as a Sexual Being

Men need to gain experience with themselves as sexual beings. For example, they need to be able to recognize and experience sexual attraction and desire. They need to be able to manage their physical functioning; specifically, they need to be able to have and sustain an erection, maintain arousal, and control orgasm. Importantly, part of gaining this experience as a sexual being is learning to manage sexual feelings and impulses. The work of Chickering (1969) relates to the managing of impulses. His Managing Emotions vector is primarily concerned with managing sexual and aggressive feelings. The first step in this process is an increased awareness of the legitimacy of these emotions, which usually requires an awareness that there are "shackles and barriers" on young adults that have taken the form of "unreasoning parents, arbitrary authorities, impersonal institutions, and inflexible rules" (Chickering, 1969, p. 40). This recognition is followed by an attempt to act on those emotions. Through the process of testing their actions and receiving feedback from others about the appropriateness of their actions, young adults learn "what can be done with whom, when, and under what circumstances" (p. 11). In this process, individuals move from a rigid control of emotions based on the external rules of their heritage (e.g., parents, religion) to a control (or wild lack of control) based on the external norms of their peer groups, to control by internal, integrated self-defined norms. Hence, boys/men seeking to resolve this NS-related task may benefit from knowledge and experiences that enable them to develop their personal norms regarding their sexual impulses.

Task 2: Gaining Experience with Interpersonal Aspects of Sexuality

There are interpersonal aspects of sexuality that need to be mastered. For example, people need to learn to attract the interest and obtain the consent of potential partners. Additionally, people need to be able to recognize, communicate about, respond to, and fulfill both their and their partners' sexual needs. This task also includes gaining experience with knowing the type(s) of individuals with whom they are compatible.

Task 3: Developing Identity

A third task concerns formation of an identity. Before the final task of this stage (intimacy) can be experienced, most men first seek to develop a clear sense of their own identity (Chickering, 1969; Erikson, 1963). In other words, males may first seek to establish "Who I am" before committing to a decision about "Who I want to be with." This sequence is frequently in contrast to the typical development of women, who may be forced to decide first "Who I will be with" prior to deciding "Who I am/going to become" (Gilligan, 1982). One vital aspect of adolescent males' sense of identity is based on their sense of themselves as men, which as noted earlier, is influenced by societal and peer group-based conceptions of masculinity.

Task 4: Developing Comfort with Interpersonal Intimacy

The final task concerns development of comfort with interpersonal intimacy. This was described as the ability to relate one's deepest hopes and fears to another person and to accept another's need for intimacy (Erikson, 1963). According to Erikson, people who successfully resolve the intimacy versus isolation stage are able to commit themselves to concrete affiliations and partnerships with others and have developed the "ethical strength to abide by such commitments" (p. 262). This process leads to solidarity between partners. The counterpart to intimacy is distantiation—the readiness to distance ourselves from others when we feel threatened by their behavior. Distantiation is a particularly common coping style when individuals' identities are developing. This identity uncertainty leaves men vulnerable to criticism, since they cannot be certain about whether the criticism is true or not. Hence, they may be prone to adopting a "lone wolf" or "I am an island" stance in order to protect themselves psychologically.

For the variety of reasons mentioned earlier (e.g., early experiences with forced separation, cultural messages about competition and aggressiveness), most men learn to stay interpersonally detached and emotionally disconnected. Noting men's lack of interpersonal connection, the developmental theorist Daniel Levinson (1978) wrote:

> friendship [among men is] largely noticeable by its absence . . . we would say that close friendship with a man or woman is rarely experienced by

American men . . . most men have not had an intimate, non-sexual friendship with a woman. We need to understand why friendship is so rare, and what consequences this deprivation has for adult life. (p. 335)

Ideally, individuals learn to assert their wants in a respectful and caring manner, to listen well to their partners, and to negotiate compromises that respect both individuals' wants and needs (Gottman, Notarius, Gonso, & Markman, 1976). Communication skills associated with conflict resolution, such as leveling and appropriate disclosure also are developed. Along with these important skill acquisitions, intimacy and commitment to relationships are enhanced. However, this increased interpersonal intimacy is not without costs. Individuals also may need to grieve giving up an individualistic, agentic, "my wants and needs are number one" orientation, so that the goals of the relationship are placed on equal footing with the needs of both individuals in the relationship. Additionally, interpersonal intimacy comes with some degree of vulnerability (i.e., voluntarily lowering one's guard and sharing one's insecurities); hence, there is an accompanying exposure to additional risk of being hurt if that intimate trust is not well cared for.

Factors Facilitating Successful Resolution of the NS Stage

As noted earlier, successful resolution of the ISR/NS stage is entry into an IRS orientation and unsuccessful resolution is reflected by a continued NS orientation. Men progress through the NS stage by mastering the developmental tasks associated with this stage. As noted earlier, this includes gaining experience as a sexual being, gaining experience with interpersonal aspects of sexuality, developing identity, and developing comfort with intimacy. Men following this route develop internally directed senses of their behavior that allow them to form and sustain intimate, caring relationships with others. This process involves a fairly sophisticated ability to understand themselves, others, and the nature of the society in which they live. Hence, the ability to perceive the relative utility of various worldviews would likely be a salient aspect of this type of NS stage resolution (i.e., more advanced stages of cognitive development [Perry, 1970]). Similarly, men's stage of moral development may also play a role in mastering tasks associated with this stage. For example, learning higher order conceptions of morality based upon notions of fairness (Kohlberg, 1980) and caring (Gilligan, 1982) could support men's successful resolution of the NS stage. Such maturation could be facilitated directly through experiences of increasing intimacy with a partner; learning the joys (and struggles) associated with the maintenance of lasting, intimate relationships and how such relationships are contrasted with the false intimacy of NS.

Two psychological "truths" have emerged over the years: (a) human behavior is multidetermined and (b) there are important differences in individuals' reactions to events. It is not surprising that there are numerous routes by which men successfully or unsuccessfully resolve the ISR/NS stage of their development. This section provides a overview of the more common factors that facilitate men's successful resolution of this stage.

For some individuals, *experience with acts of nonrelational sex* may facilitate successful resolution of this stage. This may sound like heresy to some readers, but the act of NS during adolescence may serve some useful purposes. NS (as a type of sexual activity) may allow adolescents the opportunity to reduce sexual tensions (in this case, like any form of sexual tension release, sex is a pleasurable activity). NS also allows individuals the opportunity to gain sexual experiences, refine skills associated with sexual activities, and experience different partners and behaviors, thereby reducing curiosity about different partners for the future. This would hopefully support commitment to and maintenance of a lasting relationship in the future. NS may provide opportunities for adolescents to learn about themselves in a sexual context. This type of learning may involve gaining an understanding of sexual likes and dislikes, learning how their bodies function sexually, and acquiring skills associated with satisfying sexual relations. Perhaps most importantly, experience with NS can provide important lessons about intimacy. Individuals engaging in NS may discover that while NS may meet their physical need to release sexual tension, it does not meet their needs for feelings of deep connection with others (i.e., interpersonal intimacy). In this vein, experience with NS may be useful to adolescents or young adults in determining their intimacy needs and how they may or may not achieve those needs through sexual activity.

Such "experimentation" with NS can be quite harmful to the people involved. Sexual partners are likely to be harmed if they are deceived, objectified, or exploited by individuals seeking NS. Further, individuals can be harmed if their initial "dabbling" with NS initiates a habit in which they become stuck.

An additional factor which may facilitate men's movement beyond the NS stage is *personal experience with emotional pain*. In recounting the tale of Narcissus, Pollack (1995) noted that "the root of the trouble lies in a man's self-absorption and lack of empathy, which can be remedied only by painful experience" (p. 38). For example, a man in the midst of a personal crisis (e.g., loss of employment, left by a partner, problems associated with depression and/or addiction) may want things to return to the way they were before the crisis. He desires no real changes in his life other than for the problem to go away. Conversely, a crisis may prompt a man to engage in a serious reflection of his life and of his ways of interacting with and viewing others ("existential encounter"). These changes in awareness may take the form of gradual realizations or of important, life-changing insights. This personal experience with emotional pain may break down old patterns (e.g., defensive autonomy, self-absorption, or intellectual detachment) and facilitate movement toward deeper interpersonal connection and mutuality. For men seeking to survive and grow in the midst of a difficult time, the value of such painful experiences is partially reflected in some contemporary phrases, such as "the darkest hour is just before the dawn," and "no pain, no gain." Indeed, much can be learned from personal crises and difficult times.

A related path by which men may gain awareness is through the *vicarious experience* of the painful experiences of others. By learning more about the detrimental impact of NS upon others—such as the sexual victimization of a sibling or close friend through acquaintance rape— men may gain greater appreciation of the negative consequences of NS in general and for themselves.

Similarly, friends, peers, and mentors may offer important guidance regarding the harmful consequences of an NS orientation. For example, we know of one man whose movement from NS toward ISR was prompted by a friend telling him that he was perceived as "thinking with his penis" (e.g., not attending to the effects of his NS orientation in terms of how it hurt others and himself). As a result of these caring confrontations, this man elected to change his perspectives and behavior (thus progressing to ISR). Similarly, gaining guidance and permission from men who are further along in this process can be very validating and growth-supporting. The value of a mentor in serving as a teacher and role model of more adaptive functioning has been noted (Bly, 1990; Levinson, 1978). Additionally, familial and cultural messages to start one's own family may exert direct pressure on men when they reach a certain age. Such messages may include the notion that men should stop (at least in terms of their public image) focusing on NS and progress to committed, long-term relationships. Thus, men may make progress toward ISR via developmentally-based messages from other people. *Exposure to new perspectives*—through reading, seminars and classes, and foreign travel—may also broaden men's awareness of alternatives.

Some men have medical conditions for which they feel obligated to initiate an honest dialogue with potential partners before engaging in sexual activities. The open interchange about these personal matters reduces the likelihood of nonrelational sex. For example, men who contract a chronic contagious condition such as genital herpes or HIV may be forced to face their NS pattern. Having such an incurable, infectious, sexually transmitted infection would necessitate that ethical and honest individuals have a discussion of an intimate nature (informed consent) with potential partners prior to engaging in sexual activities. Similarly, other biomedical conditions (e.g., diabetes, epilepsy, hypertension, prostate surgery) and psychosocial conditions (e.g., performance anxiety, guilt, depression) frequently affect sexual functioning. Hence, men in these situations might want to have a candid discussion and form a stronger interpersonal relationship prior to initiating sexual relations.

Biological aging and developmental processes can produce changes that affect men's stage of NS. For example, biological aging after early adulthood typically results in reductions in libido. Similarly, some developmental theorists have noted that men typically have an increased desire for interpersonal connection and intimacy during the second half of their lives (e.g., Jung, 1931/1971). Hence, a reduction in sex drive coupled with an increased interest in interpersonal connection may facilitate some men's positive movement beyond the NS stage.

Additionally, entering into psychotherapy for any reason (e.g., marital issues, including extramarital affairs, separation, and divorce; depression; substance abuse; midlife issues) can facilitate favorable resolution of NS. Therapy typically encourages reflection about what is truly important in one's life, about what one wants in life, and about societal and familial messages that may facilitate or hinder attainment of those goals (Good, Gilbert, & Scher, 1990). In the process of gaining greater awareness of their initial concerns, individuals might also gain awareness of their propensity for NS, insights about what supports NS (and/or has hindered progress toward ISR) in their lives, the deleterious consequences of NS on their and others' lives, and of their desire for greater interpersonal connection. Psychotherapy is not a value-free endeavor. Therapists have values, most of which support honest communication, interpersonal connection, and mutuality. Consequently, entering into therapy may facilitate favorable resolution of NS in part due to true increases in awareness noted earlier; additionally, part of change in clients also may result from transmission of the therapists' values to clients (e.g., Frank, 1961).

Factors Associated with Unsuccessful Resolution of ISR/NS

Men get stuck in an NS orientation for numerous reasons. At one pole, some sociobiological theorists argue for an *evolutionary basis*. This perspective holds that it is to men's evolutionary advantage (i.e., their "optimal reproductive investment") to dominate and impregnate as many women as possible, thereby increasing the number of progeny with their genes (Archer, 1996). Given a hypothesized genetic basis, such theorists might suggest that men should not be expected to move beyond it (see Hamilton & Stuart-Smith, 1995, for a rebuttal of this view). Other theorists give greater emphasis to the *cultural factors* that support NS (e.g., the contributors to this book). In our culture, engagement in NS is widely promoted as an element of masculinity. Thus far, there has not been significant media attention or marketing designed to promote alternative views of masculinity. Indeed, it appears that most men do not receive sufficient information to counter cultural/media messages and consequently fail to progress beyond this basis for their masculinity (for example, recent studies have found that a single one- to two-hour workshop does not produce lasting improvement in college men's attitudes about acquaintance rape [see Heppner et al., 1995]). Additionally, as was true for individuals who sought to oppose institutionalized racism, men who exist in highly competitive, sexist, "power-over" systems may correctly perceive that they will experience adverse consequences if they attempt to assume a more authentic, vulnerable, and relationship-oriented stance when their environment is hostile to this style and views.

Another reason for unsuccessful resolution of NS is *habitual patterns of responding*. Young men typically face many challenges while pursuing and participating in NS. Perhaps the most prototypic are the young men who enter into sexual encounters primarily for instrumental, goal-oriented sexual reasons (e.g., sexual conquest or release), while their female counterparts engage in sexual relations primarily to deepen the relationship (i.e., communal reasons). When faced with this and similar situations, young men are likely to feel off-balance and threatened. In their agentic efforts to become sexually adequate, to support their self-esteem, and to develop their personal identity, these young men are not yet willing to embrace simultaneously the challenges and responsibilities associated with interpersonal intimacy. However, if men develop patterns that emphasize "handling" women, that is to say, deceiving and manipulating women for sex, they may fail to recognize the value of intimacy and connection, as these relational styles become tainted by misuse during NS.

Men also frequently seek to *maintain grandiose self-images* (Kaschak, 1992). They want to perceive themselves as powerful and in charge. However, occasionally men glimpse their very mortal (and unacceptably deflated) real selves. During such times, men may attempt to restore their self-image through redoubling their efforts to gain power over others. These efforts may include familiar coping strategies that already had deleterious aspects to them such as displays of power over others at work or workaholism, purchasing a sports car (displays of financial/physical power), and having affairs or dating younger women (displays of sexual potence). Therefore, seeking out continued episodes of NS is one ineffective way of coping with the challenges of the NS phase.

Men may also get stuck because NS has many self-perpetuating features. These include immediate physical gratification that is completely under one's control (if based on use of pornography and masturbation) or quickly attainable (if based on the use of massage parlors or prostitutes). Relatedly, NS-based pornographic fantasies offer escape into a world in which sexual dominance and objectification are consistently glorified; one doesn't have to deal with the complexities of real life relationships in which others' needs must be taken into account (*Dreamworlds,* 1991; Stoltenberg, 1989). Pornographic fantasies may also foster the notion that women who are willing to participate in NS are desirable objects to be rewarded, whereas women who want intimacy are portrayed as controlling and annoying (bad) who should eventually be ridiculed and humiliated. NS also offers the illusion of emotional safety via minimal exposure to risk of emotional rejection or loss (i.e., "If I don't get attached I can't be hurt"). Further, having friends for whom shared NS-supportive views and/or behaviors are a part of the friendship (e.g., going to strip joints together) may serve as a shield against challenges to men's beliefs and behaviors associated with NS.

Another coping strategy for men who do not wish to face the potential threat of self-examination necessary for the successful resolution of this phase is to project blame for their discomfort and confusion onto women. Such men may conclude that successful interactions (the way they define them) are impossible, because women are fundamentally cruel and vindictive creatures. This coping mechanism is likely to become self-perpetuating, as men who hold these beliefs are likely to seek evidence in favor of them rather than against and may be drawn to women who will support this view (confirmatory bias). This view may also create a self-fulfilling prophecy in that this dynamic results in their actually collecting data to support their beliefs (e.g., women they are involved with may behave cruelly in response to their prompts). Other reasons that men do not successfully resolve NS include ineffective ways of coping, such as the excessive use of alcohol and/or drugs (avoidance and sedation) or even suicide (coping failure). In addition to harming others, men who use these later strategies to allay their distress clearly end up harming themselves.

Failing to Resolve the NS Stage

Researchers and theorists are increasingly endorsing the notion that healthy people maintain a healthy balance of "I-ness" (autonomy/individuation), as well as "We-ness" (affiliation) (e.g., Good & Mintz, 1993; Sharpe & Heppner, 1991; Sharpe, Heppner, & Dixon, 1995). Clinical reports suggest that men who do not progress beyond NS will have trouble with the "We-ness" side of themselves. Specifically, they may have less interpersonal intimacy in their relationships, greater likelihood of having affairs outside their primary relationship, and less likelihood of remaining in committed relationships than those who do resolve NS successfully. An example from author Marvin Allen illustrates the difficulty these men may have achieving intimacy within their primary relationship:

> But the real surprise for me in my marriage was that my wife wanted more from me than money and sex. It wasn't enough for her that I was working as hard as I could sixteen hours a day. It wasn't enough for her that I was an indefatigable lover. It wasn't enough for her that I had given up seeing my buddies, chasing women, playing sports, and going fishing. She wanted something more from me, something that I found impossible to give: intimacy. I was keeping such a tight rein on my feelings that there was no way I could let her get close to me. Unconsciously, I was afraid that if I let her penetrate my defenses, she would flush out some of those forbidden feelings that were threatening to blow me apart. If I was going to keep a safe distance from my feelings, I would have to keep a safe distance from her. . . . It doesn't take long for a relationship to go awry when a man doesn't know how to be intimate. (Allen & Robinson, 1993, p. 101)

Because men who do not resolve NS have difficulty with intimacy and communication, it is also likely that they will experience greater difficulty with their partners' aging process and biomedical concerns, such as having a hysterectomy or mastectomy. In *The Centerfold Syndrome*, Brooks (1995) discusses male/female relationships with a group of men. One of them, "Arthur," confesses that although his wife had a mastectomy months ago, he was never able to discuss her surgery with her. He says that he hates to think about her being "all cut up and ... mutilated" and guesses that she "talks with the girls about it" (p. 58). Arthur is an example of someone who unsuccessfully resolved the NS developmental stage and as a result, cannot accept the change in his wife's body or communicate with her about those changes. He sees the loss of her breast as a mutilation of her very being.

Not being able to achieve connection with others, men who do not resolve NS may grow accustomed to lives lacking in interpersonal intimacy. As a result, they may end up isolated, perhaps wondering what they did wrong in life. Such an existence is likely to be a lonely one, replete with feelings of disconnection, despair, and stagnation. The following quotations demonstrate the importance of connection and caring to happiness and the results of being disconnected from others. Disconnection, loneliness, violation, and dominance plant "the seeds of misery in men's lives" which lead to relationships that are not mutually empowering. "To participate in relationships that are not mutual is a source of sadness and rage that even in the dominant gender can lead over a period of time to withdrawal, stagnation, and depression, and characteristically, insecurity, aggression, and violence" (Bergman, 1995, pp. 72–73). Similarly, Pollack (1995) describes men's pattern of "defensive self-sufficiency—a pseudoautonomy in which they have been entirely dependent on others for their emotional sustenance—while denying their yearning and need for support. Their isolation in turn has caused confusion and pain ... for others and ... themselves" (p. 55). To compensate for loneliness and despair, those who do not successfully resolve NS may seek to continue the process of conquest into the world of work, seeking to accumulate additional trophies to bolster their vulnerable self-image. Men who unsuccessfully resolve NS also may fail to recognize that—at some level—life is about connecting with and caring for others. This notion is reflected in the well-known poem and song "Richard Cory" (Robinson, 1922; Simon, 1965) and in the song "Nobody knows you":

> ... But nobody knows you; nobody knows you.
> They really want to, but nobody knows you.
> ... But she doesn't know you; she doesn't know you.
> She really wants to, but she doesn't know you.

You got a good job, the best one in town.
You climb toward the top, and you never look down.
A crisis at 50, when your hair is filled with snow.
You stare at the window, and wonder 'Where did it go?'
'Cause you don't know you. You don't know you.
You really want to, but you just don't know you . . . .

(Morgan, 1980)

Unsuccessfully Resolved NS and Subsequent Developmental Tasks

Several developmental tasks of adulthood and advanced adulthood are likely to be affected by men's successful or unsuccessful resolution of the ISR/NS stage. Hence, this section examines Levinson's (1978) "seasons" of men's lives that occur during adulthood and advanced adulthood with this in mind. One of the tasks associated with the novice phase of adult development involves reexamining love relationships. According to Levinson, such reexamination is likely to occur with men between the ages of 28 and 32. Men in this phase are faced with decisions about commitment to a relationship/marriage and the type of relationship they might want to have with a life partner. Men who have successfully resolved the NS stage may be more likely to find fulfillment in a long-term committed partnership/marriage than those who have not. Men who feel isolated and disconnected from their partners (and themselves) are more likely to engage in NS outside of the committed relationship. After reexamining their love relationships, men who have successfully resolved the NS stage may try to find new ways of meeting their intimacy needs; whereas those who have not successfully resolved the stage may assess their committed relationships negatively and without hope for improvement.

Once a man has passed through the reexamination phase of early adulthood, he moves into what Levinson calls the "settling down" stage of his adult development. This stage is thought to occur in middle adulthood (roughly between the ages of 33 and 40). One of the important characteristics that marks this stage is a move toward individuation; he increasingly will think and act according to his own beliefs rather than according to the beliefs of others. It is likely that this change will be affected by individuals' experiences during the NS stage. If he has a negative and confusing experience with NS, the beliefs that are solidified may reflect negative attitudes toward sex, sexual partners, and meaningful, committed relationships with a partner.

In contrast, men who successfully resolve this stage would be expected to hold more positive views of relationships.

The next developmental phase in Levinson's model is the midlife transition in which early adulthood is reevaluated. As early adulthood ends, people are confronted with evidence of their physical decline. Faced with fears associated with getting older and becoming less powerful, some men react by attempting to reaffirm their youth, power, and desirability. Most of us are familiar with the idea of a midlife crisis that inspires stereotypic images of middle-aged men buying sports cars and running off to Maui with much younger females. Seeking out affairs and sexual adventures (typically with younger, attractive partners) are common aspects of the midlife crisis. Thus, (re-) engaging in NS is one way for middle-aged men to attempt to reclaim their fading sense of strength and influence.

In addition to coming to terms with evidence of their declining physical power, men also may face the destruction that they have purposefully or inadvertently caused others (Levinson et al., 1978). They recognize that they are capable of harming and injuring others. This reevaluation of earlier life may include examining one's earlier engagement in NS in new ways, as clearly one's behaviors associated with NS can be injurious to others. For example, men in this phase may realize the harm that they caused others (and perhaps themselves) by "using" others for gratification. As with many things, however, creation may arise from destruction. When we realize how we have caused damage in the past, we may also realize new ways to be caring and constructive in future relationships, both sexual and nonsexual.

A developmental phenomenon that begins around the time of the midlife transition and continues into the advanced years is a move toward "femininity" (Jung, 1971; Levinson et al., 1978). Earlier we discussed the forced disidentification of male children from the female sex and characteristics associated with femininity. Indeed, for most boys and men, what has been perceived as feminine was devalued in the earlier part of their lives (Levinson et al., 1978). Boys/men were encouraged to create a masculine—in direct contrast to feminine—image based on physical prowess, toughness, achievement, and strength (Thompson & Pleck, 1986). Research suggests, however, that as men age, this process is somewhat reversed and men move toward a reidentification with the "feminine" aspects of themselves (e.g., increased emotionality, expressiveness, and nurturance; Fischer & Narus, 1981). It may be that once men have reached midlife, they feel sufficiently secure in themselves and their masculinity to explore these underdeveloped "feminine" qualities. According to Levinson, this change includes learning to enjoy being dependent and interdependent and perhaps becoming more in touch with sensual and aesthetic feelings. As men indulge themselves in the nourishment of their feminine sides, they likely become more able to develop intimate relationships with women and lovers.

We hypothesize, however, that those men who unsuccessfully resolved the NS stage will find it difficult to explore of their cut-off feminine sides. Such individuals are likely to continue to emphasize differences between themselves and women; hence, they resist reidentification with characteristics perceived as "feminine" such as expressing emotions and valuing relationships in old age. Instead, they may try to reassert their power and independence, rather than allowing a degree of dependence and connection. Hence they may well miss out on gaining "wholeness" through interdependence, mutuality, and intimacy. Older men's sexual lives have been studied from several perspectives. Widespread negative societal attitudes about sexuality in old age certainly exist (Butler & Lewis, 1986). We suspect that because American society does not recognize the elderly as particularly sexual nor sexually attractive (Butler & Lewis, 1986), elderly men are expected to "age gracefully." However, a nationwide study found that 99 percent of men aged 60 to 91 reported liking sex, and 82 percent reported being satisfied with their sexual experiences (Starr & Weiner, 1981). Some older men find that physiological changes associated with aging allow them to improve their sexual functioning and intimacy (LoPiccolo, 1991; Masters & Johnson, 1966). For example, men who previously had difficulty with rapid ejaculation often find that it takes them longer to reach ejaculation as they age.

Little is known, however, about NS in men during late adulthood. Older men who have heavily endorsed traditional conceptions of masculinity may have difficulty adapting to physiological changes that accompany aging and biomedical conditions, such as slower erection response, greater need for direct physical stimulation, and decreased rigidity (LoPiccolo, 1991; Masters & Johnson, 1966; Solomon, 1982). Such men may attempt to bolster their threatened sense of sexual potency through the use of prostitutes, pornography, and searching for a perfect sexual partner. In such situations, performance pressures and anxiety are likely to further detract from sexual performance as well as interpersonal intimacy.

Additionally, in old age, what was once societally endorsed and encouraged behavior often becomes viewed as inappropriate. If elderly men use pornography, pursue sexual relations, or engage in other activities associated with NS, they may be considered "dirty old men." Fortunately, positive messages about sexuality during later adulthood are becoming more widespread (e.g., Butler & Lewis, 1977, 1986; LoPiccolo, 1991; Solomon, 1982).

Suggestions for Psychotherapists and Consumers of Psychotherapy

Therapists and others seeking to be of assistance to men stuck in NS might want to bear a few thoughts in mind. The first notion is that of the "teachable moment" (Havighurst, 1953) and the associated concept of "readiness to change" (Prochaska, Norcross, & DiClemente, 1994). The basic concept is that people are most likely to change when they are attentive to the issue and have a clearly identified reason and motivation to change. Hence, it would be hypothesized that men who are currently experiencing some distress or pain associated with their engagement in NS would be most likely to successfully change this aspect of their lives. Another potentially relevant concept is that of "plus one" programming; developmental growth may be facilitated optimally by having individuals undertake tasks and attempt risks that are one step more advanced than their current level (e.g., Baxter Magolda, 1992; King & Kitchner, 1994). Further, developmental progress is facilitated by an optimal balance of challenge and support; this might include facilitating identification of appropriate, attainable goals, and support for efforts to reach them. Group therapy also offers the opportunity to explore these issues. It may be that men optimally might begin in an all-male group where their shared issues can be explored safely. They might then progress to a mixed-sex group in which they can gain a greater range of feedback and learn directly of women's experiences. Finally, in life in general, and as it relates to sexuality and interpersonal intimacy in particular, the complex and constantly changing nature of individuals and society may qualify a specific behavior as problematic at one time or place, and as adaptive at another. In order to understand the facilitative or maladaptive value of specific behaviors, it is necessary to understand the roles they play in the healing process. Similarly, as has been noted recently by several authors, it is important to help men (and society) construct a more healthy conception of masculinity (e.g., Brooks, 1995; Good et al., 1990; Good & Mintz, 1993; Levant & Kopecky, 1995; Levant & Pollack, 1995).

Future Research

Although much information in this chapter is based on research, a large amount is derived from clinical observations, theory, and speculation; this leaves open a wide range of creative research possibilities in this area. Only a few of the many conceivable avenues of research are suggested here.

Because so little is known about NS in general and about an ISR/NS psychosocial developmental "stage" in particular, a broad, exploratory approach may be most useful to further understanding of young men's entry into and passage out of this stage (e.g., qualitative interviews). This research could also provide important information about the challenges and failures involved in both successful and unsuccessful resolution of the NS phase.

In addition to suggesting ideas for qualitative research, the ideas presented in this chapter also suggest a variety of possibilities for quantitative studies. For example, an instrument measuring attitudes toward components of NS, such as promiscuity and use of pornography, could be developed. Similarly, creation of a developmentally-based instrument would allow assessment of how far individuals have moved along the ISR/NS path. Finally, additional studies could examine the correlates of NS. Researchers may wish to correlate a measure of promiscuity with level of intimacy, or frequency of pornography consumption with its extent of sexual objectification of women.

Additionally, it is important to note that while little research has explored these developmental issues, even less has addressed how these hypothesized relations might be associated with culture, ethnicity, and sexual orientation. Such research would improve our understanding of the similarities and differences among different ethnic communities, and would contribute to the understanding of NS as a widespread phenomenon.

Conclusion

This chapter examined nonrelational sex as a developmental stage through which many men enter and through which some men progress to intimate sexual relations. A variety of factors were identified that contribute to men's successful and unsuccessful resolution of tasks associated with ISR/NS. Human development is complex and multidetermined; men's entrance into the ISR/NS stage is no exception. Chronological age per se does not initiate these stages, rather it appears that a combination of biological aging, internal psychological changes, and social experiences are associated with the onset and resolution of this stage.

It has not been our aim to promote the idea that all nonrelational sex is inherently evil, wrong, and otherwise harmful. Rather, we have sought to demonstrate that, as a whole, the unsuccessful resolution of the ISR/NS stage of development may have deleterious consequences upon individuals and others affected by their lives.

References

Allen, M., & Robinson, J. (1993). *In the company of men: A new approach to healing for husbands, fathers and friends.* New York: Random House.

Archer, J. (1996). Sex differences in social behavior. *American Psychologist, 51,* 909–917.

Baxter Magolda, M. (1992). *Knowing and reasoning in college: Gender-related patterns in students' intellectual development.* San Francisco: Jossey-Bass.

Bergman, S. J. (1995). Men's psychological development: A relational perspective. In R. F. Levant & W. S. Pollack (Eds.), *A new psychology of men* (pp. 68–90). New York: Basic Books.

Bly, R. (1990). *Iron John: A book about men.* Reading, MA: Addison-Wesley.

Brannon, R. B. (1976). The male sex role: Our culture's blueprint for manhood and what it's done for us lately. In D. S. David & R. B. Brannon (Eds.), *The forty-nine percent majority* (pp. 1–48). Reading, MA: Addison-Wesley.

Brooks, G. R. (1995). *The centerfold syndrome: How men can overcome objectification and achieve intimacy with women.* San Francisco: Jossey-Bass.

Butler, R. N., & Lewis, M. I. (1977). *Love and sex after 60.* New York: Harper & Row.

Butler, R. N., & Lewis, M. I. (1986). *Aging and mental health: Positive psychosocial and biomedical approaches* (3rd ed.). Columbus, OH: Merrill.

Chickering, A. W. (1969). *Education and identity.* San Francisco: Jossey-Bass.

Dreamworlds: Desire, sex, and power in music video. (1991). Northampton, MA: Media Education Center.

Erikson, E. H. (1963). *Childhood and society* (2nd ed.). New York: Norton.

Erikson, E. H. (1968). *Identity: Youth and crisis.* New York: Norton.

Fischer, J. L., & Narus, L. R. (1981). Sex roles and intimacy in same-sex and other-sex relationships. *Psychology of Women Quarterly, 5,* 444–455.

Frank, J. D. (1961). *Persuasion and healing.* Baltimore: Johns Hopkins University Press.

Gilligan, C. (1982). *In a different voice: Psychological theory and women's development.* Cambridge, MA: Harvard University Press.

Good, G. E., Gilbert, L. A., & Scher, M. (1990). Gender aware therapy: A synthesis of feminist therapy and knowledge about gender. *Journal of Counseling and Development, 68,* 376–380.

Good, G. E., & Mintz, L. B. (1993). Towards healthy conceptions of masculinity: Clarifying the issues. *Journal of Mental Health Counseling, 15,* 403–413.

Gottman, J., Notarius, C., Gonso, J., & Markman, H. (1976). *A couple's guide to communication.* Champaign, IL: Research Press.

Hamilton, M. C., & Stuart-Smith, S. (1995). Sociobiology revisited. In S. Ruth (Ed.), *Issues in feminism: An introduction to women's studies* (3rd ed., pp. 202–208). Mountain View, CA: Mayfield.

Havighurst, R. J. (1953). *Human development and education.* New York: Longmans, Green.

Heppner, M. J., Good, G. E., Hillenbrand, T. L., Hawkins, A. K., Hacquard, L. L., Nichols, R. K., DeBord, K. A., & Brock, K. J. (1995). Examining sex differences in altering attitudes about rape: A test of the Elaboration Likelihood Model. *Journal of Counseling and Development, 73,* 640–647.

Jung, C. G. (1971). The stages of life: Modern man in search of a soul. In J. Campbell (Ed.) & R. F. C. Hull (Trans.), *The portable Jung* (pp. 3–22). New York: Viking. (Original work published 1931)

Kaschak, E. (1992). *Engendered lives: A new psychology of women's experience.* New York: Basic Books.

Kernberg, O. (1976). *Object-relations theory and clinical psychoanalysis.* New York: Jason Aronson.

King, P. M., & Kitchner, K. S. (1994). *Developing reflective judgment: Understanding and promoting intellectual growth and critical thinking in adolescents and adults.* San Francisco: Jossey-Bass.

Kohlberg, L. A. (1980). *The meaning and measurement of moral development.* Worcester, MA: Clark University Press.

Kohut, H. (1977). *The restoration of the self.* New York: International Universities Press.

Levant, R. F. (1997). The gender socialization of nonrelational sexuality. In R. F. Levant & G. Brooks (Eds.), *Men and the problem of nonrelational sex.* New York: Wiley.

Levant, R. F., & Kopecky, G. (1995). *Masculinity reconstructed.* New York: Dutton.

Levant, R. F., & Pollack, W. S. (1995). *A new psychology of men.* New York: Basic Books.

Levinson, D. J., Darrow, C. N., Klein, E. B., Levinson, M. H., & McKee, B. (1978). *The seasons of a man's life.* New York: Knopf.

LoPiccolo, J. (1991). Counseling and therapy for sexual problems in the elderly. *Clinics in Geriatric Medicine, 7,* 161–179.

Mahler, M. (1975). *The psychological birth of the human infant.* New York: Basic Books.

Masters, W. A., & Johnson, V. E. (1966). *Human sexual response.* Boston: Little, Brown.

Morgan, G. (1980). Nobody knows you. On *It comes with the plumbing* [record]. Bellingham, WA: Nexus Records.

O'Neal, J. M. (1981). Patterns of gender role conflict and strain: Sexism and fear of femininity in men's lives. *Personnel and Guidance Journal, 69,* 203–210.

O'Neal, J. M. (1982). Gender-role conflict and strain in men's lives. In K. Solomon & N. Levy (Eds.), *Men in transition.* New York: Plenum Press.

O'Neal, J. M., Good, G. E., & Holmes, S. (1995). Fifteen years of theory and research on men's gender role conflict: New paradigms for empirical research. In R. F. Levant & W. S. Pollack (Eds.), *A new psychology of men* (pp. 164–206). New York: Basic Books.

Perry, W. (1970). *Forms of intellectual and ethical development in the college years.* New York: Holt, Rinehart and Winston.

Pleck, J. H., Sonenstein, F. L., & Ku, L. C. (1993). Masculinity ideology and its correlates. In S. Oskamp & M. Costanzo (Eds.), *Gender issues in social psychology* (pp. 85–110). Newbury Park, CA: Sage.

Pollack, W. S. (1995). No man is an island: Toward a new psychoanalytic psychology of men. In R. F. Levant & W. S. Pollack (Eds.), *A new psychology of men* (pp. 33–67). New York: Basic Books.

Prochaska, J. O., Norcross, J., & DiClemente, C. C. (1994). *Changing for good.* New York: Morrow.

Robinson, E. A. (1922). Richard Cory. In *Collected poems* (p. 82). New York: Macmillan.

Sharpe, M. J., & Heppner, P. P. (1991). Gender role, gender role conflict, and psychological well-being in men. *Journal of Counseling Psychology, 38,* 323–330.

Sharpe, M. J., Heppner, P. P., & Dixon, W. A. (1995). Gender role conflict, instrumentality, expressiveness, and well-being in adult men. *Sex Roles, 33,* 1–18.

Simon, P. (1965). Richard Cory. [Recorded by Simon and Garfunkel]. On *Sounds of silence* [record]. New York: Columbia.

Solomon, K. (1982). The older man. In K. Solmon & N. B. Levy (Eds.), *Men in therapy* (pp. 205–240). New York: Plenum Press.

Starr, B. D., & Weiner, M. B. (1981). *The Starr-Wiener Report on sex and sexuality in the mature years.* New York: Stein and Day.

Stevens, M. (1985). Rape domain. In M. Stevens & R. Gebhardt (Eds.), *Rape education for men: Curriculum guide* (Diagram I). Columbus: Rape Education and Prevention Program, Ohio State University.

Stoltenberg, J. (1989). *Refusing to be a man.* Portland, OR: Breitenbush.

Thompson, E. H., & Pleck, J. H. (1986). The structure of male role norms. *American Behavioral Scientist, 29,* 531–543.

CHAPTER 9

African American Men and Nonrelational Sex

VERNON MCCLEAN

FOR AFRICAN AMERICAN men, nonrelational sexuality can be defined as the tendency to experience sex primarily as objectification, as the inability to make love to one's partner without fantasizing about another person, sometimes of another race. There is very little emotional intimacy in nonrelational sex. Sexual compulsions or Don Juanism may develop.

Nonrelational sexuality can be intensely harmful, manifesting itself in traits such as self-hatred, anger, misogyny, heterosexism and/or psychopathology—all of which are reflected in high rates of separation and divorce. The result can sometimes be spouse abuse, sexual aggression, and rape.

An Alternative View of African American Sexuality

If we are to understand the dimensions of the attitudinal and behavioral changes necessary to ameliorate the problems associated with nonrelational sex in the African American community, it is first necessary to fully appreciate the ethnocultural context in which African American men find themselves (Majors & Gordon, 1994). As Benjamin Bowser (1991) has written:

> Sexuality is an intrinsic part of a black man's social experience. It is not isolated from his general experience or from the quality of his participation in the larger white society. If black sexuality is in some ways different than it is for whites, then there must be something different about the respective social conditions of each group. This point can be

extended to the apparent exaggerated sexuality of black men. Are there some particular conditions common to black men that might affect their sexual attitudes and behaviors? (p. 123)

I hope to answer the question Bowser raises by providing an analysis of nonrelational sex in the context of racism, sexism, and heterosexism in the African American community, with attention paid to the physical abuse of women and the vicissitudes of heterosexism.

Again, as Bowser writes,

A contextual explanation might begin by looking at the extent to which black men are able and allowed to fully play out the male normative social and economic roles. I would propose that men in all social classes who experience frustrated instrumental and expressive roles place more emphasis on their sexuality. The degree of their frustration over time directly impacts the extent to which sexuality becomes emphasized. (p. 123)

Sidney M. Jourard in his text *The Transparent Self* (1971) advanced the belief that socially defined male roles require men to appear tough, objective, striving, achieving, unexpressive, unsentimental, and emotionally unexpressive. Thus, tabloids like *The Globe* (1994) can scream that O.J. Simpson wanted to be close to his dad (a homosexual), but he also wanted to be macho. "Being thought of as tough in our neighborhood was everything." This theme was echoed in Simpson's biography, "I resented his absence. Especially when I became a teenager and was trying to find out who I was. I really needed a man around then for guidance" (p. 3).

According to Jourard (1971), "if behind his persona, a man is tender, if he weeps, for instance, he will likely be viewed as unmanly by others" (p. 87). Again, according to *The Globe* interview, "We all knew what we had to do to make it—be tougher than anyone else. If there was even an inkling that you were soft, people would make out that you were gay" (p. 4). O.J. Simpson's father worked as a chef at the Federal Reserve Bank's cafeteria in San Francisco, and later moved to that city's Haight-Ashbury section.

As early as the 1970s, Maulana Karenga listed four modes through which African American women and men engage in nonrelational sex: (a) the cash connection, (b) the flesh connection, (c) the force connection, and (d) the dependency connection (quoted in Braithwaite, 1981). Braithwaite notes that "All of these modes of connecting are related to a realization that black-on-black exploitation is prevalent in the black community" (p. 91). Because of sexism, African American men have more economic opportunities and generally are not as poor as African

American women. Thus, the "cash connection" causes African American women to compete for African American men. Every African American woman wants a BMW (**B**lack **M**an **W**orking).

When asked why he does not date African American women, the African American basketball star Dennis Rodman replied in his autobiography, *Bad as I Wanna Be:*

> Black women didn't accept me when I was younger. I wasn't attractive. I didn't have money or fancy clothes. . . . Now, though, I'm okay. Now that I have some money, some fame, the story has changed. Some of those same Black women who wouldn't talk to me years ago were rushing through the doors of my mother's house asking, "Where's your son? How's your son doing?" (Rodman & Keown, 1996, pp. 141–142)

The underlying assumption of the cash connection is that everything has a price and that money can solve all problems. Although it does not occur as frequently as in years past, many African American women still tell their daughters to find a man who can "take care" of them, as if they were disabled.

The "flesh connection" is also related to sexism. This is the belief that African American women are made up only of parts: that is, breasts, legs, and "buns" and that these are the basics of nonrelational sex bonding. This seems to be typical of all men, regardless of race. According to the actor Alan Alda, a man may be suffering from "testosterone poisoning" if he is "thing" oriented. "Do you value the parts of a woman's body more than the woman herself? Are you turned on by things that even remind you of those parts?" Humorously, he continued, "Have you ever fallen in love with a really great doorknob?" (Alda, 1993, p. 234).

The "force connection" is predicated on the violent nature of American society. The African American columnist Clarence Page (1996) has pointed out that according to federal crime statistics, more women (African American and White) are killed or injured at the hands of men than in car accidents, muggings, and rapes combined. He cites one intriguing study, conducted by researchers at Northeastern University and the University of Massachusetts, which examined 107 sexual assault cases reported at 30 Division I colleges between 1991 and 1993. The study found that while male student athletes made up only 3.3 percent of the total male enrollment, they were involved in 19 percent of the assaults (p. 29).

Finally, the "dependency connection" results from engaging in one or all of the three previously mentioned connections. In the dependency connection, the woman will not leave the man even under the worst conditions, including physical abuse (a situation discussed below). She may even justify and rationalize the abuse, in this way adopting a slave mentality.

Opposite Race Fantasy and Nonrelational Sex

Many African American men experience an inability to make love without fantasizing about the opposite race. One of the classic studies on this topic was conducted by Grier and Cobbs (1968). According to these noted psychiatrists, when an African American man and a White woman unite, one can assume that innumerable racially connected issues will arise.

For the African American man, the White woman represents the *socially identified* female ideal and thus an intensely exciting object for his sexual possession. "She has been identified as precisely the individual to whom access [for the African American male] is barred by every social institution. The forbiddenness and desirableness of the white woman make her a natural recipient of his projected Oedipal fantasies" (Grier & Cobbs, 1968, p. 91).

The African American male sees himself as finally possessing the maternal object under circumstances that reproduce the dangerous, defiant quality of Oedipal interest as experienced by the child. That is, he feels a sense of *power* at having acquired this highly valuable woman (valuable because of her skin color) and a sense of power that she finds him (as an "inferior" African American) desirable. He believes that she finds him equally or more desirable than a White man, whom the African American male both fears and admires.

Unfortunately, according to Grier and Cobbs, because the African American male perceives the White women as the embodiment of his White oppressors, the sexual act itself becomes a source of aggression against *all* White people. "The African American man then has an opportunity to live out murderous fantasies of revenge. In possessing the white woman he sees himself as degrading her . . . in this instance sharing the community's feeling that a white woman who submits to a black lover becomes as debased as he." Curiously, through having nonrelational sex with a White woman, he sees himself as getting revenge on the White man, and "thus becoming the instrument through which a white person is degraded" (Grier & Cobbs, 1968, p. 91).

Having sex with a White woman is also "good" for a *latent* African American homosexual. That is, to him the White woman is not a woman at all. He defines women as the image of his mother or his sisters. To him, the White woman is something else and it becomes easier to penetrate her (Grier & Cobbs, 1968, 1972).

Finally, and perhaps most important, the African American male who has nonrelational sex with a White woman sees himself as having bested the White man in the field of love-making "and of having rendered him impotent and castrated, for the white woman, in fantasy, at least, has embraced a white lover and then chosen a black one" (Grier & Cobbs, 1968, p. 91).

In Grier and Cobbs' view (and this relates very much to Pleck's strain theory), while in every other area of life the African American male may feel weak and powerless, at least through having sex with a White woman, "he can reverse the roles and, because of the central importance of the sexual function in human affairs, may feel that the scales are almost balanced" (1968, p. 92).

Lawrence Otis Graham, the Harvard-trained lawyer who went undercover as a busboy at an all-White country club, wrote an essay entitled, "I Never Dated a White Girl." After discussing African American opposition to interracial sex, with which he seems to agree, he muses,

> Does black opposition to intermarriage differ from the arguments made by white racists who drafted anti-miscegenation statutes a hundred years ago? Well, for one thing, the goals are different. The goal of white racists was to humiliate and to permanently label one group as "inferior" and "subhuman." (1995, p. 65)

Graham reminds us that "the primary goal of blacks supporting black-black marriages is not to develop ways to keep the races separate or to assign a status to one or another. Rather, it is to develop solutions for the loss of black mentors and role models at a time when the black community is overrun with crime" and other problems (p. 66).

This is not to say that *all* interracial sex is wrong, but suggests that it does become negative for those African American men who can *only* function sexually when their partner is of a different race.

Sexism in the African American Community

One positive outcome of the O.J. Simpson trial has been that issues surrounding nonrelational sex in the African American community have been brought into sharper focus. This trial was suffused with gut-level questions involving self-hatred, misogyny, heterosexism, African American/White sexuality, African American male sexuality, and, of course, spouse abuse. It rests squarely at the locus where racism, sexism, and heterosexism intersect. Simpson was charged with two acts that are among the most widely condemned: first, having sex with and then killing a White woman, and second, slaying the epitome of White power and patriarchy—a White man from well-to-do circumstances.

As African American men, many of us feel compelled to look at the Simpson case only from the perspective of racism. Sexism and heterosexism, however, are also intricately linked with this case. It is true that expanding an analysis of this case to include dimensions of sexism and heterosexism runs the risk of dividing people who otherwise might find a common cause around the issue of racism. But the reverse is also true—we would be making a mirror-image error of dividing people if we did *not* include the issues of sexism and heterosexism. The commonality of our struggle crosses the boundaries of race, class, and gender.

Transcending the Boundaries of Racism, Sexism, and Heterosexism

The traits attributed to African Americans, women, and gays reveal startling similarities. The interchangeability of these images provides a natural starting point to discuss nonrelational sex as a unifying focus for oppressed groups: African Americans, gays, Jews, women, the disabled.

They Are Animals—They Smell

These groups have been viewed by their oppressors as "animalistic." For example, many have characterized O.J. Simpson as a vicious Black animal. This idea of the oppressed as subhuman is hardly new. As long ago as 584 A.D., in Lyons, France, 43 Catholic bishops and 20 other White male clergy held a most peculiar—and revealing—debate. Their topic was: "Are Women Human?" After many lengthy arguments, a vote was taken. The results: 32 yes, 31 no. Women were declared human by *one vote!* (Adam, 1993).

Throughout history, there have been debates about "whether, like animals, Jews, sodomites, or savages could have souls. The sentiment is concretized in the allegation: They smell." (Adam, 1993, p. 24). While it may seem ludicrous to stigmatize an entire race, class, or gender because they "smell," this is exactly what has been done. Hitler wrote in *Mein Kampf* of his "discovery" of a supposed Jewish "smell." Charles Barkley, the all-star African American basketball player with the Houston Rockets, said that the reason he does not have sex with African American women is because they smell.

HYPERSEXUALITY

Jews were linked with witchcraft, including myths about Jewish infanticide, sadism, and blood rituals. The sixteenth-century Protestant theologian, Martin Luther, was convinced of the irresistible Jewish ability to corrupt and seduce (White) Christians. Indeed, in medieval literature, the Jew

> ... has monstrous sexual powers and his sexual powers transform him into an ogre threatening the sexual life, the existence, and very soul of his helpless primordial son. Each—the Jew as much as the Devil—runs insanely about the countryside mutilating or castrating little boys and leading Christian youths into vile debauchery. And each wantonly seduces or rapes beautiful [White] Christian virgins. (Adam, 1993, p. 25)

This theme has found a ready echo in the writing of anti-Semites throughout the ages. Hitler wrote that,

> for hours the black-haired Jew boy, diabolic joy in his face, waits in ambush for the unsuspecting girl whom he defiles with his blood and thus robs her from her people. (Adam, 1993, p. 25)

This same theme of excessive sexuality has been used to justify the persecution of African Americans. The lynching and burning of African American men in America was traditionally justified by the contention that "many Negroes were literally wild beasts with uncontrollable sexual passions and criminal natures stamped by heredity" (Adam, 1993, p. 25).

If one believes the Religious Right, gay people, as well as African Americans and women, are oversexed. What is conveniently overlooked by such "believers" is the fact that 90 percent of child molesters are heterosexual White men!

HERETICS AND CONSPIRATORS

African Americans, women, gays, Jews—all have a reputation for "offensive flamboyance." They are reputed to be loud, pushy, aggressive, extroverted, careless. Adam (1993, p. 27) notes that,

> [Albert] Memmi expresses the same anxiety in reference to Jews. "To dress in bright colors was Jewish. To speak too loudly, to call out, to gather in the streets was Jewish."

As a group, women have received more than their fair share of this prejudice. Orthodox religious doctrine holds that the natural position of women is one of inferiority to men. An Orthodox Jewish prayer says, "Blessed art thou, O Lord our God and King of the Universe, that thou didst not create me as a woman." And the Koran explicitly states that "Men are superior to women." (Note how groups that are themselves oppressed can in turn oppress others among their number—notably, their women.) According to the seventeenth-century English writer Samuel Butler, "the souls of women are so small that some believe they've none at all" (McClean & Lyles, 1993, p. 4).

Homosexuals have also been viewed as heretics and conspirators, as somehow "not normal." In his incisive essay "Some Thoughts on the Challenges Facing Black Gay Intellectuals," social critic Ron Simmons, of Howard University, documents the persistence of heterosexism in academia and elsewhere. For example, he notes that in a speech delivered at Morgan State University, Louis Farrakhan, of the Nation of Islam, ascribes African American male homosexuality to prison incarceration and the lack of positive male role models:

> Those of you who are homosexual—you weren't born [that] way, brother. You never had a strong male image . . . [these] are conditions that are forced on black men. You're filling up the jails and they're turning [you] into freaks in the jails. (Simmons, 1991, p. 213)

In the book *Afrocentricity*, Molefi Asante blames "prison breeding" for the "outburst of homosexuality among black men." To him, homosexuality is a "white decadence" that cannot be condoned or accepted. It can, however, be "tolerated until such times as our families and schools are engaged in Afrocentric instruction for males" (Asante, 1980, p. 64). And, according to Simmons, the writer Haki Madhubuti likewise states that "homosexuality is backward, abnormal" (Simmons, 1991, p. 214).

Moreover, according to Simmons, this same prejudice against gays can be seen in some of the works of Amiri Baraka. In his "A Poem for Black Hearts," Baraka (1969) praises the late Malcolm X as a "black god" whose death African American men must avenge or be called "faggots till the end of the earth." In "The Black Man Is Making New Gods," Baraka refers to the crucifixion of Christ as "The Fag's Death they give us on a cross." In plays such as "The Baptism" and "The Toilet," Baraka depicts homosexuals as degenerates and cowards. And in his "American Sexual Reference: Black Male," Baraka writes that "Most American white men are trained to be fags. . . . Their faces are weak and blank . . . that red flush, those silk blue faggot eyes" (Simmons, 1991, p. 218).

Finally, in "The System of Dante's Hell," Simmons notes that Baraka writes,

> In Chicago, I kept making the queer scene. Under the "El" with a preacher . . . [he] held my head under the quilt. The first guy . . . spoke to me grinning and I said my name was Stephen Daedalus . . . One more guy and it was over. On the train, I wrote all this down. A journal now sitting in a tray on top of the closet. . . . The journal says "Am I like that?" (Simmons, 1991, p. 219).

Racism and Heterosexism

There are many similarities between the oppression of African Americans and the oppression of gays. Both groups are viewed as subhuman. Both are viewed as deviant. Both are viewed as not possessing "family values." And both are viewed as being oversexed.

Despite this similarity of oppression, rather than seeking common cause with the gay community, many African Americans and gays seem to be pitted against each other, precisely because of racism and heterosexism. In the African American community, just about the worst thing one can be is a "faggot." The mere term ("faggot") refers to a bundle of sticks which is burned—like gay men in the Middle Ages were burned. African Americans in the American South were shot, lynched, and burned for their alleged sexual misdeeds, such as having sex with a White woman, just as gays were burned for having sex with other men.

There is a similarity of oppression throughout history: against women, gays, African Americans. All have been oppressed in similar ways and for similar reasons. As if he was being fair-minded and lenient, Thomas Jefferson proposed that the penalty for same-sex acts be reduced from death to castration! The slaveholder Jefferson was said to have had nonrelational sex with the slave Sally Hemings and to have fathered six children whom he kept in bondage (Blumenfield & Raymond, 1993, p. 258).

Many African American men practice what T. W. Adorno called scapegoating or displaced aggression. This is the tendency to take out one's frustrations or aggressions on someone other than the true source of these frustrations and aggressions (Farley, 1995; Pleck, 1981). Because we cannot easily get back at the White man, we African American men abuse our women, children, and gays. And although African American males may be "niggers," at least we are not "bitches" or "faggots." The heterosexism that many African American males exhibit oppresses us, too, as African Americans and as males.

As African American men, because of a false sense of masculinity— or a false sense of what we consider to be sexuality—we think less of an African American man if he has sex with another African American man. However, it seems that many of us are eager to see one African American man bash the head of another African American man in the boxing ring or on the football field.

Because of this false sense of masculinity and sexuality, some African American scholars have said that we should not delve into questions such as Martin Luther King's adultery and his nonrelational sex. This aversion dovetails with the view that it is a sign of masculinity to "have" many women. Not to have sex with many different women allegedly detracts from one's abilities as an African American leader. Aware of African American heterosexism and seeking to exploit it for his own ends, Adam Clayton Powell attempted to blackmail King by claiming that King and Bayard Rustin were lovers (O'Reilly, 1994).

African American gay men (perhaps overcompensating for their sexual orientation) have always been in the forefront of the civil rights movement in America, as well as in countries like South Africa. For example, Simon Nkoli, a Black gay man, was jailed by the apartheid-era government of South Africa for being in the forefront of the struggle for Black freedom. Having a White lover, he was disowned by most in the Black community for his sexual orientation as well as because of the color of his same-sex partner.

As in the United States, in South Africa homosexuality is often denigrated. It is "un-African" and a "product of the capitalist system" (Gevisser & Cameron, 1995, pp. 4–5). The issue of African American homosexuality in South Africa has been a very controversial one because in that country's worker hostels (as in American prisons) there has been situational homosexuality. Because of the policies of the current, post-apartheid South African government, South Africa is one of the few industrialized countries that have formally given equal rights to Blacks, women, and gays (Gevisser & Cameron, 1995).

Malcolm X's biographer, Bruce Perry, once interviewed a teenage friend of Malcolm's. Malcolm participated in same-sex nonrelational sex for a time. The friend said that Malcolm was reported to have said that the other man "paid Malcolm to disrobe him, place him on his bed, sprinkle him with talcum powder, and massage him until he reached his climax." (This episode is also detailed in Malcolm X's *Autobiography*, written with Alex Haley.) However, Perry emphasized that Malcolm's homosexual activities were sporadic, and that they were strictly for money-making purposes. In addition, "his male-to-male encounters, which rendered it unnecessary for him to compete for women, afforded him an opportunity for sexual release without the attendant risk of dependence on women" (Perry, 1992, p. 83).

Misogyny and Physical and Sexual Abuse

"Even though O.J. Simpson has been acquitted of the murders of Nicole Brown and Ronald Goldman, it is indisputable that he was guilty of earlier spousal abuse that was not properly addressed. The presiding judge allowed counseling by phone and by employers like Hertz and NBC who ignored his arrest for a violent crime" (Ines, 1995, p. 2). This is where we have failed. We, as African American men, must be held accountable for the sexual and physical oppression of women in our community.

According to a 1994 article in *Emerge* magazine (Briggs & Davis, 1994), nearly four million U.S. women are physically abused each year. Twenty-three percent of these battered women were pregnant. The FBI estimates that more than 1,500 women are murdered annually by their husbands or boyfriends (Briggs & Davis, 1994).

"The U.S. Surgeon General and the Department of Health and Human Services (HHS) report that domestic violence is the leading cause of injury to American women between the ages of 15 to 44—more common than automobile accidents" (Briggs & Davis, 1994, p. 50). Citing an article published in the *International Journal of Health Sciences,* these authors also report that an estimated 47 percent of murdered African American women are killed by acquaintances and 43 percent by "family members."

The murder of Nicole Brown Simpson pierced the national consciousness about domestic violence but may not have deeply affected the perspectives of African American men and women. Many African Americans see O.J. Simpson as just another African American male victimized by racism, rather than as an African American man with a history of brutalizing his wife.

"There's no widespread agreement in the black community that it's even a crime to hit a woman. We see the problem, but when you articulate it to people they say, 'Oh, you don't understand the pressure on the brother. You're a male basher'" (Briggs & Davis, 1994, p. 50). Briggs and Davis also assert that "in a society where black men are vilified as animalistic and violent, shining a light on the abuse of black women is often seen as adding fuel to the fires of racist stereotypes. The result for black women is often feeling forced to choose. Many times, the choice is race, and many times the result is silence" (p. 50).

What can be done about the problem of domestic abuse in the African American community? As vital as the African American church is to our experience, not many African American men who practice nonrelational sex and domestic abuse are likely to be involved with the church. Even so, one African American theologian reports, "The African American church is one of the most sexist institutions in the country, and part of that sexism is battering" (Briggs & Davis, 1994, p. 50).

Our children also are caught in a predicament. By observing and experiencing violence in the African American household, the stage is set. We tell our children that this is the "manly" way to solve problems. The result is violence: against African American women, African American on African American male crime, violence in sports (the recent upsurge in violent acts and "trash-talking" in the National Basketball Association being a prime example of this), and so forth.

The noted criminologist James Allan Fox observed that, as of 1992, 14- to 24-year-old African American males were just 1 percent of the population, but comprised 17 percent of the homicide victims and 30 percent of the offenders (DiIulio, 1996). In 1994, juveniles were murdered at a rate of seven per day, with most of the juveniles being between 15 and 17 years of age. Moreover, violence committed by teenagers is expected to get worse since, during the next 15 years, the number of juveniles under 17 will increase to about 74 million. Mark Fleisher, an urban ethnographer, has observed that an "abundance of scholarly evidence shows that antisocial and delinquent tendencies emerge early in the lives of neglected, abused and unloved youngsters, often by age 9" (DiIulio, 1996, p. A-15).

African American Male Sexual Life Cycle

Strong, DeVault, and Sayad (1996) document the basic elements of human sexuality that transcend race, class, and gender. From the moment we are born, we are rich in sexual and erotic potential, which begins to take shape in the sexual experimentations of our childhood. As children, we are still unformed, yet the world around us has helped shape our sexuality. In adolescence, our education has continued as a random mixture of learning and yearning.

As infants, we communicate by smiling, gesturing, crying, and so on. During infancy, we begin to learn how we "should" feel about our bodies. If a parent frowns, speaks sharply, or spanks an exploring hand, the infant quickly learns that a particular activity—touching one's genitals, for example—is "bad." The infant may or may not continue the activity, but if he or she does, it will be in secret, probably accompanied by the beginnings of guilt and shame (Strong et al., 1996).

Infants also learn about the gender role they are expected to fulfill. In our culture, African American boys are expected to be tough, while girls are often handled more gently. Girls are dressed up more and given soft toys and dolls with which to play. African American fathers rough-house their sons and speak more loudly to them than to their daughters. They will be given "boy toys"—basketballs and plastic "superheroes," many of which are violent and sexist. This gender role learning is reinforced by the larger African American community as the child grows older (Strong et al., 1996).

African American children become aware of sex and sexuality much earlier than many scholars realize. In a racist society, they generally learn to disguise their interest rather than risk the disapproval of their elders (Strong et al., 1996).

Puberty, the stage of human development when the body first becomes capable of reproduction, occurs at about the age of 12 for girls and 14 for boys. *Adolescence* is the social and psychological state that occurs during puberty. During this period, African American adolescents learn sexual roles that are similar to, but also different from those of the dominant culture (Strong et al., 1996).

Many adolescents follow a normative pattern in the sequence of their sexual behaviors: Hand-holding, embracing, kissing, petting, and intercourse. However, African American adolescents seem to speed up this process and move more quickly to intercourse. Young African Americans lose their virginity at an earlier age than do Whites. By age 15 or 16, about 1 out of every 4 Whites of both sexes have had intercourse, compared to 5 out of 10 African American females and 9 out of 10 African American males of that age group (Strong et al., 1996).

In the African American community, we are far more accepting of teenage sexual activity than are our White counterparts. There are several possible reasons for this. First, there is often a great deal of pressure among young African Americans (as well as young Whites in the lower socioeconomic status) to prove their masculinity by engaging in sexual activity. Second, African Americans (like poor Whites) *seem* to value children more highly than do average European Americans.

Furthermore, as survival is not guaranteed, African American adolescents may see no reason to wait for a future they may never have. Moreover, many African American adolescents tend to use sex exploitatively and competitively. For many, sex is not so much a means of achieving intimacy with our partners as it is a way of achieving status among our male peers—while for young African American females, having sex is a means of demonstrating their maturity, a sign of becoming an adult (Strong et al., 1996).

A high proportion of African American women are single. Because of high death rates, incarceration, and drug abuse, there are 1.5 million more African American women than African American men (Staples & Johnson, 1993). This gender imbalance is one reason *for* nonrelational sex, since it decreases opportunities for any other form of sex. African American women, if they wish to satisfy their desires in a heterosexual context, *must* participate in nonrelational sex.

MASTURBATION

Masturbation is frowned upon in the African American community far more than it is among Whites. According to Strong et al., "Whites are the most accepting of masturbation . . . while African Americans are less so" (1996, p. 247).

This difference can be explained culturally. Because Whites tend to begin coital activities later than African Americans, Whites regard masturbation as an acceptable alternative to sexual intercourse. African Americans, by contrast, accept sexual activity at an earlier age and view masturbation as sign of homosexuality and sexual inadequacy. As a result, many African Americans tend to view nonrelational sex as normal and masturbation as deviant. The result is that young Whites are most likely to have their initial ejaculation during masturbation, whereas young African Americans experience their first ejaculation during nonrelational sex (Staples & Johnson, 1993).

Beliefs and Sex Roles of the African American Male

Zilbergeld (1992) has posited that American males have certain roles and expectations. Using Zilbergeld's argument, the same can be said of African American males. The beliefs and sex roles of African American males include:

1. *John Wayne is an African American man.* African American men should emulate the John Wayne type. That is, African American

men should not be expressive. They should *not* express doubts. They should *not* be "soft." They *have* to be hard. "Softness" is often equated with impotence, or with being a "faggot."

2. *Performance is the ultimate.* Performance is all that counts, whether on the basketball field or in the bedroom. As the actor Alan Alda asked in an article on testosterone poisoning, "Do you have an intense need to win? When having sex . . . do you always ask if this time was 'the best' and gnaw on the bedpost if you get an ambiguous answer?" (1993, p. 234.)

3. *The African American male is in charge.* He must always be in control. He must be the one who wears the pants. The man initiates sex and gives the woman the orgasm. An African American man who allows the woman to dominate in any way is scorned.

4. *An African American man always wants sex and is always ready for it.* This is a stereotype. As African American men, we complain that White men view us only as sexual objects but privately we boast of our ability to satisfy a woman at any time, in any place. Alice Walker said of her father,

> My father expected all of his sons to have sex with women: "Like bulls . . . a man needs to get a little something on his stick."
>
> And so on Saturday nights, into town they went, chasing the girls. My sister was rarely allowed into town alone, and if the dress she wore fit too snugly at the waist, or if her cleavage dipped too far below her collarbone, she was made to stay home. (1983, p. 328)

5. *All physical contact leads to sex.* Touching is often viewed as the first step toward sexual intercourse, and this is why there is so little touching of other African American men, except in the sports arena or when we are ready to fight or kill another brother.

6. *Sex equals intercourse and intercourse leads to orgasm.* All erotic contact leads to sexual intercourse. Foreplay must always lead to penetration, and penetration must always lead to orgasm. On the other hand, oral sex (particularly as the active male partner) is taboo in the African American male community.

7. *Violence is part of sexuality.* This is evident in the discussion that follows on rap music, where the rapper intertwines violence with sexuality. It is also obvious in the rape of women (African American and White) by African American men and in the flippant humor of comedians like Eddie Murphy: "Remember the good old days, when you could beat up on women?" (Mithers, 1993, p. 78.)

Rap Music and Nonrelational Sex

Rap music today is a major influence on our youth; its lyrics and ideas cannot help but have a major impact. African Americans who make their living as rappers must be held accountable for their misogynistic and violence-encouraging lyrics (Osayande, 1996). And we, as their elder brothers, are responsible for them.

Ewuare Osayande of *The Philadelphia Tribune* reviewed Gil Scott-Heron's "Message to the Messengers":

> But I think you young folk need to know. Things don't go both ways, you can't talk respect on every other song or every other day. What I'm speaking on now is the raps about the women folks. On one song she is your African queen, And on the next one, she's a joke. (Osayande, 1995, p. 7-A)

Osayande reminds us that Malcolm X said that we judge how far a nation has come based on its treatment of women. "In a country that is backward/regressive, they [women] will be looked upon as a piece of meat, an object to be subjected to the desire of the men who run and benefit from the society" (Osayande, 1995, p. 7-A). In other words, they will be viewed as fitting objects for nonrelational sex.

In the spirit of transcending the perspective of nonrelational sex, we should honor our assertive sisters, rather than calling them "skeezers, bitches, and ho's." Your life may depend on it; according to Justice Department statistics, African American women kill their husbands "at about the same rate as husbands kill their wives" (Findings of family violence study, 1994, p. 26).

Within the broad category of rap is the small but profitable genre known as gangsta rap, a style that is distinguished by lyrics that graphically describe scenes of gunplay, sex, drug use, and violence, often referring to women as "ho's" and "bitches." The lyrics of gangsta rap fantasize about hurting women with the size of one's penis. To prove that we have a big penis, the woman must bleed during sex. We must inflict pain, or else we are not a "real man."

THE SHORT, BITTERSWEET LIFE OF TUPAC SHAKUR

The recently deceased gangsta rap artist Tupac Shakur is a good, albeit extreme, example of a young African American who was caught up in the web of nonrelational sex. I include him in this chapter for several reasons. First, for many young African Americans, Tupac was among the most popular of all rap artists. Second, looking at Tupac's life, we can better understand the impact of rap music and rappers on sexuality in the African American community. Moreover, a critical summation of Tupac's life and influence may alert African American youth to the negatives of irresponsible sexuality and the abuse of African American girls and women.

For many African American men, Tupac represented all of us. As one African American writer said, "Even those who never met Tupac felt like they knew him" (Yotanka, 1996, p. 27). "The internal struggle that did him in is the internal struggle many black men in America face— the battle between positive and negative, wild and refined, mature and immature: It is most frustrating. . . . Negatives seem more fun than positives" (p. 27). Finally, Tupac's history is important for us as African American people. It is tied up with the history of African American revolutionary heroes and she-roes.

The individual members of the extended clan of Tupac Shakur command almost mythic respect in the African American community, especially from African American men. This defining part of Tupac's background, incredibly, has been generally glossed over by observers trying to make sense of the stinging contradictions that permeated his life.

Tupac Amaru Shakur was born in New York City in 1971 to Afeni Shakur, a Black Panther who carried the rapper-to-be in her womb while she sat in jail awaiting trial in the famous case of the Panther 21. She and 20 codefendants were accused of conspiring to blow up several New York City department stores. She was acquitted just a month before Tupac was born.

Tupac was named for an Inca god; his surname, Shakur, is a clan name taken by a group of Black nationalists in New York including Assata Shakur (Joanne Chesimard). Although she was married to a fellow revolutionary, she acknowledged that she had nonrelational sex with two men shortly before Tupac was conceived and was never certain which man was his father.

In interviews, Tupac often said that he never knew his father. The weighty psychic burden was probably too much for the adolescent Tupac to bear. "He told MTV in a 1994 special on the controversy over 'gangsta rap' that, 'I didn't have a father and that makes me cold and bitter'" (Stephney, 1996, p. 5). Afeni Shakur subsequently moved in with her brother-in-law, Mutulu. In 1981, when Tupac was 10, Mutulu, accused of crimes including the Brink's robbery (an attempt to procure funds for the Black Liberation Army), went underground. Tupac's final album was dedicated to Mutulu, who is now serving a 60-year prison sentence.

If life for African American men having nonrelational sex is rough, it also takes a great toll on African American women, like Tupac's mother.

She turned to drugs and was unable to help him through his adolescence. Tupac often expressed ambivalence about his relationship with his mother, but earnestly wrote about the hardships of African American women who bring children that they cannot emotionally support into the world. The million-selling single "Dear Mama," an open letter to Afeni, reveals Tupac's inner conflict/love regarding his relationship with her.

Tupac's rap "Brenda's Got a Baby" tells African American girls in nonrelational sex not to despair; in a later song, "Keep Ya Head Up," he appears to be an advocate for women. But other lyrics, for example, those of "Tha' Lunatic," are degrading to women.

In 1993, a young African American woman was introduced to Tupac in a club. She charged that she went to Tupac's hotel room and was sexually assaulted by several of his bodyguards in his presence. According to Tupac, she "went down on her knees and opened his pants and performed oral sex on him right there on the dance floor." Further, "she had wanted to continue their sexual encounter, but Shakur claimed he found her repulsive and she continued to call his hotel leaving explicit messages." Tupac claimed that the police erased these tapes ("Shot in Vegas," 1996, p. 3). Ironically, Tupac died just as the appeal of his conviction was about to be heard.

The charismatic Tupac was a gangsta rapper whose life was framed by the Black nationalist movement as well as by nonrelational sex. And for those of us who are older than Tupac, the conclusions of one writer are typical:

> Hard as it may seem for older people to understand, self-destruction by causing bodily harm to others soothes pain and frustration. Drinking alcohol, sniffing coke, taking mescaline tabs [participating in nonrelational sex] and smoking embalming fluid are suicidal symptoms of a larger and more destructive disease. These activities act as placebos to ease the pain. Millions of [African American] youth engage in this type of behavior every day. Why? Because of their perceived plight, they desire to be in a place where they can have peace. (Yotanka, 1996, p. 27)

A CONCLUDING THOUGHT ON ADOLESCENT MALES

As Bill Stephney, CEO of the hip hop/r&b label Step Sun Music remarked, "Though we may be numb to the Tupac murder, it cannot be divorced from the numbness we've developed trying to come up with solutions to the larger problems of African American males in this society." He added that African Americans have transferred "our collective opinions of these men from the Evil Other to the Irrelevant Other" (Stephney, 1996, p. 5). In this context, sexual abuse among African American adolescents becomes the standard operating procedure.

Conclusion

What can we, as African American men, do to solve the problems that result from nonrelational sex? The sexuality of African American men, like that of all other men, is largely a product of male socialization. However, unlike that of White men, African American male sexuality is powerfully affected by racism, economic disadvantage, and inequities of power. Therefore, efforts to change nonrelational sexuality among African American men cannot be divorced from the general enterprise of empowering African American men and eliminating oppression. While these fundamental tasks are not the exclusive responsibility of African American men, there are, nevertheless, many things that we can do to begin to deal with this situation.

1. We need to set positive examples for our young men. When they see violence against African American women, they learn that this is appropriate behavior.
2. We need to honor the scholar as much as we honor the athlete. Schools must develop programs, including the appropriate counseling, to help African American students marry the idea of academic pursuit and African American pride. Educators must develop programs that make writing and academic pursuits into traits which are envied by young African Americans. Those we need to put on pedestals are not the Mike Tysons, but the James Baldwins and the Arthur Ashes.
3. We need to understand that the African American community must encourage inclusion. In order for us to progress, we need the help of women as well as men, of gays as well as straights, of African Americans as well as Caucasians. And as men, we need to teach our children about the contributions of women and gays to African American progress. In short, we must cast off racism, sexism, and heterosexism in our community.

4. "Assign yourself." Marian Wright Edelman tells the following story: "My daddy [an African American man] used to ask us whether the teacher gave us any homework. If we said no, he'd say, 'Well, assign yourself.'" In other words, don't wait for others to tell you what to do to help your children. As one African American man said, "For us to attack the problem we have to accept . . . ownership. If we don't want the White man to control us, what we must do is talk about these things ourselves. . . . No one has taken a black man's hand and balled it up to hit a [n African American] woman in [her] face." (Briggs & Davis, 1994, p. 50).

5. Use your political power. Go out and vote. African American women continue to make up the majority of the workers in the civil rights movement. We need to use our sisters as examples, and become more politically involved in the work of the Civil Rights Movement, including voting. Too often, we men have reaped the rewards and the leadership positions, while the sisters have done the "dirty work."

6. Attend a church, synagogue, or temple. Most of the leaders of the Civil Rights struggle (as early as Nat Turner) grew out of the African American church. This is our only independent African American institution. Why not use it to gain political and economic rights here on Earth, rather than waiting until you are dead? Again, our sisters have shown us the way. They are in the church, but we are not.

7. "Send your children to the library." Years ago, Arthur Ashe observed that African American men "expend too much time, energy, and effort raising, praising and teasing our black children as to the dubious glories of professional sport," rather than realizing that "your son has less than 1 chance in 1,000 of becoming a pro. Would you bet your son's future on something with odds of 999 to 1 against you? I wouldn't" (Ashe, 1977, p. A-30).

8. Use your economic power. As African American men, we waste too much money on sneakers, on having some White man's name on our behind (on brand-name jeans), and on legal and illegal drugs, including cigarettes and alcohol. Why not invest this money instead in our communities, in our families? Aside from the economic benefits, such action would also improve gender and household relations in our community.

9. Remember your roots. African American men (and women) have been maligned throughout history. The story is told of George Payne of Virginia, who wept when his child was sold away from him, and of another Virginia slave who chopped off his hand with

a hatchet to prevent his being sold away from his son. We need to remember our roots, and emulate our fathers in defense of our community.

10. Join a men's group. This was a suggestion made at the Million Man March in October, 1995. Gain strength from the other brothers in the struggle.

11. Don't be afraid of taking risks, of being criticized. We need a new definition of manhood in our community. This definition would include speaking up for the oppressed—women, children, the disabled, gays—in our community. This requires real courage and few of us have had this much courage as part of our arsenal of African American manhood.

An African American woman, Maya Angelou, said it best, "There is brutality against blacks, vandalism against Jews, battering against Asians and bashings against gays. And if it . . . happens to one group, the others seem to sit on their hands, not realizing that the cruelties against one are cruelties against all. And we all pay" (McClean & Lyles, 1993, p. 1).

References

Adam, B. D. (1993). Composite portrait of inferiorized people. In V. McClean & L. Lyles (Eds.), *Solutions to problems of race, class, and gender.* Dubuque, IA: Kendall/Hunt.

Alda, A. (1993). What every woman should know about men. In V. McClean & L. Lyles (Eds.), *Solutions to problems of race, class and gender.* Dubuque, IA: Kendall/Hunt.

Asante, M. K. (1980). *Afrocentricity: The theory of social change.* Buffalo, NY: Amulefi.

Ashe, A. (1977, February 6). Send your children to the library. *New York Times,* p. 23.

Baraka, A. (1969). *Black magic.* New York: Bobbs-Merrill.

Barrett, D., & Geller, D. (1996, September 14). Rapper Tupac dead. *New York Post,* p. 5.

Blumenfield, W. J., & Raymond, D. (1993). A discussion about differences: The left-hand analogy. In V. Cyrus (Ed.), *Experiencing race, class, and gender in the United States.* Mountain View, CA: Mayfield.

Bowman, M. (1993). Why we burn: Sexism exorcised. In V. McClean & L. Lyles (Eds.), *Solutions to problems of race, class, and gender.* Dubuque, IA: Kendall/Hunt.

Bowser, B. P. (1991). *Black male adolescents: Parenting and education in community context*. Lanham, MD: University Press of America.

Bowser, B. P. (1994). Black men and AIDS: Prevention and black sexuality. In R. G. Majors & J. U. Gordon (Eds.), *The American black male: His present status and his future*. Chicago: Nelson.

Braithwaite, R. L. (1981). Interpersonal relations between black males and black females. In L. E. Gary (Ed.), *Black men* (pp. 83–97). Beverly Hills, CA: Sage.

Briggs, J., & Davis, M. D. (1994, September 30). Putting domestic violence on the black agenda, the brutal truth. *Emerge*, p. 11.

Bulls' Rodman tells why he doesn't date black women. (1996, June 17). *Jet*, p. 49.

Cyrus, V. (1993). *Experiencing race, class, and gender in the United States*. Mountain View, CA: Mayfield.

DiIulio, J. J., Jr. (1996, July 31). Stop crime where it starts. *New York Times*, p. A-15.

Edelman, M. W. (1991, April 1). What can we do to help black children beat the odds. *The Black Collegian*, p. 112.

Edwards, A. F. C., & Spurlock, J. (1988). *Black families in crisis: The middle class*. New York: Brunner/Mazel.

Farley, J. E. (1995). *Majority-minority relations* (3rd ed.). Englewood Cliffs: Prentice-Hall.

Farrell, W. (1992). *The myth of male power*. New York: Simon & Schuster.

Findings of family violence study released by Justice Department. (1994, August 1). *Jet*, p. 26.

Franklin, J. H., & Moss, A. A., Jr. (1994). *From slavery to freedom: A history of African-Americans*. New York: McGraw-Hill.

Gary, L. E. (1981). *Black men*. Beverly Hills, CA: Sage.

Genovese, E. (1978). *Roll, Jordan, roll*. New York: Random House.

Gevisser, M., & Cameron, E. (1995). *Defiant desire: Gay and lesbian lives in South Africa*. New York: Routledge & Kegan Paul.

Goldstein, R. (1990, October 16). We so horny: Sado studs and sugar sluts: America's new sex 'Tude. *The Village Voice*, p. 35.

Graham, L. O. (1995). *Member of the club: Reflections on life in a racially polarized world*. New York: HarperCollins.

Grier, W. H., & Cobbs, P. M. (1968). *Black rage*. New York: Basic Books.

Grier, W. H., & Cobbs, P. M. (1972). *The Jesus bag*. New York: McGraw-Hill.

Hemphill, E. (Ed). (1991). *Brother to brother: New writings by black gay men*. Boston: Alyson.

Howell, R. (1996, September 18 to September 24). Tupac Shakur: Conflict and contribution. *City Sun*.

Hutchinson, E. O. (1996). *Beyond OJ: Race, sex, and class. Lessons for America*. CA: Middle Passage Press.

Ines, J. (1995, October 15). Simpson verdict raises awareness on domestic violence. *Oakland Post*, p. 2.

Jourard, S. M. (1971). *The transparent self.* New York: Van Nostrand-Reinhold.

Kaplan, L. (1994, June/July). Bill T. Jones on top. *Poz Magazine*, pp. 40–44.

Madhubuti, H. R. (1978). *Enemies: The class of races.* Chicago: Third World Press.

Madhubuti, H. R. (1991). *Black men: Obsolete, single, dangerous? The African American family in transition.* Chicago: Third World Press.

Majors, R. G., & Gordon, J. U. (1994). *The American black male: His present status and his future.* Chicago: Nelson-Hall.

Marriott, M. (1996, September 16). Shots silence angry voice sharpened by the streets. *New York Times*, p. A-1.

McClean, V., & Lyles, L. (Eds.). (1993). *Solutions to problems of race, class, and gender.* Dubuque, IA: Kendall/Hunt.

Mithers, C. L. (1993). The war against women. In V. McClean & L. Lyles (Eds.), *Solutions to problems of race, class, and gender.* Dubuque, IA: Kendall/Hunt.

O.J.'s dad was [a] drag queen who died of AIDS. (1994, July 12). *The Globe*, pp. 3–4.

O'Reilly, K. (1994). *Black Americans: The FBI files.* New York: Carroll & Graf.

Osayande, E. (1995, September 1). Brothers, it's time to STOP. Respect our sisters. *Philadelphia Tribune*, p. 7-A.

Osayande, E. (1996, September 18 to September 24). Tupac's death marks gangsta rap's demise. *City Sun.*

Page, C. (1996, June 17). Domestic abuse accusations. *Liberal Opinion Week*, p. 29.

Pareles, J. (1989, September 10). There's a new sound in pop music: Bigotry. *New York Times*, Sec. 2, p. 1.

Pareles, J. (1994, February 29). A little hate music please. *New York Times*, p. 23.

Perry, B. (1992). *Malcolm X: The life of a man who changed black America.* New York: Station Hill Press.

Pleck, J. (1981). *The myth of masculinity.* MA: MIT Press.

Rodman, D., & Keown, T. (1996). *Bad as I wanna be.* New York: Delacorte Press.

Shot in Vegas, Shakur has 50–50 chance to live. (1996, September 14). *Amsterdam News*, pp. 3, 30.

Simmons, R. (1991). Some thoughts on the challenges facing black gay intellectuals. In E. Hemphill (Ed.), *Brother to brother: New writings by black gay men.* Boston: Alyson.

Snake eyes. (1989, December 12). *The Village Voice*, p. 16.

Staples, R., & Johnson, L. B. (1993). *Black families at the crossroads: Challenges and prospects.* San Francisco: Jossey-Bass.

Stephney, B. (1996, September 17 to September 24). The death of Tupac Shakur. *City Sun.*

Strauss, N. (1995, June 5). Rap's a 10% slice of the recording industry pie. *New York Times*, p. D-8.

Strong, B., DeVault, C., & Sayad, B. W. (1996). *Core conceptions in human sexuality.* Mountain View, CA: Mayfield.

Tupac's death marks gangsta rap's demise. (1996, September 18 to September 24). *City Sun,* p. 4.

Walker, A. (1983). *In search of our mothers' gardens.* New York: Harcourt Brace Jovanovich.

Yotanka, D. (1996, September 18 to 24). Try to understand my brother. *The City Sun,* p. 5.

Zilbergeld, B. (1992). *Male sexuality.* Boston: Little, Brown.

CHAPTER 10

Gay Men and Nonrelational Sex

ROY SCRIVNER

THIS CHAPTER FOCUSES on nonrelational sex between gay men, from the perspective of traditional male gender role socialization. Research suggests that nearly one-third (28.5%) of gay men engage in nonrelational sex (Jay & Young, 1979). One purpose of this chapter is to bring greater attention to the less severe problems, such as sexual compulsivity, of nonrelational sex among gay men that are not as well-known as commonly recognized problems. Gay sexual compulsivity, the etiology of which includes traditional male gender role socialization, has been addressed elsewhere (Kalichman & Rompa, 1995; Pincu, 1989). This compulsivity is well-recognized as a significant problem among gay men as reflected in the large number of advertisements and related articles in gay publications that focus on treatment of the problem.

In the United States, a contextual analysis of sexual attitudes and behaviors indicates that these attitudes and behaviors are more conservative than is sometimes depicted. The negative effects of these attitudes, as well as the negative effects of heterosexism and of the traditional male gender role, on gay men and their relationships with one another will be discussed. Same-gender sexual relations in the context of different ethnic and cultural groups will also be addressed. To gain a more comprehensive understanding of gay male sexual relations, the Gay and Lesbian Couple Assessment Model (GLCAM) will be presented.

I initially agreed to write a paper on Gay and Bisexual Men and Nonrelational Sex. However, I came to the conclusion that addressing both types of men could not be done in one chapter. Therefore, I elected to write only about gay men, as I am more knowledgeable about gay than bisexual issues.

Differences between gay men and heterosexual men and women in attitudes toward casual sexual relations outside of a couple relationship will be explored. Sexual relations of single gay men will be reviewed. Some of the negative consequences related to nonrelational sex will be identified. Like sexual attitudes and practices of heterosexuals, the sexual attitudes and practices of gay men are more conservative than frequently depicted.

Recommendations will be made for empirical research that may contribute to: (a) a more comprehensive understanding of nonrelational sex among gay men; and, (b) the prevention and reduction of negative effects from this type of sexual relating.

The Broader Context—Sex in the United States

There have been numerous media reports of a sexual revolution during the 1970s in the United States. However, Klausen, Williams, Levitt, and O'Gorman (1989) and Smith (1994) document the lack of a sexual revolution during this period and a continuation of sexually conservative attitudes. Their findings conflict with the popular conception of sex in America, an image heavily influenced by sexually-explicit messages in the media, suggesting that the popular view is incorrect (Michael, Gagnon, Laumann, & Kolata, 1994). Further indications that the popular view of sex is incorrect include: (a) media reports of the resistance to sex education in the schools; (b) resistance to the use of sexually-explicit materials used in AIDS prevention; and, (c) until recently, the ban on condom advertisements on television.

Science is expected to be value-free; yet conservative sexual attitudes dominate this area (Mosher, 1989; Sonenschein, 1987). To illustrate, John Money (1986) notes that the study of reproductive behavior is considered more respectable than the study of sex. He reports that reproductive biologists and sexologists seldom attend the same meetings or publish together in the same journals.

Michael and his colleagues (1994, pp. 10–11, 27–28) chronicle the history of their initiative to study AIDS, supported by leading scientists and administrators of many federal agencies, that was refused federal funding because of sex-negative attitudes in the U.S. Congress. The study, a random survey of American attitudes toward sex, was later funded by foundations and is considered one of the best such surveys in recent history. In their study, Michael et al. (1994) divided their respondents into seven normative orientations toward sexuality based on their response to questionnaires (Table 10.1).

TABLE 10.1
Description of Seven Normative Orientations toward Sexuality

Orientation	Description
1. Traditional Conservative Pro-choice	Respondents in this group (30.6% of the sample) say that religious beliefs guide their behavior; same-gender relations are always wrong; that there should be legal restrictions on abortion; and premarital sex, teenage sex, and extramarital sex are wrong. There are two subgroups: (a) *conservative* and (b) *pro-choice*. The difference is that the pro-choice group believe a woman should be able to have an abortion.
2. Relational Religious Conventional Contemporary religious	Respondents in this group (44.3% of their sample) believe that sex should be a part of a loving relationship, but that it need not be restricted to marriage. Most respondents in this group say sex outside of a couple relationship is wrong and that they would not have sex with someone whom they did not love. There are three subgroups: (a)*religious*: tend to oppose abortions and same gender sexual relations and say that religious beliefs shape their sexual behavior; (b) *conventional*: are less influenced by religious beliefs and are more tolerant than the religious group toward teenage sex, pornography, and abortion; most in this group think that same gender sex and sex outside a couple relationship is wrong; and (c) *contemporary religious*: are much more tolerant of homosexuality and say they are guided by their religious beliefs.
3. Recreational Pro-life Libertarian	Respondents in this group (25.1% of the sample) believe that sex does not have to be restricted to a love relationship. There are two subgroups: (a) *pro-life*: oppose both same gender sex and abortion but are more accepting of teenage sex, sex outside of a couple relationship, and pornography, and (b) *libertarian*: have more accepting attitudes on all of the issues addressed in the *pro-life* group. None of the respondents in the *libertarian* group consider religion as a guide to their sexual behavior.

Michael et al. (1994) report that 60.8 percent of all respondents agree with the statement, "Premarital sex among teenagers is always wrong"; 76.7 percent agree with the statement, "Extramarital sex is always wrong"; 64 percent agree with the statement, "Same-gender sex is always wrong"; and 65.7 percent agree with the statement, "I would not have sex with someone unless I was in love with them."

The findings of Michael et al. (1994) indicate that a high percentage of individuals in the United States have sexually conservative attitudes. Additionally, the study's respondents claimed that their behavior was consistent with their beliefs about sex.

From 23.3 percent to 39.2 percent of the respondents answered the questions in a way that indicated that their sexual attitudes and behaviors were *not* conservative. Michael et al. (1994) also noted that some individuals reported having many sexual partners. These individuals tended to select partners who also had many partners and who tended not to form long-term relationships.

Predominantly conservative sexual attitudes and behaviors have created contexts that are not conducive to the open discussion of heterosexual sexuality among heterosexual men and women. This situation contributes to men's difficulty integrating their sexual and romantic feelings and to nonrelational sexuality. Because these contexts do not accept same-gender sexual relations, it is difficult for gay men to acknowledge and discuss their same-gender sexual and romantic feelings. This situation also contributes to reduced levels of relational connection in gay men's sexual interactions.

Conservative religious beliefs, because they are not accepting of same-gender sexual relations, make it difficult for gay men to find contexts to acknowledge and discuss their religious and spiritual issues (Paul, Hays, & Coates, 1995). Lacking such contexts, some partners in gay couples do not discuss the religious and spiritual aspects of their relationship, including their sexual relationship (Haldeman, 1996; Hay & Roscoe, 1996). Another factor that contributes to difficulties that gay partners may have in acknowledging and discussing the religious and spiritual aspects of their relationship is the traditional male gender role to be nonfeminine in any way and to be nonexpressive of emotions (see Levant, Chapter 1). This also can contribute to a nonrelational quality of such relationships.

SODOMY LAWS

Sodomy laws provide further evidence of the lack of acceptance of heterosexual sexual relations (except for procreation) and of same-gender sexual relations. Such laws, existent in every state in the United States until 1962, were based on religious regulations and intended to prevent nonmarital and nonprocreative sex. Today, these statutes are maintained to prohibit same-gender sexual relations (Purcell & Hicks, 1996). Fourteen states have laws prohibiting sodomy between both heterosexual and same-gender couples (Idaho, Utah, Arizona, Minnesota, Louisiana, Mississippi, Alabama, Georgia, Florida, South Carolina, North Carolina, Virginia, Massachusetts, and Michigan). Seven states have statutes prohibiting same-gender sex (Oklahoma, Nevada, Montana, Kansas, Missouri, Arizona, and Maryland). In three additional states (Texas, Kentucky, and Tennessee) the status of such statutes is unresolved (National Gay and Lesbian Task Force Policy Institute, 1996).

HOMOPHOBIA / HETEROSEXISM IN THE UNITED STATES

The words *homophobia* and *heterosexism* have come to be used to refer to negative attitudes toward same-gender sexual relations and to gay men and lesbians. There are numerous reasons why the term heterosexism is used as opposed to homophobia; for example, homophobia is not a true clinical phobia, but refers to a set of values or beliefs. Herek (1996, p. 101) defines heterosexism as "the ideological system that denies, denigrates, and stigmatizes any nonheterosexual form of behavior, identity, relationship, or community." The word *heterosexism* as just defined will be used in this chapter.

SEXUAL ORIENTATION / AFFECTIONAL ORIENTATION

Sexual orientation refers to the gender of the person(s) to whom one is sexually attracted. *Affectional orientation* refers to the gender of one's love object. For gays and lesbians, someone of the same gender is the love object. For bisexuals, it is both genders. For heterosexuals, it is someone of the opposite gender. Because the term sexual orientation focuses on an individual's sexual relations, its use contributes toward thinking of gays and lesbians only in terms of how they have sex. Therefore, the term affectional orientation is increasingly preferred, as this designation focuses on the love, as distinct from the sexual, relationships of lesbians and gay men. In this chapter, reference will be made both to same-gender sexual and same-gender affectional orientations.

Gay Men's Development of Positive Gay Gender Roles

Levant (Chapter 1) has described the male gender role in the United States, as informed by traditional masculinity ideology, as prescribing the following: Men should be strong and self-reliant, tough and aggressive, achievement-oriented and status-seeking, nonfeminine in any way, nonexpressive of emotions, nonrelational in their sexuality, and fearful and disdainful of homosexuals. Men are not only expected to be fearful and disdainful of homosexuals, but are also taught to reject any personal same-gender sexual feelings.

We have seen that the development of a positive gay gender role is a direct violation, and perhaps the most severe violation, of the traditional male gender role. Gay men who overcome this socialization and ultimately develop positive gay gender roles typically go through stages in reaching an acceptance of their same-gender sexual and affectional orientation.

Stages in the Development of a Positive Gay Gender Role

Stages in the development of a positive gay gender role have been reported by Scrivner and Eldridge (1995) and are described in Table 10.2.

Gay Adolescents

Although increasing numbers of gay and lesbian adolescents are accepting and disclosing their same-gender sexual and affectional orientation (Savin-Williams & Cohen, 1996), most gay men experience their "gay adolescence" several to many years after their chronological adolescence (as noted in the stage of Identity acceptance in Table 10.2).

There are few studies of gay adolescent affectional relations and the data are very preliminary. In one study, less than 20 percent had their first same-sex sexual experience in the context of dating or romance. A study of 29 gay adolescents by Remafedi (1987a, 1987b) found that 10 had a steady male partner and 11 had been in a gay relationship. All but 2 of the 29 hoped for a steady partner in the future. Gay and bisexual youth who have a large number of same-gender romantic relationships are high in self-esteem and are more likely to be publicly "out" to friends and families (Savin-Williams, 1996a).

TABLE 10.2
Stages in the Development of Positive Gay Identities

Stages	Description
Desensitization	In this stage, gay men develop a gender role that does not accept same-gender sexual feelings, and the meaning of the word, homosexual, is negative. Gay men may be aware of wanting a closer affectional relationship with other males than other males seem to want with them. However, this desire for a closer affectional relationship with other males is not associated with homosexuality.
Identity confusion	At the beginning of this stage, a gay male thinks of himself as heterosexual and begins to have thoughts, feelings, or behaviors that could be defined as homosexual. Very few gay men are initially comfortable with the possibility that they might be gay. Most feel shame and guilt about not conforming to a heterosexual gender role.
Identity comparison	In this stage, a gay man begins to think of himself as homosexual and perceives that all the guidelines and hopes he had for a heterosexual life may not fit. Any grief work related to giving up a heterosexual model of life may begin in this stage and may continue into later stages.

TABLE 10.2 *(continued)*
Stages in the Development of Positive Gay Identities

Stages	*Description*
Identity tolerance	In this stage, there is greater commitment to the thought, "I am probably homosexual." Feelings of shame about not living up to a heterosexual gender role may be present. This is a time of isolation, when one is not intimate about one's concerns with either heterosexuals or gays. Connecting with other gays is seen as necessary to reduce the isolation.
Identity acceptance	In this stage, a gay man develops a gay gender role accepting of same gender sexual relations and an affectional orientation for someone of the same gender. He develops an identity as a gay man that includes a social identity of being a member of a gay and lesbian minority group (Cox & Gallios, 1996). A critical evaluation of negative attitudes and incorrect information about gays and lesbians that has been introjected from the dominant culture begins. Heterosexuals typically begin to deal with their sexual and love feelings during adolescence. Most gay men do not have the opportunity to do this during their chronological adolescence. They do this from a few to many years afterward in adulthood during this stage, which is referred to as their "gay adolescence." During this period of their gay adolescence, they may exhibit signs typical of chronological heterosexual adolescents (e.g., being giddy, becoming infatuated with different people every day, and changing style of hair and clothing).
First relationships	Gay men in this stage face the developmental task of learning to function in a same-gender sexual and affectional relationship and becoming comfortable with the related intimacy. Some gay men who have related primarily on a sexual basis may have to learn to integrate their affectional and sexual feelings.
Identity commitment	In this stage, a gay man is committed to the gay gender role. Even if he could change to a heterosexual gender role, he would not do so. There may be a separation between the gay and lesbian subculture and the dominant heterosexual culture with a devaluation of heterosexuals.
Identity synthesis	In this stage, gay men are more integrated in the heterosexual dominant culture; being gay is considered only one part of one's identity. There is some criticism of the description of this stage, as it suggests that gay and lesbian leaders and gays and lesbians with a strong identity as members of a minority group may not have reached their maximal development (Cox & Gallas, 1996; Eliason, 1996). This stage was taken from Cass (1979), who developed the Stage Allocation Measure (SAM) to assess these stages. The SAM has been modified to include references to political activism supportive of gay and lesbian rights (Kahn, 1991).

Savin-Williams (1996a), in a study of gay, lesbian, and bisexual youth, reported that 90 percent of the females and two-thirds of the males stated that they had romantic relations both with same and opposite sex partners; 60 percent of these relationships were with same-gender partners. In five samples of gay and bisexual male youths, over one-half reported that they had heterosexual relations. Savin-Williams (1996a) has found that between 67 percent and 75 percent of lesbian and bisexual adolescents engaged in heterosexual sexual experiences, even though most did not find those experiences to be enjoyable.

Although many gay male adolescents want a friendship or romantic relationship with another gay youth, they must hide their sexual orientation and cannot be intimate either with heterosexual or gay peers. Their isolation may be worsened when they cannot disclose their orientation to family members.

The experience of disclosure is frequently not positive. In one study, 50 percent of gay youth who had experienced disclosure or discovery of their sexual orientation by family or friends reported that the experience was negative (Rotherman-Borus, Hunter, & Rosario, 1991). A study by Hunter (1990) reported that 46 percent of gay and lesbian adolescents reported being physically abused by family members upon disclosure of their sexual orientation. Rejection impedes intimacy with family members and peers and can inhibit the gay adolescent's individuation and separation.

Gay youth must choose from a much smaller pool of people with the same sexual and affectional orientation than is available to heterosexual youth and, therefore, may need to develop social relationships with gay adolescents who are lacking in preferred personal characteristics. The potential for developing satisfying affectional relationships with no sexual relating is decreased. When sexual relating does occur, the experience may be less than optimally satisfying due to the lower quality of the affectional relation.

Gay youths who are open about their affectional orientation must develop a positive identity in the midst of heterosexist attitudes. This is a challenge for both adults and adolescents, who lack some of the psychological assets of adults. Those who keep their orientation secret are delayed in dealing with other developmental concerns that are typical of adolescents until they reach adulthood. Some gay adolescents who first learn to relate sexually in anonymous encounters may later face another problem of learning to integrate their sexual and affectional feelings. "Coming out" and disclosing one's same-gender affectional orientation, whether during one's chronological adolescence or later during adulthood, can be related to the separation and individuation processes.

ETHNIC AND CULTURAL ISSUES

Lesbian and gays from African American and African Caribbean communities often report that these communities are extremely hetero-sexist (Greene & Boyd-Franklin, 1996), partially because of their strong conservative religious and spiritual orientations. In some ethnic groups, the male gender role is even more restrictive than the White male gen-der role (Levant & Majors, in press; Levant, Wu, & Fisher, 1996) and the consequences for violating the male gender role may be more severe (Ernst, Francis, Nevels, & Lemeh, 1991; Savin-Williams, 1996b, p. 156). Greene and Boyd-Franklin (1996) note that African Americans and Native Americans, who have faced racist genocidal practices, gave greater importance to reproduction as a means of ensuring group sur-vival than did other groups. Asian and Pacific Islander communities in the United States emphasize the obligation of men to marry to continue the family name. In these communities, homosexuality is seen as a re-jection of cultural values or as a form of social deviance that brings shame to the family (Choi, Salazar, Lew, & Coates, 1995). Thus, in African American, Native American, Asian American, and Pacific Is-lander groups in America, gay men may be under more pressure to adopt a heterosexual role and to marry and have children.

Morales (1989) describes a five-stage model for the development of positive gay gender role for men from ethnic minority groups:

- *Stage 1:* Denial of conflicts is prevalent. Individuals minimize the discrimination against their ethnic group. There may or may not be identification as lesbian or gay. If so, individuals experience their sexual orientations as having limited significance.
- *Stage 2:* Some ethnic gays prefer to identify themselves as bisexual in an effort to maintain support in both worlds. The lesbian and gay communities may be perceived as White communities, and identifica-tion with these communities could be perceived as a betrayal of alle-giance to ethnic community.
- *Stage 3:* Conflicts in allegiances deepen. Loyalty conflicts between one's ethnic group and the gay community are intensified.
- *Stage 4:* Establishing priorities in allegiances begins. Priority is often give to the ethnic group first. There may be anger and resentment to-ward this group for lack of acceptance as a gay person, as well as anger toward the White gay community for discrimination against one's ethnicity.
- *Stage 5:* The principle task of this stage is the integration of the vari-ous communities, and the development of a multicultural perspective

is the outcome. Anxiety, alienation, and isolation result when there is limited support for integration of both ethnic and gay identity.

INTERRACIAL COUPLES

In their study of African American lesbians and gays, Peplau, Cochran, and Mays (1997) found that more than a third were in interracial relationships. They attribute this, in part, to a limited number of partner choices in the African American communities and the movement of gays and lesbians into urban gay social communities that are more tolerant of interracial couples. Similar explanations have been given for reports that most gay Asian American men have partners from a different race (Nakajima, Chan, & Lee, 1996).

Greene (1997) offers additional ethnic and cultural diversity perspectives on lesbians and gay men. Scrivner and Eldridge (1995, p. 331) provide a comprehensive list of references addressing ethnic gay male and lesbian issues.

SAME-GENDER SEXUAL RELATIONS AMONG ETHNIC GROUPS IN THE UNITED STATES

Manalansan (1996) reports that some Latino, Black, and Asian men may have same-gender sexual relations and still consider themselves heterosexual. Carballo-Dieguez (1995) reports that Puerto Rican men who take the insertive role in anal and oral sex with other Puerto Rican men consider themselves heterosexual. Puerto Rican men who identify themselves as "drag queens" practice mainly receptive oral and anal sex. Those Puerto Rican men who identify as "gay" are more versatile, engaging in both receptive and insertive oral and anal sex.

SAME-GENDER SEXUAL RELATIONS AMONG MEN IN OTHER CULTURES

Among men in Mexico there is stigma toward the men who play the anal receptive role, but not toward those who play the anal insertive role (Carrier, 1995). The definition of sex differs among cultures. Among Mexicans, Nicaraguans, and Brazilians, oral sex and masturbation are seen as foreplay. If such activities do not include anal sex, the action is not considered "sex" (Carballo-Dieguez, 1995). In a study of sex in Thailand, about half of the respondents did not consider anal sex between two men to be "sex" (Jackson, 1995).

Herdt (1990) notes that sex between older males and youths is a prescribed part of development in many societies (the ancient Greeks, ancient Japan, the Azante of Africa, and New Guinea). These relations are generally part of rituals, such as initiation ceremonies. Such relations almost always occur with the understanding that the youth will later marry and have children.

Gay Male and Lesbian Couple Assessment Model

The author has developed a Gay and Lesbian Couple Assessment Model (GLCAM) for studying gay male and lesbian couple relationships. Use of this model can provide a comprehensive view of gay men's sexual relations. The GLCAM includes an integrated assessment of: (a) the stage of each partner in the development of a positive gay gender role; (b) the differentiation of each partner from family of origin; (c) the stage each partner is at in the development of a gay male or lesbian couple relationship; and (d) the systemic balance of the couple system. This model is similar to the model Schnarch (1995) developed for heterosexuals.

STAGES IN THE DEVELOPMENT OF A POSITIVE GAY GENDER ROLE

These stages have been described in Table 10.2. Partners in ongoing gay couple relationships are typically at or near the same stage of development (Scrivner & Eldridge, 1995). Couple difficulties may develop when partners are at different stages in the development of the gay gender role. Kahn (1991) has provided a measure to assess stages in the development of a positive gay gender role that can be used by therapists and researchers. The work of Kahn (1991) indicates that there is a positive correlation between stages in the development of a positive gay gender role and stages of differentiation from family of origin.

DIFFERENTIATION FROM FAMILY OF ORIGIN

Family theorists posit that two individuals in an ongoing relationship tend to be equally differentiated from their families of origin (Schnarch, 1995). There are varying degrees of empirical support for this theory (Bartle, 1993; Bayer & Day, 1995). Therapists and researchers working from this perspective may be interested in scales that have been developed to measure differentiation (Bray, Williamson, & Malone, 1984; Haber, 1993). Garbarino, Gaa, Swank, McPherson, and Gratch (1995) report gender differences in levels of differentiation.

STAGES OF GAY MALE COUPLE DEVELOPMENT

In their empirical study of gay couples, McWhirter and Mattison (1984) identified six stages (Table 10.3) in gay couple relationships from the first through the twentieth year: (a) blending, (b) nesting, (c) maintaining, (d) building, (e) releasing, and (f) renewing. In this model, individual members of a couple are assessed for the stage at which they are. They found that partners experienced difficulties when they were at different stages.

SYSTEMIC BALANCE

System theory, one of the dominant orientations in family therapy, has three core concepts (Steinglass, 1978): (a) organization, which is concerned with the consistency and patterning of family systems; (b) morphostasis, which refers to the tendency of family systems to function as steady states over time; and (c) morphogenesis, which relates to the evolution of the family system over time. Some assessment measures that are used in measuring changes in family systems include: the Structural Analysis of Social Behavior (Benjamin, 1993); the Personal Authority in the Family System (PAFS) (Bray et al., 1984); Family Adaptability and Cohesion Evaluation Scales (FACES) (Edman, Cole, & Howard, 1990); and the Beavers Systems Model (Hampson, Hulgus, & Beavers, 1991).

The systemic perspective has been criticized by feminists who argue that a typical heterosexual man and woman cannot be in a balanced relationship system because the man in the relationship has more power granted to him in a patriarchal society. Two gay men are far more likely to possess equal power. This issue needs to be assessed with each gay couple since one person may have more than his partner (Thompson, 1994).

USE OF THE GLCAM IN UNDERSTANDING GAY COUPLE SEXUAL RELATIONS

The following example of two gay couples demonstrates the use of the GLCAM:

Two gay men who have not developed a positive gay gender role and who are not well-differentiated from their families of origin form a couple relationship. Each abuses alcohol to alleviate feelings of shame and guilt about not conforming to the dominant male gender role. The alcohol also reduces inhibitions about expressing affection and relating

TABLE 10.3
Gay Male Couple Formation and Development

Stage	Characteristics
1. Blending	Blending refers to an intensity of togetherness, where similarities bind the couple and differences are minimized. The couple does everything together, often to the exclusion of others. There is a feeling of being "in love with love." Sexual activity varies but usually includes several encounters weekly and the relationship is sexually monogamous.
2. Nesting	In the second year, there is a focus on the home. Couples in this stage begin to see each other's shortcomings and discover or create complementariness that enhances compatibility. The partners' decline in being "in love with love" is usually not simultaneous and is often a cause for worry and concern.
3. Maintaining	Maintaining the relationship depends on establishing balances between individualization and togetherness, conflict and its resolution, autonomy and dependence, confusion and understanding. A reemergence of individual differences occurs. This is accompanied by some necessary risk taking, whether in outside sexual liaisons, more time apart, greater self-disclosure, or new separate friendships. Another characteristic of this stage is relying on the relationship.
4. Collaborating	Couples in this stage may unwittingly collaborate to aid the development of boredom and feelings of entrapment. After 5 years together, couples experience a new sense of security and a decreasing need to process their interactions. Collaborative adjustments often lead to effective complementarity, which yields new energy that may lead to mutual as well as individual productivity (such as business partnerships, financial dealings, estate building, or achieving personal gains).
5. Trusting	As the years pass, gay couples trust each other with greater conviction. The trust of stage 5 includes a mutual lack of possessiveness and a strong positive regard for each other. A merger of money and possessions may be a manifestation of this trust. In the latter half of stage 5, there may occur an isolation from the self as manifested by lack of feelings and inattention to personal needs, isolation from the partner by withdrawal and lack of communication and, sometimes, isolation from friends in the same ways. This type of constriction may be related to the men's ages. The relationship is taken for granted.
6. Repartnering	The 20th anniversary appears to be a special milestone for gay male couples. Couples report a renewal of their relationship. Many goals, including financial security, have often been met. Couples in this stage assume that they will be together until separated by death. Personal concerns develop, such as for health and security, fear of loneliness, and death of partner or self. Most are struck by the passage of time and reminisce about their years together.

sexually. This couple relationship is balanced from a systemic perspective and may endure for many years.

In contrast, another couple is formed by two individuals, each having differentiated from their families of origin and developed positive gay gender roles. This couple forms a long-lasting relationship that is balanced from a systemic perspective. The quality of the sexual relationship of the latter is higher than that of the couple who abuses alcohol. Each individual in the couple that abuses alcohol may be in the best type of sexual and affectional relationship in which he can function, given his stage of differentiation and stage in the development of a positive gay gender role.

Outside Sexual Relations of Partners in Gay Couples

Partners in some gay couples have sex with others outside of the primary love relationship. Disagreements about this issue can damage a relationship and may result in termination. The partners may be at different stages in the gay couple relationship. McWhirter and Mattison (1984) found that gay couples began to have outside sexual relations by the end of the maintaining stage and sometimes earlier in the preceding nesting stage. There were conflicts when one partner wanted to begin outside sexual relations earlier than the other partner. A partner in a gay couple relationship may: (a) have sex in the context of a loving relationship with his partner; (b) have sex in the context of a casual, one-time relationship; and (c) engage in nonrelational sex in which he and another person may use one another as sex objects. Some gay men engage in outside sexual relations as a part of their rejection of the values of the dominant heterosexual culture. Others may not engage in outside sexual relations on the basis of religious beliefs. Julien, Chartrand, and Begin (1996) documented that some long-lasting gay couples have outside sexual relations with no threat or harm to the primary relationship.

Comparing Gay Men and Heterosexual Men and Women

SEXUAL AND AFFECTIONAL FEELINGS

Gay and heterosexual men are typically socialized to express sexual feelings before emotional intimacy, whereas women often are socialized to prefer affectional relationships before expressing sexual feelings (Forstein, 1986). Nichols (1987) has noted that, in general, women tend to fuse sex and love. Two gay partners in a committed relationship have typically engaged in casual sexual relations prior to having sex with one another in the context of their loving relationship. Therefore, gay partners have typically had a broader range of sexual experiences that may prepare them to differentiate between casual sex and sex in the context of their love relationship. Gay casual sex outside of a couple relationship typically involves one-time experiences with different partners rather than ongoing sexual affairs with a same partner. Casual sex outside of a couple relationship may be less of an issue of disagreement in gay couple relationships than in heterosexual relationships because men have been socialized to be more comfortable with casual sex, while women have been socialized to fuse sex and love.

POWER

As noted earlier, there is generally more equity of power in gay couple relationships then in heterosexual relationships, in which women often have less power. In gay casual sexual relations, either partner, typically having equal power, may terminate sexual relations at any point. It has been noted by Brooks (Chapter 2) that women typically are the "gatekeepers" in heterosexual sex. It is questionable, however, whether heterosexual women have the same degree of power as gay men to terminate a sexual relationship. This may contribute to heterosexual women being less interested in casual sex.

DIFFERENT CONTEXTS OF GAY AND HETEROSEXUAL COUPLES

Procreation is not part of the contexts of gay male relationships while it typically is a possibility in the contexts of heterosexual sexual relations. Evolutionary psychologists (e.g., Buss, 1995) and the social constructionist view of gender relations (Levant, Chapter 1) take very different approaches to most interpersonal phenomena. They are in general agreement, however, that procreation, or childbirth and child rearing (or the decision to avoid them), are highly significant aspects of any heterosexual relationship. Therefore, it is difficult to compare the outside sexual relations of heterosexual couples, with the possibility of procreation resulting from these relations, with those outside sexual relations of gay couples, in which there is no possibility of procreation.

WAYS OF RELATING SEXUALLY

A major difference between gay and heterosexual couples is that gay men have more ways of sexual relating than do heterosexual men (Nichols, 1989). Based on a study completed prior to the AIDS epidemic, Jay and Young (1977) reported that the following were included as a part of gay male sexuality: stimulation of the penis, testicles, anus, prostate gland, buttocks, nipples, ears, neck, and toes; active and receptive oral intercourse (including ejaculating or not ejaculating into a partner's mouth and swallowing or not swallowing a partner's semen); simultaneous oral intercourse; active and receptive anal intercourse (including ejaculating into partner's rectum or receiving into one's rectum ejaculate from a partner); ejaculation during passive anal intercourse; masturbating a partner or being masturbated; mutual masturbation or rubbing penises together, any of these to the point of orgasm; frottage (two men rubbing their bodies together with penises touching, sometimes reaching orgasm, sometimes not); finger-insertion; and rubbing one's penis between the legs of a partner near the pelvic area (similar to, but not the same as, anal intercourse), sometimes to the point of orgasm, sometimes not; kissing; affection; and mutuality and compatibility.

Some of these practices have changed or been modified with the adoption of safer sex techniques (Paul et al., 1995). Bell and Weinberg (1978) found that in their study of gay men almost all of the men engaged in a variety of sexual techniques and that almost none of them had engaged exclusively in one particular form of sexual contact.

Heterosexuals may participate in some of the same types of sexual relations as do gay men, but vaginal intercourse is the dominant mode of heterosexual sexual relations. It is difficult to compare heterosexual vaginal intercourse, whether in a couple system or outside of a couple system, with the various types of and combinations of types of gay male sexual relations.

Nichols (1989) has noted that penetration is a far greater focus of heterosexual sexual relations than it is in gay male sexual relations. However, for both gays and heterosexuals, penetration may be related to level of trust in a couple system. In a couple system with a low level of trust, both gay men and heterosexual women may be more comfortable with being the recipient of oral intercourse than being penetrated. Only a minimum level of trust in a couple system may be required for both gays and heterosexuals to be comfortable with mutual masturbation.

Sexual Relations of Single Gay Men

DEVELOPMENTAL ISSUES

During their gay adolescence, many gay men seek or fantasize about a partner for a romantic and sexual relationship. They may have several sexual encounters with a minimum of affection. These men may be hurt by their emotional openness and by experiencing themselves as being used primarily as sex objects. Some gay men may conclude that "If this is what gay life is like, I don't want any part of it," and may try to live a heterosexual life. Other gay men may learn to keep their emotions closed and to relate primarily on a sexual basis. They may find this type of nonrelational relating reinforced by others seeking the same type of nonrelational sex. After relating primarily on a nonrelational basis, some gay men find it difficult to respond emotionally to someone who is interested in them for a romantic relationship. With time, some gay men can learn to do so with a caring partner whom they can trust. Others may need formal therapy in order to learn to relate to a partner on an affectional basis and to learn to integrate their sexual and affectional feelings.

Introjected heterosexism is significantly associated with greater fear of intimacy and lower self-esteem in gay men (Frederick & Gibbs, 1995). Thus, gay men who have not reached the stage of identity acceptance are more likely to engage in nonrelational sex. These men are less likely to be selected as partners by gay men with higher self-esteem who seek more intimate relating in their sexual experiences.

Gay men with lower self-esteem can be easy targets for narcissistic or sociopathic men who use them as sex objects. Being used as a sex object can reduce isolation, but comes at the expense of feeling used, humiliated, and rejected, again, by someone with whom one hoped to have an ongoing relationship. Some gay men with low self-esteem tend to develop a gay gender role of having many indiscriminate sexual relations in an attempt to find a permanent partner. Having indiscriminate sex perpetuates a self-fulfilling prophecy of not selecting a partner who might be interested in more than a one-time sexual experience. Gay men with low self-esteem often have less power than their sexual partners.

Gay men must first develop a positive gay gender role and learn to identify potential partners who have preferred personality characteristics. Next, gay men must learn to identify others who are interested in the same degree of relational connection in a sexual encounter—whether distant or close—to be mutually satisfying. If partners have different expectations and wishes about the degree of relational connection in a sexual encounter, there are more likely to be negative consequences of the encounter for at least one, and possibly both, partners.

NONVERBAL COMMUNICATION

Discussions about how gay and heterosexual men use sex as a nonverbal means of communication (Cohler & Galatzer-Levy, 1996) rarely consider the role of this communication in creating a temporary relationship between two gay men in casual and anonymous sexual relations. A physical touch may be rejected if it does not "feel right." Nonverbal communication between two prospective sexual partners is not limited to gay men. Nonverbal checking out between gay men, referred to as "cruising," is a basic skill of many gay men that is often discussed in the gay subculture and included in writings for and about gay men (Cohler & Galatzer-Levy, 1996).

Some gay sexual relations, especially anonymous or one-time experiences, may be initially perceived as two gay men using one another as sex objects. A closer examination of such sexual relations can reveal an affectional connection between two men developed by nonverbal communication.

USE OF THE GLCAM IN UNDERSTANDING SEXUAL ENCOUNTERS OF SINGLE GAY MEN

The GLCAM has previously been described as a means of more comprehensively understanding the sexual and affectional relationship of two gay partners in a committed relationship. Sexual relations between two partners who are in a one-time-only relationship can, also, be more comprehensively understood by use of the GLCAM, as shown in the following example:

> Two gay men meet. Each is equally differentiated from his family of origin, is at the stage of Identity Commitment, and has equal power in the relationship. Both partners are seeking a one-time sexual encounter with a minimum of relational connection. The two men create a temporary couple system that is balanced and enjoy sex with one another. After this encounter the two partners never see one another again.
>
> However, two gay men in a similar encounter may meet again and become long-lasting partners. Evidence that long-lasting couple relationships develop from what might be expected to be one-time encounters is provided by McWhirter and Mattison (1984, p. 210). They found that

over half of the couples that they studied met at a steambath, disco, bar, and other places such as gay beaches.

SAME-GENDER SEXUAL RELATIONS OF HETEROSEXUALLY-IDENTIFIED MEN

In some ethnic minority groups, some men have same-gender sexual relations and consider themselves heterosexual. Some of these men may be active in the gay community and others are not. Those who are not would be expected to be more likely to engage in nonrelational sex because the temporary partner relationship may be the only relationship of which each partner is capable.

Similarly, many White, heterosexually-married fathers have engaged in one-time sexual encounters for many years before falling in love with another man. Falling in love with another man is the most important factor in the decision of these men to "come out" (Patterson & Chan, 1996, p. 377). Prior to falling in love with another man, these men may be more likely to practice nonrelational sex.

Miller (1979) identified four types of gay fathers: (a) "trade" (engages in homosexual behavior but no self-recognition as being gay); (b) "homosexual" (self-recognition but no public identity); (c) "gay" (self-recognition with limited public knowledge); and (d) "faggot" (self-recognition with public identity). Trade and homosexual fathers would be expected to be more likely to engage in nonrelational sex.

Discussion

How serious is the problem of nonrelational sex among gay men? Gay male liberation of the 1970s focused on the celebration of gay male sexuality, an avoidance of constrictive gender roles, and the exploration of new ways of bonding. Sexual experimentation was seen as a way by which gay men could free themselves of societally imposed notions of guilt and shame around homoeroticism (Paul, Hays, Coates, 1995). Based, in part, on reports of some gay sexual relations from the 1970s there have been some media and other reports suggesting that, typically, gay men are: (a) sexually obsessed, (b) able to relate to one another only on a predominantly sexual basis, and (c) unable to form committed couple relationships. However, it appears that these media reports, like the media reports previously discussed which suggested a sexual revolution in America during the 1970s, provide inaccurate information about gay men and exaggerate the percentage of gay men who fit these characteristics.

In their study of gays and lesbians, Jay and Young (1979) asked the men how often they engaged in physical affection (hugging, cuddling, caressing, kissing) with their lovers or their (more casual) sex partners. In regard to "lovers," 70 percent said "always"; 18 percent said "very frequently." For "sex partners," 39 percent said "always"; 43 percent said "very frequently." In response to the question, "How important is emotional involvement in your partner?" 47 percent of gay men said "very important"; 36 percent said "somewhat important." Another question was "When you have sex, how often does it involve emotional involvement?" 13 percent said "always"; 32 percent said "very frequently," and 27 percent said "frequently." Ninety-three percent answered "yes" to the question, "Have you ever been in love?"

Peplau et al. (1996) report that both African American lesbians and gays emphasize socioemotional aspects of a relationship over economic and instrumental concerns, which is consistent with findings on a predominantly White sample of lesbians, gays, and heterosexuals. Thus, for a very high percentage of gay men, affection is an important component of their sexual relations, whether with one-time sex partners or partners in a committed relationship.

Other studies indicate that 40 percent to 60 percent of gay men are in dating or committed relationships. One national survey indicated that 97 percent of gay men had been involved in at least one ongoing relationship during the past 10 years and that 60 percent of the respondents were in a current couple relationship. A study of 500 men in San Francisco indicated that: (a) 86 percent had tried to meet a partner for a monogamous relationship, (b) 79 percent had succeeded in doing so in the past or present, and (c) 48 percent of the respondents who were currently in a relationship reported that the relationship was monogamous. Reports of sex outside of gay couple primary relationships may also be less frequent than previously considered (Green, Bettinger, & Zacks, 1996).

There are stereotypes that partners in gay couples, socialized as heterosexual men, tend to be disengaged. However, research indicates that among lesbian, gay, and heterosexual couples, lesbian couples have the highest cohesion, gay couples, the next highest, and heterosexual couples, the lowest (Green et al., 1996).

The extended, nonbiologically-related family members of choice of gay men are receiving increasing recognition and also reflect the interest of gay men in having significant affectional relationships. A relationship with a family member of choice is different from that of a primary romantic relationship and cannot offer the same type of intimacy and affection as the latter. Nevertheless, such family relationships can offer caring and long-term support for a gay man, with or without a primary partner. If without a partner, these family relationships can make it easier for a gay man to be satisfied with nonrelational sex. Family members of choice do not necessarily replace family of origin members. Some gay men have cordial to excellent relationships with biological and adoptive family members and still make a distinction between the two types of relationships (Weston, 1991).

Findings that a high percentage of gay men are interested in being coupled, that some gay couple relationships have a high degree of cohesiveness, and that some gay men have long-term supportive relationships with extended nonbiologically-related family members of choice are all consistent with other research findings indicating that gay men are less conforming to the traditional male gender role from childhood through adulthood. Green et al. (1996, p. 212) indicated that 89 percent of gay men display rates of cross-gender behavior that are above the median rate for heterosexual men. There is the possibility that gay men, particularly those in ongoing couple relationships, have distinctive relational styles, abilities, and values that differ from those of heterosexual men—or at least the traditional male gender role (Green et al., 1996).

PREVALENCE OF NONRELATIONAL SEX AND SOME RELATED PROBLEM AREAS

Jay and Young (1979) found that, in response to the question, "When you have sex, how often does it include emotional involvement?" 17 percent said "infrequently," 10 percent said "very infrequently," 0.5 percent, "once"; and 1 percent, "never." Thus, nearly one-third (28.5%) of their respondents reported that they typically engage in sex with no emotional involvement.

Thus, apparently less than one-third of gay men may fit the stereotype that gay men are predominantly involved in nonrelational sex. Of this less than one-third portion, it is unknown what percent engage in the type of nonrelational sex that is considered sexual compulsivity, previously noted as a well-documented problem area, versus other types of nonrelational sex that are less often identified. In my clinical experience, at least 15 percent to 20 percent of both individual and couple cases include issues of nonrelational sex, with varying degrees of severity, as a problem. Typically, individuals have not sought therapy with nonrelational sex as a presenting problem. Most often nonrelational sex is related to other identified problem areas (e.g., loneliness, boredom, existential dissatisfaction with apparent success in many aspects of life, difficulties in gaining or keeping relationships, sexual dysfunctions created by anxiety related to intimacy, loss of interest in a partner after the "sexual conquest," and stress reduction). Other negative aspects of nonrelational sex have been included in previous discussions of issues of gay adolescents and single gay men.

Recommendations for Future Research

Additional research is needed to estimate the number of gay men who engage in nonrelational sex, and for whom is it harmful. Research questions need to investigate the characteristics of the couple systems in which nonrelational sex occur, along variables such as level of trust, degree of mutuality, nonreciprocal relations, and the relationship of these characteristics to damage from nonrelational sex. Questions need to be asked about the specific types of gay male sexual relating. Is there more damage from nonrelational sex when one is a passive partner in anal intercourse than when one is a recipient of oral intercourse? Hodnett (1991) has noted that gay men tend to choose as partners men who are similar to themselves in terms of self-ratings of masculinity and femininity. Do more "masculine" gay men select one another as partners in nonrelational sex? Is this nonrelational sex more likely to be harmful than nonrelational sex between more feminine or more androgynous partners? While research has indicated that many gay men play a variety of sexual roles, how many gay men play predominantly the same sex roles in couple systems? Are there differences in degrees of nonrelational connection and any related negative experiences between men who play predominantly the same sexual roles and men who play a variety of sexual roles in all couple systems? Is there any relationship between cohesion in family of origin and nonrelational sexual relations? Are there any differences between gay men who engage primarily in nonrelational sex and have the support of extended, nonbiologically-related family members of choice, and those gay men who engage in nonrelational sex and who lack the support of such family members?

The preceding questions need to assess ethnic differences as well as differences between same-race and interracial couples. Peterson (1992) reports that white gay men select African American gay men as partners partly because the African American gay men are more nurturing than white gay men. The issue of nurturing among different ethnic minority groups needs to be studied and as well as the question of whether some ethnic gay men may be less involved in nonrelational sex.

Until recently, most writing on gay fathers has focused on gay men who became fathers during a heterosexual marriage. Increasing numbers of gay men are becoming fathers by adoption, use of surrogate mothers, and other means (Patterson & Chan, 1996). A cursory knowledge of what most of these gay men go through in order to become a father reveals a tremendous commitment to becoming a father. Very little is known about their sexual relations. The sexual relations of these gay fathers, as well as other significant issues of the families which they create, needs to be researched to gain a broader perspective on nonrelational sex among gay men.

A review of the history of gays, lesbians, and bisexuals in America during the last four decades indicates that between, and sometimes within, decades there have been significant changes in descriptions of these individuals. A noteworthy specific change has been the adoption of safer sex practices by gay men in response to the AIDS epidemic with significant declines in rates of all types of sexually transmitted disease. Whether changes in nonrelational sex has concurrently occurred is not known. However, a decrease in the number of sexual partners of gay men and an increase in the number of gay partners forming committed relationships has been noted (Paul et al., 1995). During the last four decades, there have also been contextual changes, reflecting increased recognition and acceptance of lesbians, gays, and bisexuals.

Existing research needs to be repeated to discover if what was true in previous decades is true for this decade. Many gay research studies have sampling problems (e.g., ethnic groups and different socioeconomic groups are under-represented or not included at all). Additional efforts need to be made toward gaining representative samples of gay men. Probability sampling offers one approach toward finding more representative samples (Harry, 1990).

Thus, the validity of the conclusions of this chapter are limited due to the research issues identified above. It is hoped this chapter will stimulate current research on these issues and bring increased awareness to the negative effects that can result from nonrelational sex among gay men and to interventions that may be used to prevent and reduce such negative effects.

References

Bartle, S. E. (1993). The degree of similarity of differentiation of self between partners in married and dating couples: Preliminary evidence. *Contemporary Family Therapy, 15*(6), 467–484.

Bayer, J. P., & Day, H. D. (1995). An empirical couple typology based on differentiation. *Contemporary Family Therapy, 17*(2), 265–271.

Bell, A. P., & Weinberg, M. S. (1978). *Homosexualities: A study of diversity among men and women.* New York: Simon & Schuster.

Benjamin, L. S. (1993). *Interpersonal diagnosis and treatment of personality disorders.* New York: Guilford Press.

Bray, J. H., Williamson, D. S., & Malone, P. E. (1984). Personal authority in the family system: Development of a questionnaire to measure personal authority in inter-generational family processes. *Journal of Marital and Family Therapy, 10,* 168–178.

Buss, D. M. (1995). Psychological sex differences: Origins through sexual selection. *American Psychologist, 50,* 164–168.

Carballo-Dieguez, A. (1995). The sexual identity and behavior of Puerto Rican men who have sex with men. In G. M. Herek & B. Greene (Eds.), *AIDS, identity, and community: The HIV epidemic and lesbians and gay men* (pp. 105–114). Thousand Oaks, CA: Sage.

Carrier, J. (1995). *De Los Otros: Intimacy and homosexuality among Mexican men.* New York: Columbia University Press.

Cass, V. C. (1979). Homosexual identity formation: A theoretical model. *Journal of Homosexuality, 4,* 219–253.

Choi, K.-H., Salazar, N., Lew, S., & Coates, T. J. (1995). AIDS risk, dual identity, and community response among gay Asian and Pacific Islander men in San Francisco. In G. M. Herek & B. Greene (Eds.), *AIDS, identity, and community: The HIV epidemic and lesbians and gay men* (pp. 115–134). Thousand Oaks, CA: Sage.

Cohler, B. J., & Galatzer-Levy, R. (1996). Self psychology and homosexuality: Sexual orientation and maintenance of personal integrity. In R. P. Cabaj & T. S. Stein (Eds.), *Textbook of homosexuality and mental heath* (pp. 207–223). Washington, DC: American Psychiatric Press.

Cox, S., & Gallois, C. (1996). Gay and lesbian identity development: A social identity perspective. *Journal of Homosexuality, 30*(4), 1–30.

Edman, S. O., Cole, D. A., & Howard, G. S. (1990). Convergent and discriminate validity of FACES-III: Family adaptability and cohesion. *Family Process, 29,* 95–103.

Eliason, M. J. (1996). Identity formation for lesbian, bisexual, and gay persons: Beyond a "Minoritizing" view. *Journal of Homosexuality, 30,* 31–58.

Ernst, F. A., Francis, R. A., Nevels, H., & Lemeh, C. A. (1991). Condemnation of homosexuality in the Black community: A gender-specific phenomenon? *Archives of Sexual Behavior, 20,* 579–585.

Forstein, M. (1986). Psychodynamic therapy with gay male couples. In R. S. Stein & C. J. Cohen (Eds.), *Contemporary perspectives on psychotherapy with lesbians and gay men* (pp. 103–137). New York: Plenum Press.

Frederick, R. J., & Gibbs, M. S. (1995). *Fear of intimacy in gay men.* Paper presented at the annual convention of the American Psychological Association, New York.

Garbarino, J., Gaa, J. P., Swank, P., McPherson, R., & Gratch, L. V. (1995). The relation of individual and psychosocial development. *Journal of Family Psychology, 9*(3), 311–318.

Green, R.-J., Bettinger, M., & Zacks, E. (1996). Are lesbian couples fused and gay male couples disengaged? Questioning gender straight-jackets. In J. Laird & R.-J. Green (Eds.), *Lesbians and gays in couples and families: A handbook for therapists* (pp. 185–230). San Francisco: Jossey-Bass.

Greene, B. (Ed.). (1997). *Psychological perspectives on lesbian and gay issues: Ethnic and cultural diversity among lesbians and gay men.* Newbury Park, CA: Sage.

Greene, B., & Boyd-Franklin, N. (1996). African lesbians: Issues in couple therapy. In J. Laird & R.-J. Green (Eds.), *Lesbians and gays in couples and families: A handbook for therapist* (pp. 251–291). San Francisco: Jossey-Bass.

Haber, J. (1993). A construct validity study of a differentiation of self scale. *Scholarly Inquiry for Nursing Practice: An International Journal, 7,* 165–182.

Haldeman, D. J. (1996). Spirituality and religion in the lives of lesbians and gay men. In R. P. Cabaj & T. S. Stein (Eds.), *Textbook of homosexuality and mental health* (pp. 881–896). Washington, DC: American Psychiatric Press.

Hampson, R. B. (1991). Comparisons of self-report measures of the Beavers Systems Model and Olson's Circumplex Model. *Journal of Family Psychology, 4,* 326–340.

Harry, J. (1990). A probability sample of gay males. *Journal of Homosexuality, 19,* 89–104.

Hay, H., & Roscoe, W. (1996). *Radically gay: Gay liberation in the words of its founder.* Boston: Beacon Press.

Herdt, G. H. (1990). Developmental discontinuities and sexual orientation across cultures. In D. P. McWhirter, S. A. Sanders, & J. M. Reinisch (Eds.), *Homosexuality/heterosexuality: Concepts of sexual orientation* (pp. 208–236). New York: Oxford University Press.

Herek, G. M. (1996). Heterosexism and homophobia. In R. P. Cabaj & T. S. Stein (Eds.), *Textbook of homosexuality and mental health* (pp. 101–113). Washington, DC: American Psychiatric Association.

Hodnett, J. H. (1991). *Correlates of relationship satisfaction in dual-career gay male couples.* Unpublished doctoral dissertation, University of Texas, Austin.

Hunter, J. (1990). Violence against lesbian and gay male youths. *Journal of Interpersonal Violence, 5,* 295–300.

Jackson, P. (1995). *Dear uncle go: Homosexual males in Thailand.* San Francisco: Bua Luang Books.

Jay, K., & Young, A. (1979). *The gay report: Lesbians and gay men speak out about sexual experiences and lifestyles.* New York: Summit.

Julien, D., Chartrand, E., & Begin, J. (1996). Male couples' dyadic adjustment and the use of safer sex within and outside of primary relationships. *Journal of Family Psychology, 10,* 97–106.

Kahn, M. J. (1991). Factors affecting the coming out process for lesbians. *Journal of Homosexuality, 21,* 47–70.

Kalichman, S. C., & Rompa, D. (1995). Sexual sensation seeking and sexual compulsivity scales: Reliability, validity, and predicting HIV risk behavior. *Journal of Personality Assessment, 65*, 586–601.

Klausen, A. D., Williams, C. J., Levitt, E. E., & O'Gorman, H. (1989). *Sex and morality in the U.S.: An empirical inquiry under the auspices of the Kinsey Institute.* Middletown, CT: Wesleyan University Press.

Levant, R. F., Wu, R., & Fisher, J. (1996). Masculinity ideology: A comparison between U.S. and Chinese young men and women. *Journal of Gender, Culture, and Health, 1*(3), 207–220.

Levant, R. F., & Majors, R. G. (in press). An investigation into variations in the construction of the male gender role among young African-American and European-American women and men. *Journal of Gender, Culture, and Health.*

Manalanse M. F., IV (1996). Double minorities: Latino, Black, and Asian men who have sex with men. In R. C. Savin-Williams & K. M. Cohen (Eds.), *The lives of lesbians, gays, and bisexuals: Children to adults* (pp. 373–415). Ft. Worth, TX: Harcourt Brace College.

McWhirter, D. P., & Mattison, A. M. (1984). *The male couple: How relationships develop.* Englewood Cliffs, NJ: Prentice-Hall.

Michael, R. T., Gagnon, J. H., Laumann, E. O., & Kolata, G. (1994). *Sex in America: A definitive survey.* New York: Little, Brown.

Miller, B. (1979). Gay fathers and their children. *The Family Coordinator, 27*, 544–552.

Money, J. (1986). *Venuses penises: Sexology, sexosophy, and exigency theory.* New York: Prometheus.

Morales, E. (1989). Ethnic minority families and minority gays and lesbians. *Marriage and Family Review, 14*, 217–239.

Mosher, D. L. (1989). Advancing sexual science: Strategic analysis and planning. *Journal of Sex Research, 26*, 1–14.

Nakajima, G. A., Chan, Y. H., & Lee, K. (1996). Mental health issues for gay and lesbian Asian Americans. In R. P. Cabaj & T. S. Stein (Eds.), *Textbook of homosexuality and mental health* (pp. 563–581). Washington, DC: American Psychiatric Press.

National Gay & Lesbian Task Force Policy Institute. (1996). Privacy project fact sheet. Washington, DC: Author.

Nichols, M. (1987). Lesbian sexuality: Issues and developing theory. In the Boston Lesbian Psychologies Collective (Eds.), *Lesbian psychologies: Explorations and challenges* (pp. 97–125). Chicago: University of Illinois Press.

Nichols, M. (1989). Sex therapy with lesbians, gay men, and bisexuals. In S. R. Leiblum & R. C. Rosen (Eds.), *Principles and practice of sex therapy: Update for the 1990s* (pp. 269–297). New York: Guilford Press.

Patterson, C. J., & Chan, R. W. (1996). Gay fathers and their children. In R. P. Cabaj & T. S. Stein (Eds.), *Textbook of homosexuality and mental health* (pp. 371–393). Washington, DC: American Psychiatric Press.

Paul, J. P., Hays, R. B., & Coates, T. J. (1995). The impact of HIV epidemic on U.S. gay male communities. In A. R. D'Augelli & C. J. Patterson (Eds.),

Lesbian, gay and bisexual identities over the lifespan: Psychological perspectives (pp. 347–397). New York: Oxford University Press.

Peplau, L. A., Cochran, S. D., & Mays, V. M. (1996). A national survey of the intimate relationships of African American lesbians and gay men: A look at commitment, satisfaction, sexual behavior and HIV disease. In B. Greene & G. Herek (Eds.), *Psychological perspectives on lesbian and gay issues: Ethnic and cultural diversity among lesbians and gay men.* Newbury Park, CA: Sage.

Peterson, J. L. (1992). Black men and their same-sex desires and behaviors. In G. Herdt (Ed.), *Gay culture in American* (pp. 174–164). Boston: Beacon Press.

Pincu, L. (1989). Sexual compulsivity in gay men: Controversy and treatment. *Journal of Counseling and Development, 68,* 63–66.

Purcell, D. W., & Hicks, D. W. (1996). Institutional discrimination against lesbians, gay men, and bisexuals: The courts, legislature, and the military. In R. P. Cabaj & T. S. Stein (Eds.), *Textbook of homosexuality and mental health* (pp. 763–782). Washington, DC: American Psychiatric Press.

Remafedi, G. (1987a). Adolescent homosexuality: Psychosocial and medical implications. *Pediatrics, 79,* 331–337.

Remafedi, G. (1987b). Homosexual youth: A challenge to contemporary society. *Journal of the American Medical Association, 258,* 222–225.

Rotherman-Borus, M. J., Hunter, J., & Rosario, M. (1991). Coming out as lesbian or gay in the era of AIDS. In G. M. Herek & B. Greene (Eds.), *AIDS, identity, and community: The HIV epidemic and lesbians and gay men* (pp. 150–168). Thousand Oaks, CA: Sage.

Savin-Williams, R. C. (1996a). Dating and romantic relationships among gay, lesbian, and bisexual youths. In R. C. Savin-Williams & K. M. Cohen (Eds.), *The lives of lesbians, gays, and bisexuals: Children to adults* (pp. 166–180). Ft. Worth, TX: Harcourt Brace College.

Savin-Williams, R. C. (1996b). Ethnic- and sexual-minority youth. In R. C. Savin-Williams & K. M. Cohen (Ed.), *The lives of lesbians, gays, and bisexuals: Children to adults* (pp. 152–165). Ft. Worth, TX: Harcourt Brace College.

Savin-Williams, R. C., & Cohen, K. M. (Eds.). (1996). *Lives of lesbians, gays, and bisexuals: Children to adults.* Ft. Worth, TX: Harcourt Brace College.

Schnarch, D. M. (1995). A family systems approach to sex therapy and intimacy. In R. H. Mikesell, D. D. Lusterman, & S. H. McDaniel (Eds.), *Integrating family therapy: Handbook of family psychology and systems theory* (pp. 239–257). Washington, DC: American Psychological Association.

Scrivner, R., & Eldridge, N. S. (1995). Lesbian and gay family psychology. In R. H. Mikesell, D. D. Lusterman, & S. H. McDaniel (Eds.), *Integrating family therapy: Handbook of family psychology and systems theory* (pp. 327–445). Washington, DC: American Psychological Association.

Smith, T. W. (1994). Attitudes towards sexual permissiveness: Trends, correlates, and behavioral conditions. In A. S. Rossi (Ed.), *Sexuality across the life course.* Chicago: University of Chicago Press.

Sonenschein, D. (1987). On having one's research seized. *Journal of Sex Research, 23,* 408–414.

Steinglass, P. (1978). Another view of family interaction and psychopathology. In T. Jacobs (Eds.), *Family interaction and psychopathology* (pp. 25–65). New York: Plenum Press.

Thompson, D. (1994). The sexual experiences of men with learning disabilities having sex with men—Issues for HIV prevention. *Sexuality and Disability, 12,* 221–242.

Weston, K. (1991). *Families we choose: Lesbians, gays, kinship.* New York: Columbia University Press.

CODA

Toward the Reconstruction of Male Sexuality: A Prescription for the Future

GARY R. BROOKS AND RONALD F. LEVANT

A S WE NOTED in the Introduction, some readers may consider this book an effort to fix something that isn't really broken. They will see it as an attack on men and an effort to deprive them of their most valued characteristics. Others will concur with our view of contemporary male sexuality, but will exhort us to accept these problems as part of biological or evolutionary reality. They will urge us to accept and celebrate men's sexual "quirks"; they may believe women should loosen up and take on male sexual habits. Finally, there will be readers who share our concerns but worry that changes are foolhardy without realistic alternatives to replace what will be lost.

We hope that the combined weight of the preceding chapters has challenged these positions and that readers will begin to consider our assertions seriously and work toward acceptable solutions.

We are very much in favor of, and sanguine about, a future of enthusiastic participation in sexuality. However, we are also highly committed to a future for men that includes greater emotional expressiveness, recognition of interpersonal needs and vulnerabilities, experiencing of empathy, and heightening of sensuality. Where we differ with others is in our conviction that these future visions must occur together. For us, nonrelational sex and disconnected lust hold far less appeal than ever before.

Changing the Culture

Because we work from a social constructionist perspective on the development of men's sexuality, we believe that the most effective change strategies must begin at the sociocultural level. Broad cultural change is difficult to initiate, but dramatic once begun. What is required is a high level of public awareness of significant problems of nonrelational sexuality and its many manifestations. A new awareness has begun to appear; we're seeing greater attention to the misbehaviors of sexually violent men, sexual harassing men, and sexually irresponsible men. Newspapers, magazines, television, and radio talk shows have been rife with castigations of these men and the problems they create. This could be an important step, but we fear that the warning signs are not being properly interpreted. When we learn of a new incident—whether a sexual indiscretion by a prominent man or a pattern of misdeeds such as widespread sexual harassment in the U.S. Army—the official analysis often misses the point. The incident may be dismissed as the product of a single "aberrant" man. Sometimes the analyst blames the extraordinary context; public life is so stressful that solid citizens are forced to resort to dysfunctional coping strategies. Of late, some analysts (Bennett, 1995; Bork, 1996) have resorted to time-worn cliches to account for these problems as symptomatic of general moral decline.

Although each of these explanatory hypotheses has some merit, they all miss the proverbial forest for the trees. *The fundamental problem is the approach to sexuality that we teach to adolescent boys and young men.* Until we reconstruct the traditional standards for male sexual conduct, we will continue to be plagued with men behaving badly.

We need a *new and different* national forum on men and sexuality. Rather than turning the podium over to those steeped in the old, and now dysfunctional, ideas about male sexuality, we need to give the microphone to those with new ideas. Those who "get it" will need to find a way to be heard over the airwaves, in print, and in public gatherings. We need to dramatically expand this public awareness effort by broadening the focus beyond the few "aberrant" men to include attention to problems inherent in the sexual socialization of *all* men. We need much more attention to how normative male socialization contributes to nonrelational sexuality in all of its forms, including the Centerfold Syndrome, pornography addiction, compulsive womanizing, promiscuity, and sexual harassment and abuse.

Legal and Legislative Remedies

Over the past two decades, several legal and legislative strategies have been implemented to "change" men's sexual behavior. Heightened awareness of the rampant problems of sexual harassment has produced legislation designed to curb this destructive aspect of some men's sexual behavior. Antipornography activists (Dworkin, 1981; MacKinnon, 1979; Russell, 1993) have exposed the most egregious offenses of pornography and, in some cases, have succeeded in passing legislation against pornographic literature. In San Francisco, California, a new program (First Offenders of Prostitution, FOP) has appeared that legally mandates "Johns" (men who have been arrested for frequenting prostitutes) to attend consciousness-raising classes. This program is being duplicated in several U.S. and Canadian cities. Marinucci (1995, p. C1) quotes researcher and program codirector Norma Hotaling, "the program is an effort to correct misconceptions about prostitution and . . . break the cycle of sexualized violence and sexually transmitted diseases."

This line of legislative activism has been controversial, sparking debate, even within groups avidly opposed to pornography, prostitution, and sexual harassment. Some fear infringement of civil liberties, while others point to the historical failure of censorship to do little except intensify the appeal of taboo materials. However, the cognitive dissonance literature and previous successful legislative activism in the Civil Rights Movement, both illustrate that attitude change *can* follow behavior change. Programs that force men to change their sexual behaviors may not only protect victims, but, in some cases, may also produce substantive changes in men.

Whatever role is to be played by legislative activism, there can be little doubt that the most comprehensive push for change will come when there is massive public awareness of the problems in the social construction of male sexuality. When there is large-scale public recognition that traditional sexual socialization of men severely limits the emotional and sexual lives of women *and* men, a fundamentally different picture will emerge. Rather than defensively wrapping themselves in the Bill of Rights, informed men will eagerly initiate the difficult task of giving up pornography and sexual objectification of women. They'll do it with dedication, because they will have realized that pornography and sexual objectification of women are not in *anybody's* best interest.

Challenging National Institutions:
Media, Sports, and Fashion

With increased awareness of the problems of nonrelational sexuality, pressure for change can be brought to bear against some major national institutions that play significant roles in the cultivation and maintenance of nonrelational sexuality, particularly the media, sports, and the fashion industry.

THE MEDIA

Because of its significant role in shaping public opinion, the national media is a logical place to start. As we know from the public reactions to televised events like *Roots*, the Super Bowl, and the O. J. Simpson trial, television has phenomenal power and immediacy. The average American child watches between 7,000 and 8,000 hours of television *commercials* between the ages of 3 and 18 (Brett & Canto, 1988). In those hours, children are continually reinforced in their views of how the world works and how women and men are supposed to conduct themselves. Content analysis research (Davis, 1990) reveals that, although there has been some change over the past two decades, television programming continues to portray men and women in traditional fashion. For example, women are now more likely to be seen as having an occupation, but they still are not as likely to be portrayed as "experts" (the voices of commercial narrators are still male voices over 90% of the time). Most importantly, women still tend to be portrayed as sex objects. The "Swedish Bikini Team" may no longer be with us, but beer commercials continue to be largely populated by semiclad and seemingly empty-headed young women.

Not only is there an unending parade of stereotyped "gorgeous babe" women, there's a dearth of alternative ideas about female attractiveness. Although attractiveness in men may come in many varieties, it comes in a narrow range for women—young, shapely, and not-too-bright. Rarely does television (or the film industry) portray older, wiser, and physically-average women as particularly attractive or sexually desirable. A broadened definition of female attractiveness is both achievable and highly desirable.

THE SPORTS INDUSTRY

For men of all ages, the sports industry is an extremely influential national institution. And, by any reasonable standard, the American sports industry is badly out of control; it has been allowed to run amok as a socializer and influencer of American men (Messner, 1992; Sabo & Runfola, 1980) Once, sports and athletics were considered useful activities to help boys learn valuable skills of group cooperation, personal challenge, physical endurance, and overcoming of adversity. But, of late, sports have gone far beyond the modest role of teaching young men about life—for many men, they've become life itself. How many times have we heard fanatical coaches and rabid athletics boosters fervently preach about how football has taught young men the most important lessons in life—to struggle always to be Number One, to never let your guard down, to never let the other guy see you sweat? In general, life becomes a giant athletic event with one ultimate goal—outperform other men and win life's most valuable commodity the "thrill of victory"—victory that brings financial success, peer respect, and trophy women.

At their best, sports have lots to teach young men *and young women.* But it's been a long time since sports have been allowed to function at their best. At high school and university levels, athletic budgets and athletic events nearly suffocate all other activities—arts, scholarship, charitable and altruistic activities. Athletic values of winning-at-all-costs, being aggressive to hurt or intimidate, and "in-your-face" taunting to demean a fallen opponent have replaced the joys of mutual participation and demonstration of athletic skill and grace.

Sports, as now experienced in American culture, perpetuate traditional ideas about masculinity and sexuality. They instill worship of big, fast, muscular, and fearless men who carry the ball and slam dunk, while they simultaneously hype bare-legged, bare-midriffed, and latex-clad young women who cheer for victory or sell beer and high-performance cars. They teach young men to seek constant validation from the applause of the crowd and the affection of women as cheerleaders. They teach men to treat each other's bodies as punching bags and blocking dummies, while teaching them that any intimacy between men is outrageous and perverted.

Sports does not have to be run this way. Parents and fans can retake control. Athletics can return to a place where people can learn to improve physical capabilities without becoming obsessed with victory or humiliated by defeat. Women, as well as men, can participate and be on center stage. Men, as well as women, can cheer, encourage, and support women performers. Bodies can be appreciated for their capacity to accomplish reasonable physical objectives and participate joyously in shared physical expression. They never should be disfigured by weights and steroids to achieve inhuman capacity in the obsession with victory.

They do not need to be molded and shaped by endless dieting, exercise, and plastic surgery to become a titillating sideshow for athletic events.

THE FASHION INDUSTRY

A third area for intervention is the fashion industry. Clothing serves multiple purposes, including provision of warmth and protection, indication of social status, and opportunity for ornamentation and adornment. With the involvement of the fashion industry, clothing has taken on an additional purpose—celebrating women's bodies, exaggerating differences among women, and contriving endlessly to drape and reveal in a manner that sexually arouses men.

According to *Vogue* magazine, fashion in the mid-1990s emphasizes "the return of glamour . . . women are more vampish and seductive" (Agins, 1995, p. B1). To accomplish this vampish look, women are being provided with clinging dresses, specially designed bras, and the return of stiletto spike heels. If ever there were an illustration of the social construction of sexual arousal, it comes in the new call for shoes that reveal "toe cleavage," that is, the cracks between the toes (Agins, 1995, p. B5).

Should women be prevented from wearing "sexy" clothes? Of course not. Once again, the issue is not one of censorship, but good sense. Women and men need to get involved and demand fashions that allow for personal expression through sensible adornment, appreciation of fabrics, colors, textures, and styles. They should not stand for being coerced, through restriction of options and hyping of the trendiest, into accepting fashions that are designed primarily to display women's body parts, tantalize men, and demoralize all but the smallest number of women.

Change at the Personal Level

Those who are interested in cultural change often differ in their emphasis—some advocate change at the individual level, while others advocate broader approaches. We believe that the effective strategy for change is one that prescribes actions at both the personal and political levels.

MEN WITH OTHER MEN

If men are to make significant changes in their sexuality, they must begin to dramatically increase the amount of talking done about sex. On the face of it, this statement appears absurd, since it has commonly seemed that sex is one of our favorite topics. In reality, men do talk about sex, but almost always in humorous, superficial, and impersonal ways. Men almost never discuss sex in a format that allows for personal revelations, admissions of insecurities and fears, and questioning about similarities in experiences. When men get together in groups, there is strong social pressure to conform to traditional norms—focus on activities, emphasize indirect communication through joking and teasing, resist direct expression of affection, and avoid deeply personal revelations (Aries, 1976; Brooks, 1996).

But this may be changing. Across the country men are getting together to share experiences with other men. Some do so in therapy groups, some in wilderness gatherings as part of the mythopoetic men's movement. Similar to women's consciousness—raising groups of the past three decades, these groups are committed to a discovering a new type of gender role, one in better harmony with contemporary times (Andronico, 1996). These men's groups seem to be more salient because they are being conducted with a different set of ground rules—ones that allow for admission of weakness, for intimate and personal conversation, for expressions of fear, anxiety, and insecurity. We are witnessing the appearance of groups that allow men to care for and nurture other men, groups that are committed to better relationships with women and to a new male sexuality. There are profeminist men's groups, mythopoetic men's groups, men-in-recovery men's groups, survivors of sexual abuse men's groups, gay men's groups, men's consciousness-raising groups, father's education groups, father's rights groups, and a variety of men's therapy groups. The groups vary greatly in their structure and their ideas about what men need most, but they share a common vision—that modern manhood is in serious transition, that modern men are seriously confused, and that new types of men's gatherings are badly needed.

Most men's groups have enormous potential benefit, particularly if they help men take steps to overturn the limited opportunities for men to relate intimately with one another. Most men are badly out of touch with other men and benefit greatly from a chance to share their distress and pain with other men. However, while most men's groups can lift spirits and boost morale, some of them seem more likely than others to offer substantive help. Some groups, such as the Christian men's group, the "Promise Keepers" (1994), have a decidedly reactionary agenda. According to their literature, this group intends to "restore traditional family values," that is, re-establish men as family leaders and women as mothers and homemakers. This is a losing formula; an important impetus for revising men's sexuality comes from groups that have a serious commitment to continued empowerment of women and resultant role freedom for men (Levant, 1997). Since traditional gender politics and nonrelational sexuality are mutually supportive, substantive change requires alteration of both areas.

MENTORING YOUTH

Although we don't agree fully with all the ideas of Robert Bly, we agree with one of the central tenets of his mythopoetic philosophy—older men have been sadly remiss in offering guidance and leadership to younger men (Bly, 1990). Far too much influence has been accorded to men with highly traditional agendas; far too few of us with commitment to change have entered the environments of adolescent males—the schools, sports teams, churches, and youth organizations.

Silverstein (1996) considers our culture to be at a point in which a "redefinition of fathering" can substantially alter the lives of succeeding generations. Silverstein argues that women's greater empowerment as workers and family leaders set the stage for men to move more fully into roles of nurturers, caretakers, and emotional participants in families.

Some profeminist men (Biernbaum & Weinberg, 1991) have begun entering all-male environments such as college fraternities, to suggest new ideas about sexuality, to counter rape mythology, prevent date rape, and teach the subtleties of sexual harassment.

Older men (fathers, uncles, big brothers, and mentors) can be models of caring, compassionate men, who are respectful of women, and who love women for their abilities and personal qualities and not for their bodies. They can provide role models of men who get their self-esteem not only from their work, but also from their roles as loving persons, fathers, and partners (Brooks, 1995; Levant & Kopecky, 1995/1996). They can encourage boys to learn to care for each other, starting a process where they will be less dependent on women for validation. They can start a process whereby toughness and stoicism are much less emphasized, while emotional vulnerability and tenderness are allowed. Finally, they can discourage sexist humor and reject all forms of exploitation of women's bodies. In this way, they can be especially active in helping young men understand the pervasive and destructive messages of pornography. Much as a feminist would try to help a young girl be attentive to the implicit disempowering messages of Cinderella or Snow White, we profeminist men must also help young men learn to decode the misogynistic and sexually inaccurate messages purveyed in pornography.

THE NEXT GENERATION—WHAT PARENTS CAN DO

One of the most exciting, yet daunting, challenges of the past several decades has been the need to incorporate the ideals of the women's movement, and the profeminist men's movement, into the practice of raising children. Child-rearing practices are heavily shaped by prevailing cultural norms, and, therefore, are usually supportive of traditional values. However, when new ideologies are fully embraced by large segments of a culture, child rearing may be a pivotal force in the reshaping of the culture itself. In the matter of raising girls to become fuller participants in work, competition, and personal self-fulfillment and raising boys to become more emotionally flexible, fuller participants in relationships and family life, substantive changes are needed. Sharply differentiated child-rearing practices must be eliminated. Just as there is a need for continued emphasis on helping young girls become better able to access instrumental and competitive skills, there is a need for corollary shifts in emphasis for young boys. There must decreased emphasis on competition and hierarchical values, with a greater emphasis on interpersonal connection and the ability to interact cooperatively. Boys' activities will need to become less gender-stereotyped, with less devaluation of "feminine" activities. Subtle forms of misogyny must be recognized and countered. Interpersonal sensitivity, empathy, and compassion can receive greater emphasis as emotional skills for young boys; self-sufficiency, toughness, and personal individuation can receive greater emphasis for young girls. For these value shifts to have the greatest chance for success, young girls need greater exposure to the hidden women "heroes" of history, to role models of competence and success. For boys, there needs to be a major reshaping of "boy-culture" (Brooks & Silverstein, 1995; Rotundo, 1993). To accomplish this, boys need access to older boys and men who model acceptance, vulnerability, and interpersonal tenderness, rather than the usual exclusive diet of those modeling competition, physical prowess, and interpersonal aggression). There must be a vigorous challenge to rampant homophobia that severely limits potential for male-male intimacy. Boys must recognize the differences between intimacy and sexuality, as a path to making it acceptable for men (whether heterosexual, gay, or bisexual) to become intimate with one another without concern that interpersonal messages will be misconstrued.

These proposed changes raise painful questions—how do we raise girls who can, if they wish, be tougher and more competitive? How do we raise boys who are more sensitive, and less "masculine," in a relatively unchanging culture? On a more personal level, do we want our daughter or son to be subject to the anguish of pioneering a new model of femininity or masculinity? These are difficult questions that point to the need for a broad systemic view of the reciprocal, and interactive, nature of this situation. Individual parents will consider new ways of raising boys and girls as they see signs that the culture will accommodate the changes; the culture will change as our children are raised in new ways.

CONVERSATIONS BETWEEN WOMEN AND MEN

The increasing realization of the considerable differences in the way women and men approach the world has given rise to a number of educational and consciousness-raising activities. Such activities help women and men understand, and in some cases, surmount these differing orientations. Much as cultural-awareness classes have been conducted in the past, these new gender communication workshops and programs are designed to help people from differing backgrounds come to appreciate the values and concerns of others. In the past, differing races and ethnic groups have had considerable success in improving cross-cultural sensitivity by clarifying misunderstandings and pointing out stylistic differences (Sue & Sue, 1990).

It may seem odd to suggest this type of activity for men and women, who, as gender groups have lived together since the beginning of time. However, despite their supposed familiarity with each other, women and men can be considered to cohabit different worlds (Philpot, Brooks, Lusterman, & Nutt, 1997). Tannen (1990, 1993) has illustrated how processes as basic as language and communication styles mirror, as well as create, marked differences between women and men. Gray (1992) may have overstated the case with his Mars and Venus analogy, but he was right to recognize that there are major chasms created by gender socialization.

Dialogues allow women and men to work collectively to identify the common satisfactions and difficulties in traditional gender arrangements. Many women and men find this process alone to be helpful, since, like the men's group activity noted earlier, it helps people recognize common issues and problems.

These groups are especially useful when they can work toward some form of resolution of relationship impasses. Frequently, this happens. Bergman and Surrey (1992) have demonstrated considerable success with their workshop format, as have O'Neil and Carroll (1988) with their Gender Role Journal Workshop, Eisler and Loye (1990) with their

Partnership Way workshops, and Walker, Gindes, Morris, Brooks, and Levant (1996) with their Inter-Gender Dialogues.

Can these activities help us overcome nonrelational sexuality and the Centerfold Syndrome? With sophisticated leadership, it seems likely that they can. These workshops are relatively inexpensive, flexible, and seem to have considerable potential to easily adapt to multiple settings—churches, schools, and community groups. As we have repeatedly emphasized, we see sexuality as integrally tied to the social constructions of masculinity and femininity. Therefore, any time vitally important issues are examined in an empathic and mutually supportive environment, positive changes cannot help but ensue.

COUPLES CHANGING TOGETHER

It is quite difficult to discuss gender-related relationships problems, particularly sexuality, in large groups of women and men. In many ways, it is even more difficult for individual couples to discuss sexuality in an open and honest fashion. It often appears that the process of seeking help for sexuality concerns is very difficult for most women and almost impossible for many men.

Over the past two decades, each author has worked extensively with widely varied populations of men and has encountered many distressed men wishing to change some aspect of the traditional male role. Many men have wanted to be better fathers. Some have wanted to be less driven by work or success obsession. Many have wished to be less emotionally isolated. Many have tried to overcome gender stresses that were severely interfering with their physical health. But when men have sought help with their sexual lives, they have generally focused on quality and quantity of orgasms. Few have directly identified nonrelational sex as a significant problem. Women are far more likely to recognize the necessary connection between sexuality and intimacy, more likely to discontinue sexual activity when the relationship goes awry, and more likely to complain about a male partner's casual attitude toward sex. As a result, the woman in a heterosexual partnership may be the person most likely to seek change.

Because a woman usually is the "customer" for change from problems of nonrelational sexuality, her perspective needs to be supported. She needs to know that although many cultural forces are invested in silencing the recognition of men's sexual problems, she must persevere. At the same time, however, male partners must be helped to understand that a critical perspective on normative male sexuality is not designed to vilify him as a man. The emphasis is not to dwell on the problems of the past (although past injuries must be recognized), but to build a new future by crafting a new and more functional sexuality. Once couples become committed to change, the essential task is to replace dysfunctional sexual patterns with more intimate and adaptive ones. Here the primary objective is to replace an overly agentic, voyeuristic, phallocentric, and compulsive sexuality with one that is more relaxed, tactile, sensual, and intimate. Of all that has previously been written about sexual enhancement techniques, the sensuality exercises (Comfort, 1972, 1991; Zilbergeld, 1992) seem to have the most central role.

To develop new channels of sexual arousal, couples can focus on helping each other try new ways to experience pleasure. Couples can touch and fondle each other, openly communicating about sensations and pleasures. They can open up their sensory channels through music, massage, bathing, and hugging. To avoid maladaptive habits of emotional disconnection and stranger fantasies, a man can concentrate on looking directly into the eyes of his partner, studying her facial expressions, participating intimately in her sensual pleasure. He can learn to appreciate the subtle signs of her pleasure—goosebumps, erect nipples, more rapid heart rate, or labial engorgement. He can become more attuned to the corresponding sensual sensation in his own body—his breathing or his increased tactile sensitivity. Couples do well to allow time to participate leisurely in relearning sexual arousal, without needing to rush into intercourse and orgasm.

Couples are encouraged to give high priority to their intimacy needs. Special efforts are made to create both psychological and physical space for relationship maintenance, since the ultimate objective is to integrate sexuality and all other aspects of a couple's life. Some couples might benefit from a gender-aware form of couples therapy (Silverstein & Levant, 1996).

INDIVIDUAL MEN

Both Levant (Levant & Kopecky, 1995/1996) and Brooks (1995) have addressed the matter of how individual men can change their own lives. In suggesting a path to "reconstruct masculinity," Levant suggests that each man should (a) re-examine his beliefs about manhood; (b) separate out the still-valuable aspects of his traditional male code; (c) identify those parts of his masculine code that are obsolete or dysfunctional; (d) apply his strengths to the task of developing the skills that make up *emotional intelligence*—particularly emotional empathy and emotional self-awareness; and (e) use these skills to make the changes needed in his relational and sexual life.

Brooks (1995) also suggested several steps to overcome nonrelational sexuality (in the form of the Centerfold Syndrome). First, he suggested that self-evaluation is needed to determine the relative amounts of voyeuristic practices, dysfunctional masturbatory habits, and intimacy-avoidant fantasies. He suggested that a man then review his sexual heritage, with particular attention to sexual myths and anachronistic macho attitudes. In particular, a man is encouraged to explore his tolerance for emotional and sexual intimacy. If a man discovers troublesome symptoms of the Centerfold Syndrome, Brooks suggests that he work to (a) develop new visual habits and new ways to "look" at women; (b) discontinue masturbatory practices that focus on "others" rather than self; (c) replace destructive and misogynistic "self-talk" with more functional self-talk; and (d) work to develop intimate, but nonsexual relationships with women *and* men.

The Payoff for Men

In the briefest form, here are few of the outcomes that can occur for men if they make a concerted effort to reconstruct their sexuality:

- Freedom from the distracting and anxiety-inducing aspects of voyeurism.
- Decreased reactivity to media manipulations of attention and emotional state.
- Increased sense of mastery of sexual arousal and less reactivity to sexual fetishes.
- Freedom from obsession with pornography.
- Greater appreciation of women based on mutual interests and emotional compatibility.
- Less anxiety about rating one's sexual performance.
- Greater confidence in the underpinnings of relationships with less possessiveness and jealousy.
- Greater comfort with a loved one's changing physical appearance.
- Greater chance for greater sexual harmony and emotional connection with one's partner.
- Increased possibilities for nonsexual yet intimate relations with women and men.
- Masturbation that leaves one feeling pleasured instead of guilty and alienated.

- Fewer sexual fantasies of strangers interfering with our intimate moments with a loved one.
- Sexual intercourse that leaves one closer to a partner, rather than more distant.

We hear a lot of calls for us to give up things we like because they are bad for us—tasteless humor, cigarettes, cigars, alcohol, cholesterol, unsaturated fat, salt, and sugar. The last thing we need now is a suggestion that we should do away with the best parts of male sexuality—no more girl watching, no more magazines, no more recreational sex. This book is not about eliminating male sexuality—but it is about overhauling it. It's about replacing irresponsible, detached, compulsive, and alienated sexuality with a type of sexuality that is ethically responsible, compassionate for the well-being of participants, and sexually empowering of men.

To accomplish our goals we'll need to modify what we expect of women and men. We'll need to value women for more than physical attractiveness—for their personal strengths, talents, and intelligence. Our models of competent men will also need to evolve. The old idea of masculinity being judged by the capacity to "score" will need to be replaced with models of men who are sensitive and understanding. We'll need to question the concept that manhood must be proven and regularly measured by a man's acquisitions and symbols of success. We must grasp the idea that many men can be more by doing less. We can help men be more fulfilled when we can help them give up the need always to be in the driver's seat (literally and figuratively), and more frequently go along for the ride, enjoy the scenery, talk to the kids, and allow themselves to appreciate the talents of the woman who will share driving. In this way, we will all come out ahead.

References

Agins, T. (1995, January 20). Fashion slaves get kicks from spike heels. *Wall Street Journal*, pp. B1, B5.

Andronico, M. (Ed.). (1996). *Men in groups: Insights, interventions, and psychoeducational work.* Washington, DC: American Psychiatric Association Press.

Aries, E. (1976). Interaction patterns and themes of male, female, and mixed groups. *Small Group Behavior, 7,* 7–18.

Bennett, W. J. (1995). *The book of virtues.* New York: Silver Burdett.

Bergman, S. J., & Surrey, J. (1992). *The woman-man relationship: Impasses and possibilities* (Working Paper No. 55). Wellesley, MA: The Robert S. and Grace W. Stone Center for Developmental Services and Studies.

Biernbaum, M., & Weinberg, J. (1991). Men unlearning rape. *Changing Men, 22,* 22–25.

Bly, R. (1990). *Iron John: A book about men.* New York: Vintage Books.

Bork, R. H. (1996). *Slouching towards Gomorrah.* New York: Regan.

Brett, D. J., & Canto, J. (1988). The portrayal of men and women in U.S. television commercials: A recent content analysis and trends over 15 years. *Sex Roles, 18,* 595–609.

Brooks, G. R. (1995). *The centerfold syndrome: How men can overcome objectification and achieve intimacy with women.* San Francisco: Jossey-Bass.

Brooks, G. R. (1996). Treatment for therapy-resistant men. In M. Andronico (Ed.), *Men in groups: Insights, interventions, and psychoeducational work* (pp. 7–19). Washington, DC: American Psychiatric Association Press.

Brooks, G. R., & Silverstein, L. B. (1995). Understanding the dark side of masculinity: An integrative systems model. In R. F. Levant & W. S. Pollack (Eds.), *A new psychology of men* (pp. 280–333). New York: Basic Books.

Comfort, A. (1972). *The joy of sex.* New York: Simon & Schuster.

Comfort, A. (1991). *The new joy of sex: A gourmet's guide to sex in the nineties.* New York: Crown.

Davis, D. M. (1990). Portrayals of women in prime-time network television: Some demographic characteristics. *Sex Roles, 23,* 325–332.

Dworkin, A. (1981). *Pornography: Men possessing women.* London: Women's Press.

Eisler, R., & Loye, D. (1990). *The partnership way: New tools for living and learning, healing our families, our communities, and our world.* San Francisco: Harper.

Gray, J. (1992). *Men are from Mars, women are from Venus.* New York: HarperCollins.

Levant, R. F., Kopeckly, G. (1995/1996). *Masculinity reconstructed: Changing the rules of manhood—at work, in relationships, and in family life.* New York: Dutton/Plume.

Levant, R. F. (in press). The masculinity crisis. *Journal of Men's Studies.*

MacKinnon, C. A. (1979). *Sexual harassment of working women.* New Haven, CT: Yale University Press.

Marinucci, C. (1995, April 16). School for johns. *San Francisco Examiner,* C1–5.

Messner, M. (1992). *Power at play: Sports and the problem of masculinity.* Boston: Beacon Press.

O'Neil, J. M., & Roberts Carroll, M. R. (1988). A gender role workshop focused on sexism, gender role conflict, and the gender role journey. *Journal of Counseling and Development, 67,* 193–197.

Philpot, C., Brooks, G. R., Lusterman, D. D., & Nutt, R. (1997). *Bridging separate gender worlds.* Washington, DC: American Psychological Association Press.

Promise Keepers. (1994). *Seven promises of a promise-keeper.* Colorado Springs, CO: Focus on the Family.

Rotundo, E. A. (1993). *American manhood: Transformations in masculinity from the revolution to the modern era.* New York: Basic Books.

Russell, D. E. H. (1993). *Against pornography: The evidence of harm.* Berkeley, CA: Russell.

Sabo, D., & Runfola, R. (1980). *Jock: Sports and male identity*. Englewood Cliffs, NJ: Prentice-Hall.

Silverstein, L. S. (1996). Fathering is a feminist issue. *Psychology of Women Quarterly, 20*, 3–37.

Silverstein, L. S., & Levant, R. F. (1996, August 12) *Bridging the gap from Mars to Venus: Treating couples impasses*. Paper presented at the annual convention of the American Psychological Association, Toronto, Ontario, Canada.

Sue, D. W., & Sue, D. (1990). *Counseling the culturally different: Theory and practice*. New York: Wiley.

Tannen, D. (1990). *You just don't understand: Women and men in conversation*. New York: Morrow.

Tannen, D. (1993). *Gender and conversational interaction*. New York: Oxford University Press.

Walker, L., Gindes, M., Morris, L., Brooks, G., & Levant, R. (1996). Inter-gender dialogues. *The Independent Practitioner, 16*, 167–170.

Zilbergeld, B. (1992). *The new male sexuality: The truth about men, sex, and pleasure*. New York: Bantam Books.

Index